The Early Public Theatre in France

The Early
Public Theatre
in France

By W. L. WILEY

HARVARD UNIVERSITY PRESS · CAMBRIDGE

MCMLX

Distributed in Great Britain by Oxford University Press, London

Publication of this book has been aided by a grant from the
Ford Foundation

Library of Congress Catalog Card Number 60-11561

Printed in the United States of America

FOR MY GRANDSON

WILLIAM LEE WILEY, JUNIOR

PREFACE

The idea of *The Early Public Theatre in France* has stemmed from over twenty years of interest in French drama, and from the questions of many of my students about the whole broad field. As a generality, these more than two decades of contact with the theatrical history of France have led to the conclusion that the fifty years from around 1580 to a little beyond 1630 needed further study. The Middle Ages have been carefully examined, and scholars like Emile Faguet and Raymond Lebègue have looked into the sixteenth century; Henry Carrington Lancaster's fine series of volumes was primarily concerned with dramatic material after 1620. There has been something of a gap (partially filled by the late nineteenth-century studies of Eugène Rigal and the more recent work of Madame Deierkauf-Holsboer), then, in investigations into the half-century of the French theatre ending around 1630. This is particularly true in regard to the milieu of plays and players, and the problems of the first professional companies. It is hoped that *The Early Public Theatre* in France will help to fill in this interlude.

Active work on the project was begun in Paris during the summer of 1954; further delving into French libraries, museums, and archives (national and provincial) was carried on for some nine months in 1957, and in the summer of 1959. These periods of necessary research in France were made possible by grants from the Carnegie Foundation, from the Institute for Research in Social Science at the University of North Carolina, and by a Kenan Leave for one semester in 1957. For the latter I am grateful to the Administration of the University of North Carolina, and to the Chairman of the Department of Romance Languages, Professor Sterling

A. Stoudemire, and to my colleagues who made possible the absorption of my academic duties during this interval.

Specific debts of gratitude are due Joseph Fuchs, archivist of Strasbourg, who was my guide through the Archives Municipales of that city; Michel le Moël, archivist in charge of *cartes et plans* at the Archives Nationales in Paris, who helped me locate some rare maps and celebrated with me the rediscovery of a lost one with an early-morning *apéritif*; Roger-Armand Weigert, Conservateur au Cabinet des Estampes at the Bibliothèque Nationale, who assisted me in finding several sixteenth- and seventeenth-century engravings; Mademoiselle Madeleine Chabrier, the head of the photographic and microfilming service of the Bibliothèque Nationale; Madame Monval of the Bibliothèque de l'Arsenal and the staff of the Bibliothèque de la Comédie Française. I am greatly indebted to Raymond Lebègue, Professeur à la Faculté des Lettres, Université de Paris, for giving me ready access to his latest discoveries on the French theatre. And without the efficiency and good disposition of Mrs. Evelyn Graham the manuscript would never have appeared in any sort of readable form.

The translations in the body of the text are my own. Some of the passages in the original French have been included in the notes; in most cases, for the sake of brevity, this has not been done, though every effort has been made to give exact references to sources. Sixteen- and seventeenth-century French spellings in quoted material in the notes have generally been put into modern French. When there has been no modernization, it has been indicated.

The Early Public Theatre in France is being dedicated to a young man who is now a little more than one year old. Perhaps some day he, too, will love the land of France.

Chapel Hill, North Carolina   W. L. W.
January 16, 1960

CONTENTS

ILLUSTRATIONS

The Early Public Theatre in France

INTRODUCTION

France was late in having a theatre of professional caliber, but this was not because Frenchmen did not like plays. Throughout the Middle Ages there had been a varied and colorful offering of dramatic productions, in the provinces as well as in Paris. A wandering *jongleur* could recite a monologue in which he played several parts, a group in the town of Arras might get together to produce a comedy under a brush arbor, or an organization made up of bourgeois and a few clerics in Paris might give an elaborate staging of the Passion of the Saviour. There were miracle plays, fools' plays, moralities, mysteries, and farces. The peak of this communal dramatic activity was reached in the fifteenth century; by the middle of the sixteenth century it had nearly ceased, except for the tenacious comic genre, the farce. The large semiprofessional societies of Paris, Rouen, and other cities had almost stopped producing the older medieval forms, and writers of plays began to imitate the tragedies and comedies of the Greeks and Romans. These were seldom performed except in schoolrooms or adjacent courtyards, and by schoolboys playing both masculine and feminine roles. Or, occasionally there might be a representation at some château of a play based on ancient material, and with young ladies and gentlemen of the Court taking the parts. The tragedies and comedies of youthful writers like Jodelle, Grévin, La Péruse, and others were destined primarily for reading and would have scarcely appealed to a professional company of actors if such had existed.

A major blow was dealt the development of the theatre when Catherine de' Medici removed her support from the performance of serious plays at Court, though the Queen continued her interest in ballet and the lighter Italian *commedia dell' arte.* Catherine had sponsored tragedy along with other court entertainment until her husband, Henry II, was killed by the broken lance of Count Montgommery in the ill-fated jousting match of 1559. After this real tragedy in her life, she became progressively more superstitious, and listened more and more to soothsayers, alchemists, and astrologers. A tragedy on the stage came for her to be symbolic of the death of a dynasty in the world of reality. The sixteenth-century gossip, Brantôme, who had a great deal to say about Catherine de' Medici, stated that after Trissino's *Sofonisba* (in Melin de Saint-Gelais' version) had been "very well staged by the ladies and young ladies and gentlemen of her Court," she would have nothing further to do with tragedy: "she used to like very much to see comedies and tragedies performed; but since *Sophonisbe*, she has had the opinion that tragedy brought bad luck to the affairs of the kingdom — as indeed it turned out; she had no more of them played, but continued comedies and tragi-comedies, and even the antics of *Zani* and *Pantalone.*" [1]

The professional stage would have had a hard time coming alive during the Renaissance, with or without the approval of Catherine de' Medici. The Protestants disapproved of the general idea of the theatre as a public amusement, and there were many followers of Calvin and Luther at the time. Some Catholics had similar feelings and believed that professional acting was a continuation of the decadent paganism of Rome. Also, it must be remembered that the Wars of Religion which went on inside France during the thirty years that Catherine's three weak sons, Francis II, Charles IX, and Henry III, were kings left little time for gaiety or established institutions of amusement. The Valois line ended in 1589 in weakness and in death, even as Catherine de' Medici had feared. It needed no play-actor to symbolize its demise.

The first professional actors to perform in France were the Italians, and they came in under the last of the Valois. One company of Italians, *I Gelosi*, was invited by Henry III to give their repertory of the *commedia dell' arte* at Blois in the great *Salle des Etats*, where the States-General held its sessions. The actors so pleased the frivolous king that he allowed them to perform in Paris at the Hôtel de Bourbon. They opened on Sunday, May 19, 1577, and, according to the oft-quoted report of the sober and somber Pierre de l'Estoile, there was a "concourse and affluence of people such as the four best preachers of Paris never had." The Parlement de Paris in the following July forbade performances by *I Gelosi*, even though they had letters of permission from the King — and Parlement threatened to impose on the comedians ten thousand livres fine. In spite of all this, they were still giving performances at the Hôtel de Bourbon in September 1577, "by the express permission and authorization of the King, the corruption of this era being such that farce-players, buffoons, prostitutes, and mignons are in full control." ² It will be noticed at what general level of the social scale actors were put. French actors had not yet appeared in companies and as professionals, but they too were to be regarded for a long time as low specimens of society.

The story of the first gropings toward a professional theatre in France was left in many and varied places. Parts of it were included in memoirs, journals, and diaries of the late sixteenth and early seventeenth centuries; parts of it are in the actual plays of the period, and the prefaces and letters accompanying them. Other portions of it are in the leases of the theatrical halls, contractual agreements between acting companies, and in the records of the owners of the first public theatre, the Hôtel de Bourgogne. Much information on the theatre is to be found in seventeenth-century historians of the city of Paris, as well as on contemporary maps of the French capital. A great deal of pictorial material like engravings, sketches, paintings, and medallions of the period still exists, and illustrates vividly many phases of the developing public theatre and the participants in its flowering. Much of this accumulation, whether written or representational, has not been put in a book before; on the other hand, free use has been made in the present study of the discoveries of earlier researchers in theatrical history and of the patient delvers into the National Archives in Paris. The sum-total of this collection, it is to be hoped, has been blended into a recounting that will have appeal not only for the specialist in French literary matters, but also for those citizens of the world who love both France and the theatre.

The interval of time involved for this examination is a little more than fifty years, and it extended from around 1580 to a little past 1630. During this period the theatre as a public institution in France came into existence. It was of greatest importance in Paris, though the provinces were used as training grounds for actors. There were both outdoor and indoor performances; and there were street entertainers, singers with herb salesmen, marionnette manipulators, and rope walkers of the fairs, as well as performers of tragedy, comedy, and farce. All of these will be classified as professionals if their operations were for the purpose of earning a living. It will be noted that usually the early professionals found a welcome in the provinces before they were accepted in Paris. Also, this interlude of time will show a change from official disapproval or indifference to the hearty approbation of the idea of the theatre by Richelieu and his recognition of it as a social force. By the early 1630's there were two thriving public theatres in Paris, and all classes of society were seeing Corneille's first plays. It should be a pleasant task to follow the threads of this half-century of theatrical history.

I

THE SETTING

THE LAND OF FRANCE WAS NOT A VERY HAPPY land as the sixteenth century drew to its close. Her strife-torn provinces and her great and turbulent capital city faced too many real problems to have much leisure or enthusiasm for the illusion of the theatre. Catholics and Protestants continued a bitter civil war that was political as well as religious, and many inhabitants of Paris recalled the vivid spectacle of the Massacre of Saint Bartholomew which had taken place in 1572 near the east gate of the Louvre during the reign of Charles IX. Conditions certainly were not improved when the third of Catherine's sons came to the throne in 1574. This last of the Valois monarchs, Henry III, was frail and weak, dressed effeminately and reeked of perfume, and lacked control of his realm. But there still lingered over the Court a tradition of artistic and literary patronage begun under Francis I and Henry II, when the Valois kings were sturdy and strong. As for Henry III, he was intelligent enough to see that his kingdom was crumbling around his feet and that the leader of the Catholic League and tough man of war, Henri duc de Guise, would be glad to push him aside and found a new dynasty in France. There was some popular support for this move, particularly after Guise had defeated the German Protestants in 1587 and had ridden triumphantly into Paris, sitting his horse tall and straight, his proud saber-scar of battle marking his cheek.

Henry III and his Queen, Louise de Vaudémont, had produced no children — a somewhat understandable deficiency but one that gave considerable aid to Guise in his plans. In this time of tension, with the people of Paris barricading their streets and shouting their allegiance to the duc de Guise, the King slipped out of the Louvre through a gate along the Seine and fled to Rambouillet and Chartres. After such a humiliating abandonment of the royal seat of Government, it is rather remarkable that Henry III, even with concessions, was able to slow down Guise's juggernaut and call a meeting of the States-General at Blois in the autumn of 1588. Guise attended as Commander-in-Chief of the armies of France, and as Grand Master of the Order of the Holy Ghost; he occupied a seat at the assemblies just a little below that of the King. Guise's insolence toward his monarch continued to manifest itself, so Henry III made a move that he had been planning at least for some months: he called on nine of his special guard of forty-five gentlemen, mostly hard and seasoned soldiers from Gascony, to assassinate the duc de Guise. Guise was stabbed to death according to plan early in the morning of the twenty-third of December 1588, in the great château of Blois. He died bravely, after a night of revelry that had kept him occupied until the near dawn. On the floor of the hall in which he received the dagger-thrusts — it has a door leading from it into Henry III's *cabinet de travail* — even now on a foggy winter's day there seems to linger the stickiness and clamminess of Guise's blood. Thus in the historic setting of Blois, where had been seen earlier in the century Francis I fight against a wild boar, and where the staging of the tragic love of the Carthaginian lady, Sophonisba, had taken place, now was enacted a somber drama that made these previous diversions seem pale and inconsequential.

Before the removal of the duc de Guise, Henry III had already leaned toward his distant cousin, the mighty warrior from the south, Henry of Navarre, who was next in line for the throne. It looked as though Henry, King of Navarre, would never become King of France because his religion was

Protestant. Nevertheless, Henry III arranged a meeting with his cousin in the latter part of April 1589, at the château of Plessis-lès-Tours in Touraine, to discuss matters of political and religious adjustment. And, when in his turn Henry III was stabbed to death by a Dominican fanatic on the first of August 1589, this last and weakest of the Valois kings before dying handed over his crown to Henry of Navarre. The able and veteran campaigner of the religious wars, who was to rule France as Henry IV, found that his kingdom would have to be won and that much more fighting lay ahead.

Henry IV was too busy with the internal problems of France to pay much attention to arts and letters — though as will be seen he did enjoy from time to time a good belly laugh in watching a rough-and-tumble farce. The Catholics most naturally were unwilling to accept a Protestant king, even when Henry indicated early in his reign his willingness to give up the Huguenot faith. The Catholic cities and strongholds of the north denied him entry. He was repulsed at Rouen by the forces of the duc de Mayenne, but later in March 1590, Mayenne was soundly defeated at Ivry, with Henry rallying his tattered soldiers to a great victory. Paris still refused to open her gates to him, the King of Spain would gladly have taken over France to save the nation from the Protestant heretic, and the Pope looked disapprovingly upon Henry's proposed conversion. Nevertheless, after a conference with the bishops at Saint Denis, Henry became a Catholic on July 25, 1592, and his religious ordination as King of France took place at Chartres on February 27, 1594. Along the way, Henry continued to win more and more Frenchmen to him because of his real love for France, and on March 22, 1594, he entered Paris in triumph, his white plume flying proudly in the breeze.

Paris showed the marks of siege and her citizens had suffered from lack of food (they ate dogs and candle wax) and a skyrocketing of prices, much of which was described by

Pierre de l'Estoile who was there and kept a record of it all.[1]
By 1600, the Pope had granted Henry absolution, the Spaniards had been driven across the frontiers, and peace had been
established once again in the land. Now came the moment of
rebuilding and reconstruction after several decades of internal
struggle. Henry was assisted in this by M. de Rosny, a Huguenot, who became duc de Sully in 1606. Sully was an honest
and upright man, whose unrelenting financial accounting built
up funds for the depleted royal treasury. Industry and manufacturing — in glass, silk, and tapestry, for example — were
encouraged, and the road system began to be improved, especially the main roads leading into Paris. The reparation of
the transport network — bridges, canals, and main arteries of
communication — allowed the early traveling dramatic companies to practice their profession a little easier, though it was
a hard one at best. The project of rebuilding France and
Paris after so many years of destruction was enormous and
continued throughout the first half of the seventeenth century.

Henry IV, with genuine broad-mindedness and good
humor, sought to resolve the physical, religious, and moral
problems of his nation. In 1598 the famous Edict of Nantes
gave rights of worship to the Protestants, in spite of Catholic
opposition. And in 1603 the Jesuits, with their excellent staging of plays, were permitted to return to France, over the
opposition of the Huguenots and others. Between 1604 and
1608 foreign colonization was to be encouraged; Champlain
founded Quebec, and a pageant in Canada in 1606 depicted
the glories of "la Nouvelle France."

Henry, the tireless Vert Galant, could spend the whole day
working, fighting, or hunting, and the whole night making
love. Despite a certain gamy flavor that persistently attached
itself to his person, he never lacked for the society of women.
After the annulment of his marriage to Marguerite de Valois
(a move that suited them both, since neither had been re-

motely faithful to the other) and the death of his favorite
Gabrielle d'Estrées in childbirth at the age of twenty-five,
Henry married in 1600 the healthy and plump niece of the
grand duke of Tuscany, Marie de' Medici. Other feminine
interests continued to crop up, including an infatuation for
the fifteen-year-old Charlotte de Montmorency at the moment of his death. He was slain on May 14, 1610, by one Ra-
vaillac while the King was on the way to the Arsenal to see
Sully; it happened at the corner of the rue de la Ferronerie
and the rue Saint Honoré in Paris. The whole realm realized
the greatness of Henry IV after his death — his love of
France, his bravery, his camaraderie with all classes, his gaiety,
his fierce dignity, his gentleness and his *politesse*; in the words
of a present-day historian, "vraiment il avait été un roi." [2]

   In 1601 Marie de' Medici gave birth at Fontainebleau to a
son who was destined to be the future Louis XIII. According
to the court physician who looked after the royal heir and
chronicled his every move for more than twenty years,[3]
young Louis was a lusty and even sexually precocious child —
while in the nursery he was fascinated by the handsome and
visible bosom of mademoiselle de Guise — but such reports
were a bit optimistic. The young Dauphin, in any case, idol-
ized his father and played with toy soldiers and guns in anticipation of military exploits, but he was never to be the
captain, the athlete, or the master of the boudoir that Henry
IV was. Louis was very early exposed to plays and players
both in palaces like the Louvre or Fontainebleau, and at the
public theatre of the Hôtel de Bourgogne, all of which was
hopeful for the development of drama during his reign.

   After the assassination of Henry IV, Marie de' Medici as
Regent began to spend money lavishly and get rid of the ad-
visers of her husband, including Sully who had filled up the
royal coffers. The young King was treated very much as an
imbecile by his Mother, who was strongly under the influence
of Concini, Maréchal d'Ancre, and his wife, a former lady

of the queen's bedchamber. Louis had been betrothed to Anne of Austria, the granddaughter of Philip II of Spain, and the marriage took place in Bordeaux on November 28, 1615. Concini's influence over Marie de' Medici continued to mount, in spite of his unpopularity with the French nobility, who did not dare to oppose him. During these years he treated Louis XIII as an immature weakling who could be ignored. Louis, now a youth of no more than sixteen years, realized that he had to break the yoke of dominion of his mother and her favorites, and that he would have to do it almost alone. He acted with energy, and arranged the assassination of Concini by the marquis de Vitry of the royal guards, on April 24, 1617. France was pleased at this display of action on the part of its courageous if not intellectually brilliant young King. Marie de' Medici was sent to Blois in practical exile, and was not even allowed to be present at the marriage of her daughter Christine to Charles Emmanuel de Savoie in 1619. There was never to be any final reconciliation between Marie de' Medici and her son who was now exercising to the fullest extent of his powers his responsibility of being King of France. Louis received very little help either from his mother or his wife, Anne of Austria, in the governing of his domain. Anne became involved in a trivial incident with the English Duke of Buckingham, and later showed great indiscretion by writing to madame de Chevreuse letters destined to give the Spaniards secret information about affairs in France. Under these conditions, Louis saw very little of his wife, and it was only because of a storm that he spent a night in December 1637, at the Louvre instead of going on to his proposed destination of Versailles. The future Louis XIV was born on September 5, 1638.

There was less privilege of free-thinking and religious deviation during Louis XIII's reign than in the time of Henry IV. A greater emphasis on devoutness was present, in literature and at the Court. Various religious societies came into existence, and they were in general opposed to the profession of the theatre. The Protestants continued to cause trouble, but were administered a crushing defeat when their stronghold of La Rochelle fell after a long siege in 1628. The resolution of the political strength of the Protestants and the containment of the House of Austria were two of the prime accomplishments of Louis's thirty-three years as King. As a fair man, he maintained the individual rights of worship promised to the Huguenots in the Edict of Nantes. It is incorrect, then, to think of Louis XIII as a sad and ridiculous puppet, who dressed drably, danced poorly (he loved ballet), and stumbled around under his big head and nose and slightly pendant lower lip. He was a brave if mediocre soldier, and realistic enough to recognize the superior abilities of Richelieu and therefore to call him in as minister of state. Louis XIII had the heart of a great sovereign if not the mind or body. He died on May 14, 1643 around three o'clock in the afternoon, on the same day in May that had seen an assassin's hand destroy his father more than thirty years before. If the father could well be called Henri le Grand, the son deserved the title of Louis le Juste. Louis' death came a little less than six months after that of the man whose brilliance had dimmed royal authority — Armand du Plessis, Cardinal de Richelieu.

Richelieu, Bishop of Luçon in 1606 when he was only twenty years old, was really a protégé of Marie de' Medici, though before the end of his career he fell out of the favor of this strange woman. Louis XIII, who had no personal admiration for Richelieu but respected his abilities, called him into the government in 1624. Thereafter, for almost twenty years the Cardinal molded the destiny of France with keen intelligence, ruthlessness, and amazing intuition. His interests were legion, embraced literature and literary patronage, and during the last ten years of his life major reforms in the theatre. There is no need to retell the full story of his political accomplishments or to examine again the astuteness of his diplomacy by which he subordinated the powers of the nobles, strengthened the monarchy, and made France the most feared nation of Europe. The remarkable feature of his career is that with all the official demands upon his day, he found time for literature, authors, and plays — and possibly did some creative writing himself. He loved the luxuries and displays of the world, and had no hesitancy in spending his vast wealth in external revelation of the grandeur of his position. He had all the vanities which included a rather stylized admiration for women, most of whom did not care for him. Few people except His Gray Eminence, Father Joseph liked Richelieu. His portrait, as well as the decoration of the private apartments in his palace, were done by the fine artist, Philippe de Champaigne. According to the fine description given of him in the seventeenth century by the Cardinal de Retz, he "had enough religion for this world." [4]

Richelieu had read an enormous number of books, especially in the field of history. He had a solid training in Latin, which he spoke and wrote with facility. He also knew Spanish, Italian, and some Greek; he had a great love for verses and for the theatre, and his prose style was clean and clear. This astounding man drove himself into all avenues of culture, in spite of being sick most of his life with headaches, boils, hemorrhoids, and such things. His tremendous energy, far from being used up by his other myriad activities, allowed him to build the gigantic palace and gardens known in his time as the Palais Cardinal, now the Palais Royal. Richelieu, the "inexorable Cardinal," died bravely on December 4, 1642, and passed off the stage like a hero out of a tragedy of Corneille. [5]

No glance at France, a nation of some fifteen million souls during the period from around 1580 into the 1630's, would be complete without a look at the physical and cultural appearance of the great and cosmopolitan city of Paris, resting on both sides of the Seine and cradling her two islands, the Ile de la Cité and the Ile Saint Louis (then the Ile Notre-Dame or the Ile aux Vaches because of the grazing land thereon), on the bosom of the river. Paris may have contained as many as a million persons if the faubourgs were counted, and undoubtedly half a million in her central quarters. In any case, even as today, Paris belonged to the world, and everybody wanted to be there at the beginning of the seventeenth century, just as they had in the Middle Ages. In Paris one lived life fully in an atmosphere that combined both universality and anonymity; and all of this in spite of the mud and debris of her streets, the smell of her open sewers, the number of her beggars, and the noise of her wandering peddlers. The city was still girded by the walls built in the fourteenth century, but they were crumbling and the area of the metropolis increased by one third during the first part of the seventeenth century.

Paris at this time had three major divisions — the *Cité* on the island which was marked by the cathedral of Notre Dame and the Palais de Justice, the *Ville* to the north, and the *Université* to the south.* There were several faubourgs outside the city, among them Saint Germain, Saint Michel, Saint Honoré, and Saint Antoine. Saint Germain was a small city in itself, with indoor tennis courts, or *jeux de paume*, and other buildings that could easily be converted into theatres; and the famous Foire Saint Germain, with its variety of entertainment for all classes. The Foire Saint Germain had a definite influence upon the progress of the theatre during this period and also later in the century. Also, the Faubourg Saint Antoine turned out to be a very fertile piece of theatrical terrain.

Henry IV, who loved the city he had had such a hard time winning, evolved before his assassination a large plan for the beautification and urbanization of Paris. This comprised the creation of a number of fine squares, the building of beautiful *hôtels* (or town houses) by and for the important families

* These divisions were marked on seventeenth-century maps of Paris, though the limits between the city proper and the faubourgs were not sharply drawn.

of the realm, and the regularizing of all architecture. There were to be no plowed fields or marshes inside the walls; one of the dried-up and reclaimed areas became the well-known Marais quarter, popular for its theatres and other amusements during the century. Henry also had many ideas for constructing quays along the river and a building scheme of interlocking brick and stone for houses on the Ile de la Cité, a most effective design which is still visible in some of the structures on this island. The most notable result of the combination of brick and stone occurred in the buildings surrounding the almost perfect Place Royale, which was to become celebrated in song, story, and play.

Two of the most notable of Henry IV's physical reforms of Paris were the completion of the Pont Neuf across the western tip of the Ile de la Cité and the fashioning of the "triangular square," the Place Dauphine, on the island just east of the Pont Neuf — both of which regions became prime rendezvous for charlatans, herb and nostrum salesmen, and street entertainers of all kinds. The Pont Neuf was begun in 1578, according to the plans of the great Renaissance architect and designer, Androuet du Cerceau, and with Henry III laying the first stone. Henry IV completed the splendid and stable structure in 1604 and its durability is indicated by the French expression of solid well-being, "se porter comme le Pont Neuf." The bridge was not encumbered with houses, as previous wooden ones had been, and gave an open view of the river. It also had sidewalks on both sides, with little shops and tooth-pullers (painless, in theory) and dealers in old books. Everybody loved it and walked back and forth across it; there was a saying during the century that at any hour of the day on the Pont Neuf could be seen "a monk, a white horse, and a prostitute." And the mountebanks never lacked for an audience to listen to their spirited harangues.

In 1607 Henry IV handed over to Achille de Harlay, the first president of the Parlement de Paris, the triangular strip of terrain between the Palais de Justice and the Pont Neuf for the creation of a new "square," with uniform and regularized houses around its sides. It was called the Place Dauphine in honor of the future Louis XIII, then six years of age. Some remnants of the original houses still stand, though the greater part of this construction was torn away in the nineteenth century to reveal the new façade of the Palais de Justice. In the seventeenth century the Place Dauphine overflowed with crowds and was the favorite stamping ground of one of the town's most famous entertainers and *opérateurs*, Tabarin. Right in the middle of the Pont Neuf, overlooking the Place Dauphine, was erected in 1615 the statute of Henry IV sitting on a horse of bronze. It was the first statue set up in the city for the glorification of a mortal, and none was more deserving of it. The lusty Vert Galant must have enjoyed looking out across the Pont Neuf to the Place Dauphine and watching the raucous and noisy goings-on of the people he loved.

Louis XIII, with the approval of his *conseil* in 1611, proceeded to carry on the renovation of the city begun by his father. He wished to extend the walls, which were never finished as such but became some of the present-day boulevards. Richelieu obtained the terrain for what was to be the Palais Cardinal, and many streets in this sector of the *Ville* were opened up. The Marais quarter * was further developed by turning some of the vegetable gardens into building lots and the Marais thus continued its evolution into a fashionable section of Paris, with its fine *hôtels*, a few theatres, and an occasional house of ill-repute. The city went on growing, even though the royal *conseil* tried to stop it on the theory that too many people were hard to govern and that the disposal of garbage was already too much of a problem. However, the building of the Pont Marie and the proposed Pont de la Tournelle were aimed at opening up the Ile Saint Louis for houses where before there had been cows grazing and a few fields under cultivation.

There were over five hundred streets in Paris during Louis

* For a fuller description of the Marais quarter, see Chapter V.

XIII's time, but there were only twenty-four major sewage drains and these were usually stopped up and smelly. The streets were more than full during the day with foot and carriage traffic, and street vendors who blocked them with displays of their wares. There were no street numbers, but every variety of sign was hung out, all of which gave a picturesque but cluttered appearance and made an awful banging when the wind blew. Paris was not a safe place to wander about in at night, although the bourgeois were supposed to hang out lanterns in front of their houses as darkness came on. This frequently was not done and, in any event, the candles burned out shortly after midnight. Under these conditions there was good reason for not having theatrical entertainment after dark. The Guet, or Night Watch, patrolled the city after sundown, but there were many robberies and killings in the small hours before dawn. It was impossible for the thirty-two horsemen and two hundred archers on foot to answer every call for help when the city became stygian as the lanterns burned to blackness. In the seventeenth century the Night Watch was particularly busy on ceremonial days, days of the fair, and days of the big open markets.

Horses and their riders had always been the enemy of pedestrians in the narrow city streets. To the horsemen were added in the sixteenth century the carriages of the nobles, which were impressive but dangerously cumbersome. They bumped into everybody and everything, and tangled in their own wheels. The Maréchal de Bassompierre, favorite of Henry IV and fashionable man about town, describes in his *Mémoires* an incident that took place in Paris in January 1611: "The Prince de Conty and the Comte de Soissons, his brother, got into a quarrel because their carriages, in passing each other, had collided and their coachmen had had a fight." [6] There were also sedan chairs with their porters, and then a certain monsieur Sauvage, living at the Hôtel Saint-Fiacre, began to offer carriages for rental — which came to be called *fiacres*.

By 1617 *chaises à porteurs* were available for rent and before the middle of the century some clever fellow had put wheels on them. The streets of Paris were completely cosmopolitan in their collection of noise, dirt, and entertainment. In the general hubbub, it was hard to keep any clear distinction of social rank or class. There was something for everybody, and everybody was there.

The Seine, in addition to being a dumping place for garbage and something of a community sewer, was an important avenue of traffic. It was constantly filled with all kinds of boats, which brought in a large portion of the city's supplies. The limited number of quays were often so jammed that footbridges for unloading cargo had to be built across the boats into the river. Paris ate and drank well in the time of Louis XIII, but the question of getting food and drink to demanding gullets was not of the simplest. In any case, there was no lack of inns, cabarets, and restaurants. The cabaret of La Pomme de Pin, rue de la Juiverie on the Cité, made its place in literature, and the restaurant of La Boisselière near the Louvre was both famous and expensive. Paris consumed a great deal of meat — freshly slaughtered beeves, cooked pork products for sale on the streets, and a lot of salt herring as well as fresh (at least moderately fresh) fish. Vegetables, salads (which were supposed to calm the ardors of Venus), and cheeses were in demand, but there was a dearth of fruits. At any rate, the population of Paris spent a large portion of its time in the streets and public squares, eating, drinking, and seeking diversion. It was a propitious setting for the development of a professional theatre.

The great public market of Paris, Les Halles, had since the fifteenth century been associated with the production of plays. It was there that a fool's-play or farce might be given by a group of semiprofessional actors in some unoccupied stall. In the Middle Ages merchants brought their produce to the three gates of Paris and sold it. During the twelfth century Louis VI set aside some fields a little northeast of the Châtelet for a market on Mondays, Wednesdays, and Saturdays. It became so popular that houses were built around it, with streets appropriately named — rue de la Fromagerie, rue de la Cordonnerie, and so on. Philippe-Auguste built a splendid hall, the Halle au Blé, for the sale of grain. It was still there during the reign of Louis XIII. Louis IX built two more *halles*, for fresh fish and for salt fish. Thus there were three halls, or Les Halles. By the early seventeenth century, everything was being sold in this central market — candles, clothes, shoes, and the like as well as food — and the noise and crowds were something to hear and see. The wholesale operations of Les Halles began about three o'clock in the morning with the arrival of produce from outside the city, and lasted until around eight. From then on there were retail sales at higher figures, with much bartering and bickering over the price of a limp fish or a pair of second-hand shoes. Many of the costumes used by the early dramatic companies were obtained from the old-clothes dealers on the rues de la Petite or Grande Friperie, or on the rue de la Tonnellerie, all adjacent to Les Halles. Such garments were likely to be a little less than clean, and no pleasure to the sense of smell. But there was always excitement around Les Halles, plenty to eat, and much rough amusement.

Much of the selling in Les Halles, particularly of fish and vegetables, was done by women, and these *femmes des Halles* were a noisy and rough outfit of fishwives. Their language was their own, and in heaping vituperation upon a non-purchasing customer, it was both colorful and incisive. An edict was passed late in the sixteenth century aimed at making them treat with a little more consideration "damoiselles et bourgeoises" who came shopping, but it was to little avail. The *femmes des Halles* continued to heap insults upon a client who refused to buy, and left no doubt as to their estimate of his or her ancestry and social standing. These tirades, however, had a certain artistry, and attracted the attention of any and every connoisseur of invective. They also had their influence upon the harangues of charlatans and street entertainers, and upon some spirited passages of the farces which were so popular in the early part of the seventeenth century. The whole district around Les Halles, in fact, was steeped in a tradition of dramatic skits and players since medieval times, either at an open spot on the corner of a street or in an empty covered market. And a little more than two blocks north of Les Halles stood the first theatre to be used by the budding professional companies, the famous and dilapidated Hôtel de Bourgogne.

EARLY ACTORS
AND THEIR COMPANIES

PARIS AND ITS ENVIRONS BELONGED almost completely to the Italian actors and their companies until very nearly 1600. The fortunes of the Italians, though not the primary concern here, will be tied up with those of French actors well into the eighteenth century; therefore, they should have a brief review, a review that will go a little past Henry IV's reign to around 1615. It was natural that the two Medici queens, Catherine and Marie, should enjoy theatrical entertainment in their own language and consequently encourage troups of Italian actors to come to the French Court. With royal backing, the Italians were gradually able to lease halls and give performances open to the public at large. The remarkable thing is that Frenchmen all over France, and Parisian audiences in particular, in spite of linguistic difficulties, seemed very much delighted with the imported plays. The reason must have been the Italians' ability at pantomime, the reappearance over and over again of a series of stock characters, and the spirit of slapstick and buffoonery that pervaded all the *commedia dell' arte*. In the sad closing years of the sixteenth century Frenchmen did not mind having transported into their land a touch of something that was light and gay.

It was around the middle of the sixteenth century that Italian entertainers began to divert royal audiences in France, and one of the earliest diversions was a play presented by Italian actors at Lyon in 1548 for the entrée into the city of

Henry II and Catherine de' Medici, a splendorous occasion well described by chroniclers of the time. Catherine's continued interest encouraged the *commedia dell' arte*, said the theatrical historian Beauchamps in the eighteenth century, and thus the Italians "have pretended to be our masters." However, no real troupes came up from Italy before the time of Charles IX. In 1571 a well-organized company of Italian comedians performed for the duc de Nevers in Paris — probably the first time that such a group had appeared in the French capital — and a little later in the same year *I Gelosi* ("The Jealous of Pleasing Ones") performed for a royal audience at Nogent-le-Roi, a château near Chartres. This first troupe of *I Gelosi* was not permitted by Parlement to bring their comedies into Paris and charge admission for them, so they wandered south before the end of the year. It is likely that this was the troupe that was giving the *commedia dell' arte* in Lyon during the month of December 1571. Other Italian comedians came to France in 1572 and with them was the good actor, Alberto Ganassa. They gave their repertory in Paris — Parlement evidently allowed them entry — and Charles IX hired them to come to Blois for a series of "comedies and acrobatics." [1]

Henry III saw the new company of *I Gelosi* in Italy in 1574 and was very much pleased with them. They finally crossed into France in 1576, were seized in the south by the Huguenots, ransomed by Henry III, and appeared at Blois in January 1577. This was the group that aroused the ire of Pierre de l'Estoile and attracted so much attention in Paris. They were giving their gay repertory at the Hôtel de Bourbon in September 1577, but disappeared shortly thereafter despite the favor of Henry III. During 1578–1579 there is evidence that Catherine de' Medici was amused by some Italian actors in Nérac, and their offerings were paid for by that good Protestant, Henry of Navarre. An interesting tidbit which shows that another troupe of Italians was in Paris in 1583 is the record of the Confrérie (or Brotherhood) de la Passion, the sole masters of the Hôtel de Bourgogne, being privileged to seize the belongings of one Battista Lazzaro (evidently the leader of the troupe) as security for a half-crown due weekly to the Confrérie. This was a standard amount that the Confrérie was permitted to collect from dramatic companies performing outside the Hôtel de Bourgogne, and was a piece of racketeering on the part of the Brotherhood of the Passion that had official sanction.[2]

Another Italian troupe was reported to have come in 1588 to amuse what remained of the House of Valois, but it was not a healthy time to be in France. About ten more years were required before Henry IV had restored order, and quite understandably during this decade there was little dramatic activity of any sort in the land. The Hôtel de Bourgogne was practically a dramatic desert, the Confrérie seldom rented it or put on plays in it themselves, and there was talk of turning it into a *collège* for the Jesuits. By 1598, as a result of Henry IV's vigorous program of rehabilitation, conditions had begun to improve and the Confrérie could rent again the Hôtel de Bourgogne to a variety of troupes that made their way to Paris. An indication of this is seen in the decree from the court of the Châtelet on April 28, 1599, prohibiting a troupe of "Italians who call themselves the King's comedians" or any other actors from performing in any place except the Hôtel de Bourgogne. In vivid evidence of the Confrérie de la Passion's monopoly, a lease was signed between the Italians and the Confrérie on this date. In December 1599, Henry IV invited Arlequin — there were many Arlequins in the history of the *commedia dell' arte* but this one was the famous Tristano Martinelli — and his company to come to France. This troupe was patronized in Italy by the Duke of Mantua and was called the *Accesi*. Henry IV was delighted with the gaudy antics and familiarities of Tristano Martinelli, and felt that he did much to relieve the boredom of the new Italian

Queen of France, Marie de' Medici. Arlequin was audacious enough to give Henry the title of "Secret Secretary of the Secret Cabinet of the Madame Marie de' Medici" as well as the more practical one of "Grand Treasurer of the Italian Comedians." Arlequin and his company, possibly because their repertory had dulled or on account of recall from their patrons at home, seem to have been back in Italy before the end of 1601.[3]

A new Italian troupe visited the French Court in 1603, having been invited there by the King and Queen. This organization included in its personnel the notable husband and wife team of Francesco and Isabella Andreini. The wife made the name of Isabelle a famous one even in French comedy, and she is also most likely the central figure in the early seventeenth-century painting of Italian comedians now at the Musée Carnavalet (see Figure 1). The company first played at Fontainebleau, where they were well paid by Their Majesties for some thirty-six days sojourn in the atmosphere of the Court. Then the Italians performed from the end of 1603 until April 1604 at the Hôtel de Bourgogne. After these months in Paris they left for Italy, with letters of safe conduct from the King. Isabella, however, died in Lyon in June 1604, where she was given a fine funeral, a courtesy and a tribute rather unexpectedly extended at this time to an actress. A contemporary historian said that if she had lived in Greece in the great epoch of the theatre, statues would have been erected in her honor.[4]

The comedians of the Duke of Mantua returned to France in 1608 under the leadership of the actor Fritellino. The King and Marie de' Medici wanted to see Arlequin again, but the Duke of Mantua said he was too old and that one Cola would be sent in Arlequin's place. The troupe traveled through a terrible winter to arrive at the French Court in early February with their baggage and gaiety, and Henry IV was accused of not allowing the company to present their repertory in

Paris before a general and paying public. However, a lease was signed February 16, 1608, between the Confrérie and Fritellino's company, who later in May objected to giving a free loge to the official *contrôleur des comédiens*, since the Confrérie already had six loges at their disposal and it was suggested that the *contrôleur* occupy one of these. The Italians must have been drawing good houses in Paris for such an argument to arise over one loge. The popularity of the acrobat Cola is shown by many references to him in unexpected spots. Pierre de l'Estoile put him in a poem and the Dauphin Louis used his name as a password. An idea of Cola's technique may be derived from the description of him when the company performed at Fontainebleau on July 3, 1608: Cola was "that admirable acrobat who climbed straight up a ladder that was not leaning against anything, and he fell its full length doing somersaults without getting a scratch." The Duke of Mantua himself came to spend three weeks in France during this period, and, in the midst of much wining and dining, received many compliments on his troupe. It returned to Italy in 1608, with the good wishes of Their Majesties and the hope on the part of Marie de' Medici that it would return the following year.[5]

Something of a time gap now occurred in the visits of the Italians to the French Court and the French capital, though in January 1610, young Louis in his own quarters saw "an Italian named Simon" play five or six characters all by himself — and Marie de' Medici had her son put on a costume at times to "dance Pantalone" before her. The whole theatrical as well as the real world was undoubtedly made somber by the assassination of Henry IV in May 1610. But Marie de' Medici could not forget the incomparable Arlequin, Tristano Martinelli, and began in 1611 a long correspondence that eventually brought him back to France. In the meantime, a lease of March 9, 1612, shows that another Italian troupe under Jehan Alfieri was at the Hôtel de Bourgogne and alternated for several weeks there with some French actors. Finally the favorite Arlequin of Marie de' Medici reëntered France in 1613, and picked up some nice profits in Savoy and Lyon on his way north. His troupe first performed at Fontainebleau and then rented the Hôtel de Bourgogne from October 1613, to the end of March 1614, for twelve hundred livres — a long lease and indicative of a profitable season in Paris. During 1614 Louis XIII also helped with the finances and gave Arlequin three hundred livres a month to play for him. Shorter leases on the Hôtel de Bourgogne were taken out by the Italians in 1614, but they left for Italy in July of that year, after a most successful invasion of France. No other Italian troupes of actors crossed the Alps into France until after 1620, so this first phase of Italian influence in the French public theatre may be said to have ended before 1615.

The *commedia dell' arte* did not mean an "art comedy" but simply a situation and improvized comedy produced by a guild of actors, with the same characters used over and over. The appeal that it had for the French is worth a moment's glance. Arlequin (Arlecchino), the agile servant of Pantalone and clothed in a clown's patchwork costume with black mask and wooden sword (see Figures 2 and 3), was the favorite in France. He became the suitor of the charming Colombine, whom he had taken away from the pathetically appealing Pedrolino, or Pierrot. There were other characters like Scapin, the blustering Capitaine Matamore, and the clowning and slapstick specialists, the Zanni. Arlequin, with an added finesse and turn of wit around the end of the sixteenth century (probably as a result of the interpretation given him by Tristano Martinelli), took on the features that were to mark the later Arlequins all over Europe. In any case, the French enjoyed the *commedia dell' arte*. An eighteenth-century critic, who was still able to see the Italians in Paris in his day, described their early success as follows: "The Italians introduced pantomimes in their plays, so that like the ancient *histrions*, they made a mixture of speeches and of gesticulations and of acrobatic twists — which first attracted to them large crowds, but public order could not allow their performances for a very long time." [6]

A most complete story of an Italian company's offerings is found in the travel log of two students from Bâle, Felix and Thomas Platter, who were journeying through southern France at the end of the sixteenth century. They were in Avignon at the end of 1598 and saw there many "very agreeable comedies," usually given by Italian companies, especially "that of Zan Bragetta, composed of four actors and two actresses." This group gave their repertory in "the hall of the indoor tennis court which they had rented for several weeks." Their "very gay pieces, performed on a scaffold stage, lasted sometimes until nightfall, so that they were obliged to finish them by the light of candles." All sorts of clever tricks were done: birds and animals were imitated most realistically, and sometimes an actress' head would be cut off right in front of everybody! Pantalone and the Zanni were particularly good, and the language of the plays was a "mixed jargon of Italian and Provençal." When the rental of a hall was too expensive, the Italians set up their trestles in the public square, where they performed "before a thousand spectators." The show began right after lunch, with a comedy that lasted an hour or two, and then the Zanni and the Doctor (Pantalone) got talking about a lot of "remedies" that were in a big box. After considerable discussion of the amazing qualities of these remedies, they finally decided to sell them — very cheap, in view of the splendid qualities of the splendid audience. The spectators then passed up their handkerchiefs with a few coins therein for the purchase of the incredible medicaments, and the actresses might possibly send back to certain favored gentlemen little *billets*, "to set the time and place for a rendezvous." After some days, the audience became smaller and smaller, so the actors moved on to another town — "but they rarely became rich, since their money was more quickly spent than made." [7]

A year or so later the Italians were doing some remarkable things in Paris: "In this month of June 1601, there was seen, at the Hôtel de Bourgogne where Arlequin was playing, a sight as rare and marvelous as could be imagined; it was a young Italian girl about thirteen years of age, who for a full quarter of an hour, danced to the steady cadence of violins, on a cord (the cord was of the thickness of an arm) stretched very high in the air, moving backward and forward, with as much calmness as if she had been in the middle of a hall." This act was followed by that of two young men, twenty-five and thirty years of age, who did all sorts of tricks like hanging by their toes, "and several other things terrifying and incomprehensible to those who saw them." At the same time, "in the courtyard of the Palais" another Italian attracted a crowd by pulling teeth painlessly and by running a sword through his body without injury since he covered the wound immediately with a special "oil." The doctors of Paris chased him away from the Palais — this would be the Palais de Justice on the Ile de la Cité — but he went back to his house "behind the Hôtel de Bourgogne" and carried on his demonstrations. And such is a story taken from the *Mémoires-Journaux* of Pierre de l'Estoile, who saw all this and who had so scathingly denounced the idea of *I Gelosi* being allowed to appear in Paris a few years earlier. [8]

Arlequin, in the personality given him by Tristano Martinelli, could be very familiar with kings, if the story told about his swiping Henry IV's chair has any truth in it: "Arlequin and his troupe came to Paris at that time,* and when he went to pay his respects to the King, he chose the moment so very well — being a very clever fellow — that when His Majesty was out of his chair, Arlequin took possession of it and speaking as though he was the King said [to Henry IV]:

* The time was not given but it was the early 1600's.

'Very well, Arlequin, you and your troupe have come here to amuse me; I am delighted that you have, I promise to protect you and give you a good pension, and other things too.' The King did not contradict any of Arlequin's remarks, but said to him: 'You have been playing my role for some time; suppose you let me do it for a while." In view of the bluff good nature of Henry IV, it would not have been impossible for such an incident to take place.[9] Frenchmen knew the Italian actors both in France and in Italy. Bassompierre on the way north from Rome stopped over in Florence where he did some riding, went to a few weddings, and "saw some comedies" — and undoubtedly some charming ladies. Louis XIII knew the *commedia dell' arte* from his earliest childhood, and one entry from the good Doctor Héroard's diary in 1609 would suggest that the young Dauphin saw an Italian comedy at the public theatre when the Italians were not, according to the records, supposed to be in Paris. Héroard says that on Sunday, February 8, 1609, young Louis was "taken to the Hôtel de Bourgogne * at three-forty-five; he began to laugh loudly and said: 'Monsieur de Souvré [his companion], I am laughing so that everybody will think that I understand Italian.' He was brought back at six-thirty." In any event, Louis XIII saw some Italian comedy in 1613, and a great deal of it in 1614 — January 15, 21, 26, 30, February 4, 6, and June 26, 28, 29 — according to Héroard's *Journal*. There is no doubt that Louis found relaxation from the affairs of state in the gay triflings of the Italian comedians.[10]

By the end of the first years of the seventeenth century the Italians had done a great deal to spread a taste for the theatre all over France, and in this they rendered a service to the French actors as well as to themselves. They had become so well known that the prologuist Bruscambille could make

* For further details on young Louis' visits to the Hôtel de Bourgogne, see Chapter VIII.

references in his harangues to "those who pay a *teston* to see the Italians dance the sarabande at the Hôtel de Bourgogne," or a satiric poet like Claude d'Esternod could say "je fay de l'arlequin" or "I twist my nose *comme arlequin*" (both times with a lower case *arlequin*) — and there was no question of misunderstanding. Or, in a slightly earlier poetic satire, *Les Comédiens de la Cour*, the King could be directed without explanation to look around his Court for a Pedrolino, a Pantalone, some Zanni, a Capitaine, and an Isabelle, all of whom would "do better than the Italians" and would not "cost a sou." The Italians, then, had left their imprint as personalities and as dramatic characters upon France by the end of the reign of Henry IV. The seventeenth-century writer, Charles Sorel, said that Frenchmen liked them because of their "graceful use of a foreign language," their "simple and absurd actions," their ability to make an audience laugh even in the midst of a serious play, and their numerous gestures which made a piece understandable even when the language was not. The French actors most certainly owed them a debt for helping clear the way for a public theatre.[11]

Though there were no "acteurs de profession" in the real sense of the word in France during the late Middle Ages and the first part of the Renaissance, a pick-up group of amateur or semiprofessional performers would at times receive some sort of recompense for their services. This was most likely to happen in the provinces where the medieval dramatic forms, both serious and comic, aroused community interest long after the more sophisticated Parisian had become bored with all the older plays except the farce. The city of Dijon, for example, put on a Biblical play, the *Histoire d'Assuaire et de la Royne Esther* (a subject later treated by Montchrétien and Racine), in 1497 with the city fathers assuming financial responsibility for the representation. They gave fifteen francs to the actors, whoever they were, and as a further inducement to bring out their histrionic best, set aside for the performers "two puncheons of red wine which cost eight francs." It is not recorded whether the "vin vermeil" was consumed before or after the show. In Amiens in 1499 the town gave to "sire Pierre Bonnart, a priest, who in the Lord's play did the role of Lucifer and to his companions who played the roles of the devils in the same play, thirty-five sous, *pour boire.*" The city of Metz to the northeast gave three plays — a mystery, a miracle, and a morality — in 1513 with a considerable display of fire, boiling cauldrons, and hail. The actors were paid thirty-three francs for it. It is more than clear from a number of provincial records that well on into the sixteenth century municipalities rewarded the somewhat casual groups of actors with money or wine, or both, for their operations. The amateurs would often go from town to town in the same region and there were courtesy exchanges of dramatics between "companions" of two adjacent municipal areas such as, for illustration, between Abbeville and Amiens in Picardy. Farces were likely to be given more frequently than the serious plays, though some names of the performers in all genres have come down. One interesting detail is in the archives of Amiens, where in the early 1500's twenty-two sous and six farthings were given to "six companions and a *fille* for having played several gay pieces before Messieurs." This must have been a series of special showings for the town council, and is one of the first references to an actress appearing with a dramatic group.[12]

The city authorities had a problem in keeping the audience under control, even when the play was a community project. The French audience was probably boisterous from the earliest Middle Ages just as it can be today. At a fifteenth-century Passion Play in Metz, with visitors around from Germany and other countries, the police had to take vigorous measures to prevent the noise of the spectators: ten "livres de Metz" fine, whether the offender was a man or woman; or, in place of the fine, if the offender had no money, a dipping in the town sewer. At a performance of a farce in the Place des Cordeliers of Dijon in 1511, a "certain Girart" played his part so badly that a "young girl of marriageable age" laughed at him fit to kill. She laughed so loudly and with such derision that Girart's wife, who heard the whole thing, gave the girl a sound thrashing — all of which caused a very bitter lawsuit. Things were so bad around the middle of the sixteenth century in the cathedral town of Beauvais that the Cardinal de Châtillon, Bishop of Beauvais, issued an edict against clerics being present at any sort of dramatic production — and this included listening to tavern singers. One of the most raucous affairs happened in Bordeaux in 1578 during the festival of Saint John the Baptist. The Biblical scene of John the Baptist and the Saviour baptizing each other was enacted on a stage built up in one of the city squares, with the Apostles assembled below the stage: Saint Peter with the keys, Saint Paul with a sword, and Saint Andrew with a cross. By this date the whole serious ceremony was performed by laymen — carpenters and artisans — and they had given to it a tone of satire and burlesque. However, people came "in great multitude to see the spectacle, in which they took great pleasure because of the grimacing and gestures of the crude actors." The audience, obviously, was just as lacking in dignity as were the performers, and also contained some unbelievers who played their part in the following episode: "Several priests and holy men, desiring to see this baptism, took their places right next to the stage; the heretics [of the audience] by means of money handed over to these rascally actors persuaded them to drench the priests and holy men thoroughly with the full buckets of water that had been prepared for the mystery play, and all this with mockery and laughter." It is easy to understand why the Mystery of Saint John the Baptist, having descended to this undignified and farcical level, was abolished in Bordeaux in the year 1578.[13]

The colleges of Paris had given plays in the Middle Ages and continued to do so into later centuries. The students at times also would mix in with the medieval acting organizations like that of the lawclerks around the Palais de Justice, the Basoche; or with the fool's-play group, the Enfants sans Souci, and with the more august and monopolistic Confrérie de la Passion. The activities of the collegians, as in any age, were hard to regulate, but in 1515 the Parlement de Paris passed on to the principals of the various colleges the responsibility for preventing their students' giving any play attacking established authority — "any farce, sottie, or other type of *jeu* against the honor of the King." If such were done, there was official "threat of punishment." In any case, students all over France enjoyed getting together to put on shows and they must have been encouraged to do so by their masters because the boys became quite good performers. During vacations they even wandered around in groups resembling summer stock companies. The city of Poitiers was entertained in the month of July 1581, by a group of "schoolboys performing tragedies, comedies, and farces." They gave their repertory from a Wednesday through Sunday, and "they left two or three days later." Such barnstorming must have helped in creating a clientele for the professionals. The story has been told many times of Etienne Jodelle's *Cléopâtre*, the first tragedy to be written in France in imitation of the ancients, and its performance in 1552 by Jodelle and his student friends. The King, Henry II, liked it so much that he gave Jodelle a bag of *écus*, and at the Collège de Boncourt performance people hung out the windows to see it, with Jodelle himself possibly playing the title role. The boys apparently had a good time indulging in histrionics over the tragic fates of Cleopatra and Marc Antony — who, incidentally, got on stage only as a ghost. Ronsard and other friends of Jodelle gave him a big party afterward in the little town of Arcueil outside Paris, with much wining and dining and a goat for a prize, in the best traditions of the festivals to Dionysus in ancient Athens. The whole thing had been a great success, much more so than an earlier presentation in Latin of Terence's *Andria* by schoolboys in the Cour de l'Evêché of Metz, when the audience, irritated by the foreign language,[14] chased the youngsters off stage.

As late as Garnier's tragicomedy, *Bradamante*, in 1582 it was assumed that plays borrowed from or in imitation of antiquity would be performed under the direction of the colleges and by the *collégiens*. Garnier indicates himself in a preliminary discourse at the head of *Bradamante* that in his time theatrical pieces belonged to whoever wanted to put them on and that normally it was in the colleges that they were staged. This is an interesting commentary in view of the fact that the first professional companies most likely put *Bradamante* in their repertory for at least two reasons: it could be staged without paying anything to the author, and a heroine who could ride and joust the way Bradamante did around Charlemagne's court must have struck popular fancy. For their part the schoolboys did not neglect the exciting story of Bradamante entering the lists against her beloved Roger who was disguised as another man. The Collège de Chabeuil in Dauphiné presented in 1602 an *Histoire de Bradamante* — probably an adaptation of the Garnier work — for which the principal of the college received from the municipality eleven crowns, thirty sous. Six sous of this sum were designated as payment for "the beards of Aymon and Charlemagne." The schoolboys gave plays all over France * up to the seventeenth century — in Rouen, in Besançon, in Aix-en-Provence, and elsewhere. They gave a *Clytemnestra*, of unknown authorship, at Besançon in 1580 and one is inclined to wonder what beardless youth essayed the portrayal of the mightiest and most ruthless woman of Greek tragedy. In any event, the

---

* The same was true of French schools in Holland, despite opposition from the Reformed Church.

schoolboys must have had more of a public than just proud
fathers and doting mothers. From the archives of Aix-en-
Provence of June 1, 1608, comes the statement that "after
dinner on the festival of Corpus Christi, the students staged
a comedy to add to the entertainment, to amuse the public,
and to fill in the emptiness of the day." And the regents of the
college were given by the town of Aix some sixty livres for
"representations during the year." Also, there must have been
competition for the various roles in these schoolboy productions. In a Biblical tragedy on Cain and Abel presented in
Rouen, all the parts had been assigned, much to the irritation
of an important lady whose son had been left out of the cast.
In order to appease her he was allowed to portray "the blood
of Abel." Therefore, "he was put in a red bag of crimson
satin, rolled on from the back of the stage, shouting 'Vengeance, Vengeance.' " [15]

One of the attractions of the plays staged in the colleges was
the fact that there was no admission charge, and seldom was
a collection plate of any type passed among the spectators.
The dramatic offerings sponsored by the pedagogues and
classical scholars, however, were likely to be of the serious
variety and maybe even in Latin — which could have scared
away a popular audience that had been brought up on the
medieval mystery plays. And, too, the novelty of the rather
stilted and formalized Renaissance tragedy introduced by
Jodelle wore off after some fifteen years or so, certainly as
far as the nobility was concerned. They returned to other
diversions and were soon occupied with the Wars of Religion.
But a free show in the colleges was a free show, without the
restriction of the Confrérie de la Passion in their Hôtel de
Bourgogne. The production of these plays, even if directed
by a professor, must have helped to build a public for the
later serious drama of the seventeenth century.

The Jesuits in their schools did their part in keeping alive
the idea that plays should be staged and not just read. Their

1. *Painting of the Italian comedians*

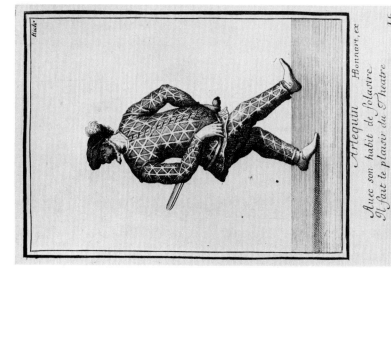

HABIT D'ARLEQUIN ANCIEN *Boullar Sculp.*

Comme il est represente dans un livre imprimé du
temps d'Henry quatre.

2. *An Arlequin of Henry IV's time*

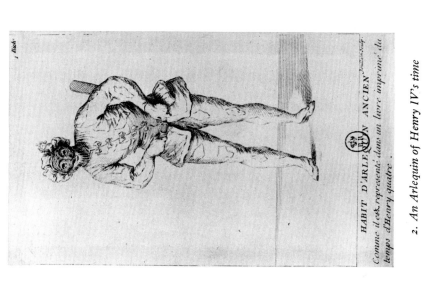

15

Arlequin   Bonnart, ex

Auec son habit de Jelousie.
Il fait le plaisir du Theatre

3. *Another early Arlequin*

whole program of instruction was clever and suave, and aimed at giving their pupils — who came mainly from the upper classes — easy good manners, a literary culture based on antiquity, and a graceful facility with words. Plays were produced, therefore, to assist in training the memory to recall beautiful verses and the tongue to release them in the later world of society. Henry IV sought toward the end of the sixteenth century to revise the other schools in France to bring their program a little nearer that of the Jesuits. The Jesuits had opened their first school in Paris in 1564, with the permission of Parlement and despite the opposition of the Sorbonne. They made it clear that they wanted to vivify religion, avoid the abstractions of the Sorbonne in their instruction, and to make study a pleasure. They shortly produced at the Collège de Clermont a play about Herod, which may not have vivified religion but which must have trained the memory. In their *Ratio Studiorum*, the program of instruction set up for all their schools in Europe, the Jesuits' policy on play-acting was stated. Both comedies and tragedies might be presented if they were in Latin and decent in tone. There were to be no female characters, and no performances inside churches. No priestly vestments could be used, and the production was limited to four hours. Some of these limitations were irregularly observed, since at the college of Pont-à-Mousson a tragedy on Joan of Arc was presented in French in 1580. Musical interludes were later permitted and pastorals were performed under Jesuit auspices when the form became popular early in the seventeenth century. Unfortunately, very few of the Jesuit plays have come down because they were infrequently published. But Jesuit performances could be quite elaborate, and they must have been well attended, since according to plan separate ones were given for *Dames* and *Messieurs*. In Pau the Jesuits used a theatre with a curtain, and costuming in many cases could be rather ornate. On occasion they would set up a stage in a courtyard, or by the invitation of some noble would perform in his château. It will be remembered that young Louis XIII went at times to see "les Jésuites," and at least once saw them in Rouen where they continued the dramatic tradition already begun by a principal of the Collège de Bons Enfants in the 1590's. The Jesuits were, if not wandering actors, at least mobile actors. They helped, too, in creating a public for the struggling professionals as they began their difficult migrations over France.[16]

The earliest professional was most likely a lone wolf, and a descendant of the medieval *jongleur* who had wandered around from court to court doing his tricks and reciting from his extensive stock of stories and dramatic monologues. He was very probably a street entertainer who hoped to draw a few precarious coppers from the passers-by in return for his stunts and patter. Seventeenth-century men of the theatre like the Abbé d'Aubignac and Bruscambille called him a *bâteleur* as distinguished from a *comédien*, and it was a "pile of little bâteleurs usurping the quality of comédien" who brought the theatre into disrepute. In antiquity, says d'Aubignac, the mimes (the equivalent of the French *bâteleurs*) were held in low regard, while the legitimate actor, the *comédien*, was highly esteemed as he would be today if the stigma of these "lost and debauched souls" did not carry over to him. The *bâteleurs*, who were splendid acrobats, came in a large degree from Picardy. Whatever their origin, they were agile performers: *a bâteleur* from Meaux early in the sixteenth century in the city of Metz stretched his cords, banged on his big tambourine to assemble a crowd, and danced on a rope with feet weighted on balls and his eyes banded. Another *bâteleur* on the same program of events slid on his head down a rope from the tower of the cathedral to a post on the ground, just "as though he were an eagle or a buzzard." In a slightly higher category would be Jean de Pontalais, one of the first named performers of the sixteenth century and one who put on his plays in the district of Les Halles. It was said

by the storyteller Bonaventure des Périers that Jean de Pontalais was making so much noise with his tambourine outside
the church of Saint Eustache that the curate came out and
smashed the tambourine — whereupon Jean looped it around
the curate's head. Other rather detached professionals whose
names got into print during the sixteenth century were Jean
Serre, described by the poet, Clément Marot, as an excellent
player of farces, and Chasteauvieux who amused Charles IX
and Henry III.[17]

A few troupes of actors which came near to being professional in organization if not in performance began to circulate
in the provinces of France after 1550. Little is known about
them; they may well have been remnants — diehard extro-
verts deeply bitten by the bug of the theatre — of the medieval semiprofessional societies in Paris. Members of the
Confrérie de la Passion of Paris before 1550 at times went to
areas outside the city to produce a mystery for hire. This was
done by "poor fellows who worked for pay," and such a type
of operation may have started the smaller groups of professionals on their way. In any case, a troupe of comedians came
into Rouen in October 1556, and set up shop "in the jeu de
paume where hangs the sign of the Port-de-Salut." The archives of Rouen have retained a record of their personnel and
their activities. They were under the direction of Pierre Lepardonneur, who had as actors in his company Toussaint
Langlois, Nicolas Lecomte (could he have been a relative of
the famous Valleran le Conte, later at the Hôtel de Bourgogne?), Jacques Langlois, Nicolas Transcart, and Robert
Hurel. They also had with them "three children who sang."
The first two days' performances went off pleasantly, but on
the third day the play, the *Life of Jacob*, was interrupted and
the audience told by two police officers to retire. The audience had "paid for its seats" and raised a big hubbub about
the stopping of the show. Lepardonneur and his actors went
to the Palais de Justice and protested to the Parlement of

Rouen as follows: "Noble Sirs, since our occupancy of the Port-de-Salut up to the present moment we have conducted ourselves honorably and beyond criticism. We have made for the entertainment of the inhabitants of this city great expenditures for which we are still in debt; among other things, we have had to buy silk cloth, hangings and a quantity of other things for the decorations — which are not paid for but which would have been if we had not been interrupted. We beg you then, Noble Sirs, to permit us to finish our play, and we promise for the future not to have a tambourine or any other noise-making instrument sounded throughout the city; and also we will inform any person you may designate of the play we intend to give."

A fairer statement could scarcely be imagined, and the Parlement of Rouen not being automatically hostile to the theatre, it appointed a committee to look into the matter: "Since this is the first time [in Rouen] that a [dramatic] troupe has made its presentations in public for pay, the Court orders that brother Mathieu des Landes, from the district of Carmes, and Jehan Lambert, canon and master of the confessional of Notre-Dame, go examine the moralities and farces that the petitioners propose to perform." It will be noted what types of dramas were in Lepardonneur's repertory. The Committee appointed by Parlement made its report and Parlement rendered a decision: "It is permitted to the petitioners to carry on their productions as they have begun them, provided they stage their plays on Sunday only after Vespers and sound no tambourine or any other noise-making instrument to assemble the audience; and also provided they do not offer the farce, Le Retour de Mariage, and that all their plays up to their completion be performed decently and modestly. And when the said moralities are finished, it is forbidden to play any others without further permission." Lepardonneur evidently did well under these conditions, and obeyed all the edicts concerning censorship and noise-making. Unfortunately, the farce that was rejected has not been saved for posterity, but it probably was a tough morsel that deserved to be taken off the theatrical menu. Lepardonneur came back to Rouen in 1558 with three new actors — Nicolas Michel, called Martainville, Nicolas Roquevent, called Leboursier, and Jacques Caillart. This assuming of stage names was to be a common practice of later professionals. Rouen was disturbed in 1558 by a pestilence, religious problems, and general misery. Parlement therefore forbade the staging of farces and moralities in the city, because they led to "vain and useless expenditures." Lepardonneur and his aggregation thus left the town and it is doubtful — unless further digging in the archives brings up something new * — that any other French troupe of comedians visited Rouen during the sixteenth century.[18]

Other provincial cities had calls from wandering actors, but none left so intriguing a record as that of Lepardonneur in Rouen. On August 3, 1559, the city of Amiens gave authorization to "Roland Guibert and his companions to present moralities, farces, violins, and music, for no longer than ten days, on the condition that they perform first in the Council Chamber and that they submit the moralities for inspection at least one day before putting them on the stage." The farces seem to have been left out of the inspection, but it is hard to believe they did not need it. In September 1561, "Jehan Poignant, called abbé de la Lune, and his companions, players of tragedies, moralities, and farces" asked permission to entertain the citizens of Amiens. Did these fellows really produce a tragedy — and if so, what was its name and subject matter? The records omit such details. Other fragments of information, sometimes frustratingly small, are to be found here and there to add to our knowledge of the developing spirit of the theatre. The municipal magistrates of Dijon were asked in 1577 to treat kindly some "players of comedies" who wanted to perform there. Nothing further is known

---

* There is a possibility that Valleran le Conte was in Rouen in 1593.

about this company, whether it was well received or thrown out of the city — nor is much of anything on record concerning the theatre in Dijon until several decades later. In 1585, the consuls of Agen permitted one Guillaume Marteau and "his companion comedians to play some of their comedy" in the town "for eight days" if they did it "without any scandal." If things were not done in proper fashion, and this decree appears a trifle harsh, Marteau would have to answer "with his life and those of his companions." In 1609, when there were more companies of professionals moving about the land, the consuls of Agen had a chance to rent the city hall instead of a *jeu de paume* to some "comedians passing through this city." Such a rental would bring in enough money to fix the roof and repair the floor of the municipal building. Nevertheless, a citizens' committee — and their names are all listed — "opined one after the other" that it was not a good thing to permit "comedians or players of farces and dramatic trash to perform in the city hall, or any place else in the city, if it is possible to prevent them from doing it." A number of the inhabitants of Agen most obviously were not very fond of actors. On the other hand, the authorities of Beauvais were a trifle more generous toward nomadic entertainers in the early years of the seventeenth century. According to police regulations in Beauvais, rope dancers, marionnette manipulators, and comedians might come into the town and charge two farthings per person for their acts, "because it is necessary sometimes to offer something for the relaxation of the public." But everything had to be done with "much circumspection," and the performers could stay in the city only one or two weeks or "a month at most." All of which is rather liberal and somewhat different from earlier churchly and official attitudes in Beauvais toward popular diversions.[19]

Paris was the ultimate ambition of the practitioner in France of any profession, including the oldest. The wandering dramatic companies hoped, then, to find at the end of their weary road the city on the Seine, with its life and people and opportunity. Few, if any, of the little French troupes traveling around the provinces in the sixteenth century ever got there. None of the names of those already mentioned has been found in any Parisian record indicating that the group operated in the capital city. Nor has any contemporary memoir, diary, or bit of poetic doggerel — which was the good fortune of some other actors — connected them with Paris for later centuries to see. There is no doubt that, all told, the provinces were more considerate than Paris of the loosely organized companies which were trying to be professionals. Also, for a long time (well into the seventeenth century) provincial audiences were more likely to permit dramatic experimentation and give a new type of play a patient hearing. Paris, with the complications of its troubled existence, was a hard place to penetrate. It was doubly so for a troupe of comedians because of the Confrérie de la Passion's monopolistic control of the mechanics of theatrical production.

The Confrérie was willing late in the sixteenth century to rent out the Hôtel de Bourgogne, after its own productions of mystery plays had been restricted by the Parlement de Paris and after the plays themselves had, in addition, ceased to have much appeal for Paris audiences. Of these declining mysteries the theatrical historians, the Frères Parfaict — whose dating of performances is often open to question but whose criticism is sometimes quite astute — had nothing good to say. They suggested that any play presented by a visiting band of comedians, if it did not have "more art" than the Brotherhood's offerings, would in all likelihood have "more good sense." There was every reason, then, for injecting some vitalizing energy, which the Italians had already begun to do, into the dramatic life of Paris. The first problem for any aspiring troupe was to acquire the only theatre in Paris, the Hôtel de Bourgogne, from the Confrérie and at a reasonable figure;

or, if this were not possible, to find some makeshift hall in which to set up their offerings. In the latter case the Confrérie had the legal authority to demand a fee from any group of actors *not* occupying the Hôtel de Bourgogne. The next problem was to interest the Paris audience, which could be either boisterous or apathetic. It was all rather complicated, and made more so by the Confrérie which was stubborn and Gothic-minded and much concerned with money. In 1571, it threatened a group of young men with fine, corporal punishment, and imprisonment for putting on a few farces. Anyway, the Confrérie recognized before 1600 that tastes had changed and felt that more money could be made by renting their theatre than by performing in it themselves.[20]

In the inventory of the papers of the Hôtel de Bourgogne, there is a record of an agreement on July 28, 1578 between the masters of the building (the Confrérie) and Agnan Sarat, Pierre Dubuc, and "other companion comedians" by which "the companion comedians promise to present comedies according to the terms mentioned in the said contract." This is the first known document showing the rental by the Confrérie of their theatre to a specific company of actors — and some critics would doubt that Agnan Sarat and his cohorts actually mounted the boards at the Hôtel de Bourgogne. Yet there is evidence to suggest that he did. In a bit of doggerel, published in 1600, about the silk breeches of a courtier are the following verses:

> How many times did your silken finery
> Clothe the King of Troy
> And the chivalric knights of Amadis
> When Agnan with his ugly face
> Played at the Hôtel de Bourgogne
> Some tale of long ago.

It will be remembered that the struggling actors in this period frequently got their costumes from some old-clothes dealer around Les Halles. Nothing is certain about Agnan's repertory, but he might have essayed some piece concerning Priam or Hector or an episode from the Spanish *Amadís de Gaula*, which novel of chivalry had been popular in France since the time of Henry II. How long Agnan performed in Paris is not known, but these verses would imply that he was still remembered in the seventeenth century. Further support for this point of view came later in the century when the chattering Tallemant des Réaux began his little story of the principal comedians of France with: "Agnan was the first who had any reputation in Paris." However, Tallemant lived too late to have remembered much about Agnan, and the gossip columnist was notoriously lax in documentation.[21]

Some contemporary engravings (see Figure 4) give another slant on Agnan. In these he is playing the role of a shepherd and is mixed into an episode with Arlequin. The verses underneath the pictures explain the story: Arlequin, a glass dealer, steals the shepherd's awl while Agnan receives the gift of a magic flute, instead of money, from the Nymph. Agnan then plays the flute which makes everybody dance; the Milkmaid breaks her eggs and spills her milk, and Arlequin drops his glassware in the spirited stepping. He begs Agnan to stop playing and promises to return the awl. Such a playlet would intimate that Agnan was associated with the Italian actors — and that his name as well as his role of a shepherd might be associated with *agneau*, "lamb." Or it all might be a manifestation of the quirks of the artist's imagination.

In 1584, a troupe of comedians came into Paris, according to the Frères Parfaict, and rented the Hôtel de Cluny on the rue des Mathurins (not the present-day rue des Mathurins, which is on the Right Bank) — "on its own authority" and ignoring the Confrèrie's concessionary rights. The comedians had had some success in the provinces, and their "novelty" caused them to be well received in Paris, but not for long. After one week the Parlement de Paris threw them out of the Hôtel de Cluny, and forbade their performances anywhere in the city or faubourgs. The concierge of the Hôtel de Cluny was ordered to close the place to the troupe, under threat of one thousand crowns fine. The decree was dated October 6, 1584, and is included by the Frères Parfaict as a note. The Hôtel de Cluny, part of which is preserved today in the Musée de Cluny, was a large Gothic pile about one hundred yards north of the Sorbonne and important enough to be put on seventeenth-century maps. It had a courtyard and in its day (it was built in 1505) was considered an "edifice of consequence." By the next century it was regarded as being "remarkable only for its solidity" and not habitable "according to the fashion which reigns at present." It undoubtedly had in it one or more reception halls which would have been spacious enough for a theatre — a bleak, dark, and damp one. The names of the actors who occupied it in 1584 are buried in the past, nor is it known what happened to them after the concierge locked the Hôtel de Cluny up.[22]

In 1588, say the Frères Parfaict, the Confrérie was obliged to start renting the Hôtel de Bourgogne; the signing of the lease by Agnan Sarat in 1578 is ignored by the chroniclers. The Confrérie also was probably seeking to revive some of its own creations at this time, but "the best people had abandoned its spectacles." A French troupe, as well as an Italian one, appeared in 1588 — and "this first French troupe," though there are no "specific memoirs" for exact details, must have had a hard time. The general as well as theatrical situation in Paris continued to be bad until 1593, when the "sweetness of the reign" of Henry IV commenced to be felt. On the 1588 company of comedians the memory and therefore the dates of the Frères Parfaict may have slipped a trifle, since no record of a lease of the Hôtel de Bourgogne by this troupe has been discovered in the archives.[23]

Dramatic activity in Paris became quiescent until 1595 — a comprehensible situation in view of the trials and tribulations the city was undergoing — when things began to come to life. At this time Jehan Courtin and Nicolas Poteau, "chiefs of an ambulatory troupe," were giving performances at the Fair of Saint Germain. The Confrérie objected, but the court of the Châtelet allowed Courtin and Poteau to "play and represent secular, licit, and correct mysteries" for just the time that the Fair was open, and provided they pay the Confrérie two crowns. Also, Courtin, Poteau, and company were forbidden to "hurl any insults into the Hôtel de Bourgogne, nor throw stones, powder, or anything else which could cause people to riot." This was in a decree of February 5, 1596, and was to be announced to "the sound of a trumpet at the said Hôtel de Bourgogne on the day of the presentation of the said plays." Evidently the two companies were putting on their shows, possibly of the same type, at the same time, and some rather drastic means were being used to avoid competition. On December 11, 1596, the masters of the Hôtel de Bourgogne filed an official complaint against Nicolas Potrau (it must be the Poteau mentioned above) to make him and his "companion French comedians" present "plays and farces" at the Hôtel according to agreement — all of which shows a shift from the status of things as it existed earlier in the year. In 1597, the Confrérie apparently went back into the production business, because on April 12, 1597, it was given official permission to present "comedies in the Hôtel de Bourgogne on the proper days for a theatre to be open." On this occasion, the Confrérie asked the Provost of Paris and the Civil Lieutenant for protection against those who would "interfere with the performances of the actors of the said Hôtel." The Confrérie's life before the dramatic public was scarcely a happy one. Shortly thereafter they ceased to be anything but landlords.[24]

Some English actors came to Paris in 1598, and one wonders how many of the natives understood the foreign tongue from across the Channel. English actors had begun to perform in Europe late in the sixteenth century; one Robert Browne and company was in Holland in 1590, with a repertory that included farces and acrobatics. It will be recalled that at the age of three the future Louis XIII saw "tragedy presented by some English actors," which he listened to with "calmness, gravity, and patience until the time came to cut off the head of one of the characters." Some days later he wanted to dress up as an actor, and strode around the royal nursery saying "tiph, toph, milord." In any event, on May 25, 1598, a lease was made to "Jehan Sehais, English comedian, of the great hall and stage of the said Hôtel de Bourgogne." It may have been Jehan Sehais' company which appeared in Rouen toward the end of January 1598, since Rouen would have been on the normal route from London to Paris. However, by a decree of January 30, 1598, the Parlement of Rouen threw these British-ers out of the city. They would thus have had some time to kill before showing up in Paris in the latter part of May, if Jehan Sehais' group it was. The troupe of Jehan Sehais apparently was unhappy in the Confrérie's theatre, because there was a sentence of the Châtelet court on June 4, 1598 directed against the "English comedians" for playing outside the Hôtel de Bourgogne. They must not have had too pleasant a sojourn in the French capital; later English companies were to have a little stronger support from royalty before invading the land of France.[25]

The most influential of the early French professional actors, Valleran le Conte, came to Paris in 1598. His effect upon the development of the public theatre in France was strong and lasting. More is known about him than the comedians that have crossed the scene up to now, but his life story still has many details in it that are missing. He seems to have come from Amiens or Montdidier in Picardy, that spawning ground of actors and acrobats, but the date of his birth remains on some undiscovered parish or town record. He most likely became interested in the theatre early in his youth, since he lived in an area so much given over to histrionics. In any case, he was a thoroughly established performer by 1592, at which time he was with a company of actors in Bordeaux and doing splendidly. This is evidenced in the *Chronicle of Bordeaux* written by the Bordelais Jean de Gaufreteau, who was prominent in and proud of his city. Portions of the Gaufreteau commentary on Valleran are so informative about him and other phases of the theatre that they deserve quoting again: "In that year (1592), Valeran,* a notable French comedian, came to Bordeaux and presented there a number of tragedies and farces, with a very fine applause from the spectators. It is to be noted that he was not married nor did he bear the title of chief of the troupe (another did that), although he was the soul and leader of it." The chronicle goes on to describe a beautiful and chaste actress of the company, who played serious roles and of whom Valleran was enamored. Valleran was also "marvelous in his parts," and especially so when he played opposite the beautiful actress and bestowed upon her "sighs and soul-stirring glances that were not pretended." There has been much theorizing as to who this anonymous beauty was. Gaufreteau states that she was invited into the best Bordeaux homes, and that after the death of her husband she returned to Paris where she lived "correctly and honorably." From the warmth of his discussion of her, Gaufreteau might well have been in love with her himself. One recent opinion is that she stayed with the company and subsequently married Valleran, but there is little tangible evidence to support this conclusion. Gaufreteau, who may have been prejudiced because of his own feelings, states that she gave no signs of reciprocating Valleran's affection. At any rate, it is quite provocative to find this paragon of feminine charm and virtue playing classic roles in the provinces so many years before actresses appeared on the Paris stage.[26]

---

* In his leases and contracts he signed himself Valleran le Conte, and not Valleran Lecomte, a spelling sometimes given to his name. Gaufreteau calls the actor Valeran.

With Paris in turmoil Valleran made no effort to take his
company there — he must have become *chef de troupe* by
the end of 1592 — after his successful season in Bordeaux.
He made the long and arduous journey north and then turned
east toward the frontier, possibly taking a little repose along
the way in his native Picardy. According to his own statement, he had before 1593 performed in "Angres," or Angers,
Rouen (though the record of this is still to be found), and
Strasbourg, in a repertory consisting of biblical pieces and
the plays of Jodelle. The archives of Strasbourg show that he
was there. At the end of March 1593, he was playing in Frankfort-on-Main a French program of "biblical tragedies and
comedies," which may have included Garnier's *Les Juives*,
Louis des Masures trilogy on David, and Théodore de Bèze's
tragedy on Abraham. These plays would have appealed to
the large crowds, many of whom were French-speaking
Protestants, that he attracted. He was allowed by the city
council to charge a maximum of four pfennigs a person as
the price of admission. On June 21, 1593, the local authorities
of Strasbourg refused him reëntry for the presentation of
"several beautiful comedies sacred as well as profane." For
almost five years after the Strasbourg rejection, as far as the
records are concerned, Valleran le Conte was lost.[27]

Valleran was too good and too tenacious a man of the
theatre to have given it up, so he must have during these
"lost" years kept the framework of his company intact and
even improved its organization. In any event, the next record
shows that his itinerary has brought him to Paris along with
a number of other comedians who have begun to have names.
On March 16, 1598, Valleran le Conte and his "troupe du
Roi" signed a contract with Adrien Talmy and his "compagnie de comédiens français." Valleran and his company
were called "comédiens du roi" and they were living on the
"rue Merdet paroisse Saint Eustache," so evidently they had
some permanence of residence in Paris. This is the first docu-

ment that has come to light in which the coveted title of
"comédiens du roi" has been used and it would imply that the
troupe had already gained some reputation in the eyes of the
King. The Bordeaux troupe of 1592 would scarcely have had
enough royal recognition to call themselves "comédiens du
roi," though they have been so designated in present-day
criticism. The contract was drawn up, then, for three years —
an optimistic attitude toward theatrical conditions — and
stipulated that the two companies would perform together
either in Paris or the provinces. Valleran was responsible for
costumes, music, and transport, for which services he was to
receive one quarter of the receipts. The year 1598 was a busy
one for the Paris stage. It will be recalled that the English
company of Jehan Sehais came, however briefly, at this time.
And on December 21, 1598, the Confrérie made demands on
one Benoist Petit and his troupe that they perform at the
Hôtel de Bourgogne on the day specified in their contract
and that they give the same play as advertised. The particular
importance of this document is that it mentions among Benoist
Petit's comedians the name of Robert Guérin, the earliest
known reference to the actor who was to become famous in
Paris as the farce-player, Gros Guillaume. Valleran was most
likely still in Paris with his group, but had rented some hall
other than the Hôtel de Bourgogne. He must have been close
at hand because on January 4, 1599, he and Benoist Petit
signed an agreement by which they would alternate with
their companies at the Hôtel de Bourgogne, unless Valleran
had started a "romance" which needed to be completed in
successive performances. Valleran was now living on the
rue Montorgueil, near the Hôtel de Bourgogne. They agreed
to help each other by filling in parts when necessary — and
Valleran promised to furnish the farce, the usual conclusion
of the program. Less than two weeks later, on January 16,
1599, Valleran amended the above agreement slightly by
declaring he would like to substitute a tragedy for the romance

which he had not received from Benoist in time to get ready.[28]

On May 1, 1599, the Hôtel de Bourgogne was leased to Valleran and his companions, "comédiens français ordinaires du Roi." The lease was renewed on October 2, 1599, which would indicate that it had been a pretty good year for plays and players. Further proof of success was the contract made by Valleran on October 5, 1599, with two decorators to furnish some stage sets, all freshly painted, for the sum of eighty crowns. These sets were to be used in "romans, comi-tragédies, pastoralles, et comédies," all probably written by the prolific Alexandre Hardy, who became Valleran's paid furnisher of plays in 1597 or 1598. Crowds were pushing around outside the Bourgogne according to a document of October 6, 1599; it must have been a satisfactory season. And on November 24, 1599, the wife * of Valleran renounced dowry rights from her deceased first husband, added support for the belief that the financial position of the actor-manager was as solid as the Pont Neuf.[29]

But the year 1600 was a different matter and showed that only optimists gamble their money on what the theatrical public will like. The new tragedies and pastorals of Hardy did not catch popular fancy, even when helped by handsome and expensive décors. By January 26, 1600, Robert Guérin and two other actors were doubling as collectors of the sparse admissions "at the doors of the said Hôtel de Bourgogne" — and counting the money in front of Valleran, which would intimate that nobody had any confidence in anybody. The situation continued to get worse, so on February 25, 1600, Valleran and Savinien Bony, one of his actors, signed an agreement to share the Hôtel de Bourgogne with what must have been a pick-up Italian company, since one of them could not even write his name. This move displeased some of the other

---

* Madame Deierkauf-Holsboer, the Dutch critic of the seventeenth-century French theatre, thinks that Valleran's wife might have been the beautiful actress from Bordeaux (*Vie d'Alexandre Hardy*, p. 342).

actors in Valleran's company, but it became more and more obvious that Parisian audiences preferred the Italians or farce-players to the more serious and ornate plays of Valleran and company. Valleran, nevertheless, on May 17, 1600, signed a contract to have a stage constructed in a courtyard, with an entrance on the rue du Coq, to give plays outdoors for fifteen days. This move was a futile gesture, as was signalized on October 30, 1600, when Robert Guérin and troupe — the great and corpulent farce-player, Gros Guillaume, now had formed his own company — leased the Hôtel de Bourgogne to "present comedies." Under these conditions, Valleran and his companions abandoned the theatrical world of Paris to the *commedia dell' arte* and Gros Guillaume, and took to the road. They were not to be back in the capital city for around five years.[30]

Valleran was a stubborn and dedicated man, for in the latter part of 1605 he decided to have another look at Paris. On January 4, 1606 he signed a contract engaging the young actor, Estienne de Ruffin, to play with his company for two years in return for six hundred livres of Tours and food and lodging. Valleran was unable to meet the financial obligation. 1606 was a difficult year for him and so was 1607, with debts accumulating and actors leaving the company. On the first of December 1607, he formed a new association, with Nicolas Gasteau, Ruffin, Hugues Guéru (who was to become famous as the long and lank farce-player, Gautier Garguille), and two actresses, Rachel Trépeau and an unnamed girl. These are the first actresses to be identified with the Paris stage, but it is doubtful that they were very active in the era that favored farces. Gros Guillaume was not associated with this group, but with some other actors he joined Mathieu Le Febvre, called Laporte, and his wife, Marie Venier, in a two-year contract on February 21, 1608. Laporte had been with Valleran as recently as January 1608. Gros Guillaume and Laporte, leaving the serious drama to Hardy and Valleran, planned to specialize on farces. Valleran probably spent most of 1608 in the provinces, but was back in Paris in 1609 where he took many youngsters into his company as apprentices and gave them dramatic training. Among these was Pierre le Messier, who was destined to gain fame at the Hôtel de Bourgogne under his stage name of Bellerose. By 1610, many of the competing actors were together again, and on March 29, 1610, a two-year contract put Valleran, Laporte and his wife, Gros Guillaume, Gautier Garguille, Nicolas Gasteau, Bellerose (whose star continued to rise), and some others in the same company. Valleran was now living on the rue Peronet, in the parish of Saint Eustache. Before the end of the year the actors began to break apart, and by March 1611, Valleran was deeply in debt to his landlord for a variety of services, including the funeral of Valleran's sister. In early December 1611, all the loges of the Hôtel de Bourgogne, except those reserved for officials and the masters of the Confrérie, were leased to a responsible bourgeois who was to collect the revenue from them in an effort to pay Valleran's debt to his landlord. Never could the financial affairs of an organization have been in worse shape.[31]

The year 1612 was little better for Valleran, even though at the end of 1611 Alexandre Hardy had been pressed into service as a comedian. Early in 1612 Valleran joined forces with the Italian troupe of Jehan Alfieri, "chevalier de l'empereur," at the Hôtel de Bourgogne in producing French and Italian plays one after the other on the same program. Parisian audiences had little liking for the double features, a situation that was reflected most depressingly at the ticket office. On February 14, 1612, Valleran and the Italians agreed, rather pitifully, to allow the masters of the Hôtel de Bourgogne to open the strongbox containing the receipts of the preceding performance and take out the money due them. The masters, among whom was the former actor Benoist Petit, had previously demanded an official impounding of the actors' collections. One sad if realistic note in the contract of the joined companies was the statement that the other actors would not be expected to come in aid if any funds of "the said Le Conte and his consorts" were seized by creditors. Though Valleran and Alfieri signed another lease on March 7, 1612, it was not to keep them together very long. Gros Guillaume and Gautier Garguille, the prime farce-players, were not associated with this combined Franco-Italian operation, which broke up before the end of March 1612. Gros Guillaume picked up the French pieces of it for a new combination stressing rough and bawdy farces and did what the "comedies, tragicomedies, pastorals, and other plays" of Valleran and Hardy had been unable to do: he for the next few years packed the Hôtel de Bourgogne.[32]

Valleran, his spirit battered but unbroken, by an act of association dated March 31, 1612, formed a new company made up of young actors and actresses. Valleran was to get two shares of the profits for his various services, and a certain Gillebertz, "called Mondaury," was to receive one-half of a share — and here is an early mention of Montdory, later to become famous as the chief of the Marais troupe in Paris. After this contract Valleran apparently decided to have nothing more to do with the theatrical difficulties of the capital city since there is no further listing of his name on the notaries' records of the Hôtel de Bourgogne or on any official document in Paris. He left immediately with his new company for the provinces, where he could reminisce happily over his earlier successes. His route is hard to trace, but on May 2, 1613, he got quick permission from the city fathers of Leyden in Holland to play there, supported by the recommendation of the Prince of Nassau, before whom he must have performed previously in The Hague. The archives of Leyden speak of him as "Master Valleran and his consorts," so he undoubtedly was well known in the city. The Leyden permit is the last documentary evidence on the career of Valleran le Conte. He probably died before the end of 1613, on tour like the trooper he was, covered by his companions with an alien soil "in a corner soon to be forgotten." [33]

The exact moment of Valleran's demise may always remain a mystery, but several of his near contemporaries commented on his particular skills and the theatrical situation of his era. Tallemant des Réaux, in his rather offhand way, puts him right after Agnan Sarat; "Next came Valeran [sic], who was a tall man of fine appearance; he was the chief of the troupe; he did not know what to give to each one of his actors, and he took up the money himself at the door." And thus Tallemant disposes of Valleran. In the *Memoirs* of Michel de Marolles, Abbé de Villeloin — which were written in 1656 when the author was getting near the age of sixty — several events of the early seventeenth century are recalled. Marolles comments upon his schooldays, when he had a friend with more wit and money than piety, who on occasions took a favored few of his mates to a game of court tennis or, sometimes, to the theatre. The "comédie" was preferred "when that famous actress called Laporte * was still appearing on the stage and when she along with Valleran was eliciting the admiration of everybody." Marolles continues with the statement that they also saw "Perrine and Gaultier" whom "nobody has been able to imitate." These two would be Gaultier Garguille and his stage-wife, Perrine (regularly played by a man), in a gross and rough farce following the comedy. Marolles places the date of his excursions to the theatre at 1616, but his faulty memory should have put them four or five years earlier.[34]

The best observation on Valleran's technique and the theatrical world of Paris around 1600 comes from Thomas Platter, previously noted with his brother in Avignon. His whole trip over England, Holland, France, and Spain took from 1595 to 1600. The descriptions he gives of what he

---

* Marie Venier, already seen as the wife of Mathieu Le Febvre called Laporte.

saw in Paris are colorful and acute, and he did not miss the theatre: "At the Hôtel de Bourgogne, there is a comedian named Valeran, engaged by the King. He plays every day * right after lunch a comedy in French verse and offers after it a farce based on whatever amusing episode may have happened in Paris, amorous or otherwise. He does so well this recital in blank verse or prose, embroidering it so clearly with funny jokes, that a person cannot keep from laughing, especially if he knows the story or the individuals involved. For everything extraordinary that goes on in Paris, as soon as it happens, Valleran gets hold of it. He makes a play out of it and everybody runs to hear the farce that he presents at the end of his show." All of which happened in 1599, when Valleran was younger and gayer and more willing to conform to the tastes of the time.[35]

Other comedians passed on and off the French stage before 1615, but none was the solid professional that was Valleran le Conte. They all had their ups and downs and the developing theatre was far from being a dependable source of income. Some, like Charles Chautron, seem to have stayed in the provinces and thus are not on the Paris records. Variations of social and political conditions had a tremendous effect on the actors' fortunes. After the death of Henry IV, for example, Tallemant says they left Paris: "It happened that after the death of the King, the comedians, not daring to perform in Paris where everybody was is such consternation, went into the provinces and finally to Bordeaux." It was definitely a precarious profession. In a moment of rare concession, Valleran and Laporte, his partner at the moment, early in 1608 were given a deduction on a lease of the Hôtel de Bourgogne "in consideration of the heavy freezes which have taken place during the said time, because of which very few people have gone to the plays which were being offered at the said place." On the other hand, Claude Husson, who had the approval of

* Two or three times a week would be more likely.

the Prince de Condé, was fined sixty sous a day in 1610 for playing in the faubourg Saint-Germain-des-Près instead of the Hôtel de Bourgogne. And Laporte and his companion comedians were fined during the same year sixty sous a day for operating in the Hôtel d'Argent,[36] a dilapidated edifice just across the river on the Right Bank near the Place de la Grève.*

By 1615 the land of France and its capital city knew what a professional troupe of actors was. It had required several decades for this generic evolution to take place, and the professional entertainer's position in society was to be debated for a still longer time. Nevertheless, after the labors of Valleran le Conte and his fellows there was no reason to confuse the professionals with the medieval societies who did some avocational acting, or even with the rather tentative wanderers of the sixteenth century. The mechanics of troupe organization, shares, and profits (if any), distribution of roles, selection of repertory, and many other basic problems had been examined if not conquered. The matter of the tastes and desires of the public was difficult then even as now. Valleran guessed completely wrong in seeking to displace farce for the Parisians and substitute for it the more literary plays of Alexandre Hardy. It was to be a long time yet before the rough and lusty farce was swept off the boards of the Paris theatre. The farce-players were to be on stage for more than another decade because much of the public wanted them there. The moment had not yet come for the balanced couplets of Pierre Corneille, and even less for the subtleties of a Jean Racine.

* Today the general site of the Hôtel de Ville and the square in front of it.

III

FARCE-PLAYERS AND STREET ENTERTAINERS

THE NOBLES LIKE TRAGEDY because their sentiments are lofty, but the populace sunken in the mire and accustomed to crude concepts and conversation prefer the "miserable buffooneries of our farces." Farce has corrupted the idea of comedy, which has become this "impertinent clowning that our theatres have suffered to be performed after the tragedy." Farces are "works unworthy to be put in the rank of dramatic poems." They are "without art, without composition, contrary to good sense" and "recommendable only to ignoramuses and scum because of the rough language and vile actions which form the basis of their attraction." Such were the opinions expressed around the middle of the seventeenth century by that solid critic of the theatre, the Abbé d'Aubignac. A similar conclusion was recorded toward the end of the sixteenth century by the political theorist, Jean Bodin, who said that farces were being put on at the end of tragedies — which would show that tragedies were played at this time — and were like "poison in the meat." Others felt that farces were displacing the serious drama, were corrupting the youth of the land, and shocked God with their profanation and blasphemy. About the only virtue most critics granted them was that they were less dirty than the plays staged by the Italians.[1]

But the French liked farces, and it would be difficult to prove that these raucous and satiric playlets appealed only to

the lower element of society. Their comic relief had originally been the "stuffing" (the literal meaning of the word may
still be seen in such a combination as *tomate farcie*, "stuffed
tomato") in the long and cumbersome mysteries, and they
evidently still leavened a pastoral or tragedy in the sixteenth
and seventeenth centuries. Until 1625 they tended to steal
the show, and thirty or forty years later they were to receive
more finished literary treatment in the hands of Molière.
Henry IV, who made no pretense to refinement of literary
taste, loved them. The story was told by a contemporary
chronicler of Henry's visit, with all his royal retinue, to the
Hôtel de Bourgogne on January 26, 1607, to see a "pleasant
farce." It opened with a wife's attack on her husband — a
favorite theme of even the earliest farces was that of the
henpecked husband — for not working and for spending his
time in a tavern. He replied that his relaxing in a public house
had no effect on their financial condition since the King got
all the money in taxes anyway. At this juncture three of the
King's functionaries arrived, demanded the payment of a poll
tax, and forced the wife to open up a chest in which they
thought some money was hidden. When the cover was lifted
three devils jumped out, seized the royal functionaries and
locked them in the chest. The farce ended with one private
citizen (and three devils) defeating the machinery of the
government, a situation which has always been satisfactory to
Frenchmen. But this was not the end of the affair: after the
performance the players were arrested by the Conseillers des
Aydes and imprisoned for insulting His Majesty's servants.
Henry IV released the actors and pardoned them, "since they
had made him laugh so much, even to tears." Everybody
agreed that there never had been a better farce. Another
favorite of Henry IV and some of his courtiers was the *Farce
of the Gascon Gentleman*, a piece that has come down in
name only. Henry IV was having Gros Guillaume and his
companions give the play at a private session when the

Maréchal de Roquelaure jumped up as though he meant to strike Gros Guillaume, but the portly farce-player calmed things down with: "Take it easy, Cousin." The farce may have contained some caustic material on Southerners — which both Henry and Roquelaure were. After Henry IV's assassination and the comedians had left Paris, Roquelaure had them stage the *Farce of the Gascon Gentleman* in Bordeaux, but he could not enjoy it so soon after Henry's death and left before the performance was over.[2]

Very few farces from this period in French dramatic history have been saved for later generations to see. This is understandable since they were of no great literary value, repeated the same incident and events over and over, and depended for many of their effects upon the improvisations of the farce-players. In this respect, as well as others, they resembled the plays of the Italians, and it was hard to tell which was the pot and which was the kettle. Many were nothing more than short skits that could be played indoors or outdoors, and in some there is a mixture of French and Italian. Such is the case with the four extant little farces performed by the street entertainer, Tabarin (see Figure 9). They are of unknown authorship, and have been catalogued simply as *farces tabariniques*. One of them has in it the feminine characters Francisquine and Isabelle — borrowed from the Italians — as well as a captain and two fellows who get tied up in a sack. Another is of some interest because it is very similar to one used by the farce-players of the Hôtel de Bourgogne. In the Tabarin version one Lucas says he is going to India to make money and leaves his daughter, Isabelle, in the charge of Tabarin. Isabelle is in love with the soldier, Rodomont, and sends him a ring. Tabarin persuades Rodomont to get into a sack, and after much confusion the play ends in noise and the beating of Lucas who has changed places with Rodomont in the sack. The other play was put by the Frères Parfaict in their history of the theatre because "these types of pieces are extremely rare." It is called simply a *Pleasant and Delightful Farce* and adds a few touches to the Tabarin story which it probably copied: Gautier Garguille is going on a business trip to India and leaves his daughter, Florentine, with Turlupin (see Figure 5), the third of the famous farce-players at the Hôtel de Bourgogne. Turlupin would like to seduce Florentine, but she is in love with Horace, "the flower of the army." Florentine entrusts Turlupin with a ring to give to Horace, and Horace gives Turlupin a gold chain for Florentine. Turlupin keeps them both. Gautier Garguille returns from his trip, is disgusted with affairs in his house, and promises both Florentine and Turlupin a thrashing. These two farces are bright and rough in language and situation: there are feminine roles in each one but it is not likely that an actress was in the Bourgogne version. In the *Pleasant and Delightful Farce*, Gautier Garguille is worried about the shattering of his daughter's honor, which is already "cracked." Florentine would like to have Turlupin "do her a favor" (it is a question of the ring being delivered to Horace). Turlupin is quite willing and says "lie down right over here." These little masterpieces would probably date from around 1617 or a trifle later. None of them is as coarse as the *Farce of Perrine*, wherein Gautier Garguille quarrels with his wife, Perrine, over her being a prostitute — this was the play admired by Michel de Marolles when he was a schoolboy. Perrine is adamantine about carrying on in her profession and boasts of the profits of her "front." The quarrel is submitted to judicial opinion and Perrine wins. The play was later than 1613 since that date is referred to in it. A few farces, at least, have come down from the reign of Henry IV, but whether or not they were staged is another question, since they are more in the manner of medieval treatments of the genre. Two farces from around 1612 or 1614 were somewhat airily called "tragicomedies": the *Pleasant and Facetious Tragicomedy . . . of Franfreluche and Gaudichon*, in which Franfreluche is carried off by the devil; and the *Tragicomedy of the Children of Turlupin, Cursed by Nature.* The latter is in twelve-syllable verses and four short acts. It tells the story of Turlupin's marriage to a hideous old gossip to whom, he fears, Gautier Garguille is paying intimate attention. Nevertheless, Turlupin and Gautier Garguille go out and have a drink together. This creation must have been played by the two prime *farceurs* of the Hôtel de Bourgogne whose names are in it. Other farces certainly existed, as is suggested by contemporary references and visual evidence of excerpts from them on prints and engravings. However, the collection that has come down to the twentieth century is pitifully small. It was too fast-moving a genre to take time out to get into the domain of books. If the story is true concerning Valleran le Conte's fitting the sprightly daily events of Paris into farces, it is easy to see why they would be considered too stale for printing a week later.[3]

Whether they were worth printing or not, the theatrical public of Paris before 1630 was inclined to label the farces as the best part of the program. Even a courtly audience at Fontainebleau in 1611, after being regaled with a French pastoral, then watched a farce. At the Hôtel de Bourgogne, Bruscambille who controlled a restive audience there with his racy prologues during the years, approximately, from 1609 to 1620, attained a modicum of quiet by promising the crowd a "lively farce." Yet Bruscambille recognized that purists and detractors of the theatre, though they admitted that tragedies and comedies were "tolerable," estimated that a "farce with its filthy language spoiled everything" and that like a "poisonous rain it shriveled our most beautiful flowers." If the spectators would permit it, said Bruscambille, the company would be glad to remove the farce from the day's entertainment, but there was a "popular superstition that the rest of the show would not be worth anything without it, and that there would be no enjoyment in getting only half value for the price of admission" — and here the question of money reared its ugly and noncritical head. Bruscambille went on to say that the actors, for their part, would be willing to bury the farce in a "perpetual oblivion," since it has been an "unbearable burden" and "prejudicial to professional renown." Nevertheless, it must be conceded that the "most chaste Italian comedy is more depraved in words and actions than any one of these farces." The whole situation, therefore, was relative; and the French actors were a long way from giving up the lucrative farces. Also, the taste of the public, which in general the theatre follows rather than creates, was not yet ready for refinements that ultimately would come.[4]

Few of the farces of the early seventeenth century may have been deemed worthy to carry over to future generations, but the attitude was different in regard to the farce-players. Their names were kept alive in prose, in verse, and in the drawings and engravings of a variety of artists. The same, as far as pictorial evidence is concerned, cannot be said for the more serious actors of the period. No sketches or engravings of Valleran le Conte, Bellerose, and Montdory have come to light to compare with those which Abraham Bosse and other artists made of Gros Guillaume, Gautier Garguille, Turlupin, Tabarin, Jodelet, and even minor farce-players. Possibly drawing on the popular engravings, the historian of the city of Paris at the end of the seventeenth century, Henri Sauval, described in detail the famous trio of *farceurs* at the Hôtel de Bourgogne — Turlupin, Gautier Garguille, and Gros Guillaume — and also Gautier Garguille's successor, Guillot-Gorju. Sauval was later copied by the Frères Parfaict. The portrayals of Sauval form much of the basis for our knowledge of the personalities of these notable actors of farce. Turlupin, in a slight violation of chronology according to the records in the archives, was treated first by Sauval. Henri le Grand was Turlupin's real name, and he was called Belleville in serious plays; but it was as Turlupin — which as a common noun, *turlupin*, meant a "sorry fellow" — that he gained his fame. He wore the dress of the Italian Brighella and the same sort of mask. "Never has anybody better composed, acted, or arranged a farce than Turlupin," said Sauval, and he had "wit, fire, and judgment" though he lacked a little in "simplicity." However, everyone admitted he "never had his equal," even if he was not so good a serious actor as he was a *farceur*. He was clever and agreeable in conversation, and he mounted the stage at the Hôtel de Bourgogne "as soon as he could talk and did not come off it until he went to his tomb." His widow remarried an actor in the Marais troupe. Gautier Garguille (see Figure 6), whose real name was Hugues Guéru, was known in serious drama as Fléchelles — but his reputation did not come from this stage name, although he played kings in a long dressing gown and mask. He was able to twist like a "real marionnette," with his "lean body, long, straight and thin legs, and heavy face." He never wore a mask in his farcical roles, but a pointed beard and a black cap. Nobody could look at him without laughing and it was delightful at the Hôtel de Bourgogne when he, Turlupin, and Gros Guillaume burst into a song — "a lot of people went to the Hôtel de Bourgogne just to hear it." Gautier, according to Sauval, died at the age of sixty; Emile Magne, in his biography of the actor, says it was in 1633.[5]

Gros Guillaume (see Figure 7) received less courteous treatment from Sauval. His real name, as has been seen from the leases of the Hôtel de Bourgogne and other contracts, was Robert Guérin, and he was in serious plays called La Fleur. Sauval said he was once a baker, then an actor, and "always a big drunk" — and in general a low type of fellow who married late in life when he was an "old sinner." He was so fat that he "walked along a considerable time after his belly." Two belts were wrapped around his torso, one below the navel and the other high on his chest, and he looked like a large wine cask in motion. He never wore a mask but always covered his face with flour, which enabled him just by moving his lips to whiten all those who were speaking to him. Kidney stones bothered him all his life and at times on stage he was in such great pain that he wept, but "his face bathed in tears and his countenance so sad" still amused the audience. In spite of his maladies he lived until he was almost eighty years old and left one poverty-stricken daughter behind. Guillot-Gorju (see Figure 8), to whom Gautier Garguille handed over the responsibility of continuing the tradition of the farce, was in the opinion of Sauval a big ugly man. Guillot-Gorju had studied medicine and played the "ridiculous doctor" so well that even the doctors laughed. After performing as a *farceur* for some eight years, he practiced medicine in the town of Melun, but became so bored that he came back to Paris and lived on the rue Montorgueil near the Hôtel de Bourgogne. He died at the age of fifty in 1648 — and when he came off the stage, "farce came down with him." [6]

Other stories were told about the three primary *farceurs* who worked together at the Hôtel de Bourgogne. Lemazurier, the theatrical historian of the early nineteenth century — notably inaccurate on the matter of dates — stated that Gros Guillaume died at the age of eighty because a lawyer whom he had satirized put him in a dungeon and that Gautier Garguille and Turlupin died the same week out of sympathy. Lemazurier thought also that the three friends had a little hall at the Porte Saint Jacques, where they performed from one to two o'clock in the afternoon with such skill that Richelieu invited them to the Hôtel de Bourgogne! All these bits of gossip show simply how well known they were. Tallemant des Réaux said that Gautier Garguille was such a comedian that a better one could not be found, and that he took his profession quite seriously, so much so that when a "man of quality" invited him to dinner he refused because he "was studying." Turlupin normally played the role of "a rascal," though in private life he lived very neatly in a well furnished room. Gros Guillaume said "almost nothing" when he was on stage but he declaimed it with such naïveté and had such an amusing face that the spectators could not stop laughing when they looked at him. This was the golden age of French farce and it was illustrated by an accomplished triumvirate. The likelihood is that Gautier Garguille died first in 1633, Gros Guillaume in 1634, and Turlupin possibly as late as 1637.[7]

The farce-players were invited to private parties and gave relaxation, as has been seen in the case of both Henry IV and Louis XIII, to persons in high station. Also, their reputations and mannerisms were so much a matter of public property that they were frequently imitated by amateur performers. On one occasion, "in a social group of the Saint André quarter, at the home of a certain Monsieur Guiet," a few young ladies and gentlemen presented the celebrated pastoral of Racan, *Les Bergeries* — which would put the date of the affair later than 1620. After the pastoral it was decided rather suddenly to give a farce by "one Montgazon." All the roles were quickly assigned and "a gentleman from Brie" played Gros Guillaume so ably that "in one spot in the piece" he surpassed the corpulent *farceur*. D'Ablancourt, a popular young man about town, was made up like Gautier Garguille, and "in the judgment of everybody outdid by far Gautier Garguille, whose costume he had imitated." The farce, in any case, was a huge success. Then there was the accusation made against Laffemas, an important and feared agent of Richelieu, to the effect that the Cardinal's man had once been a professional actor and had "worn the flour" of farce. Laffemas admitted that he *had* played Gros Guillaume and very well — in fact, he had done so "several times, but in private as anybody could do." There was no doubt that all Paris knew the farce-players.[8]

And, too, their names were mixed in all sorts of prose and poetry. In one of the plays of the dramatist, Du Ryer, the prologue points out that it is to be acted by children:

> Messieurs, it is not Bruscambille
> Turlupin or Gautier Garguille
> That you will see coming out on stage —
> It is a band of youngsters
> Full of eagerness and joy. . . .

Then the rough burlesque and satiric poet, Sigogne, began an epigram against a chattering female with:

> I never saw a mountebank,
> Gipsy, lawyer, booby,
> Or Guillaume, Gautier, or Garguille
> Rattle on as does this *fille*. . . .

Such verses as these, which date from around 1616, were in like spirit to those of about the same period by Charles d'Esternod, who in his second satire speaks of several poets and actors and how they praise a kindly old bawd. A whole list of performers at the Hôtel de Bourgogne before 1619 is included:

> And in the Hôtel de Bourgogne,
> Vautret, Valerant, and Gasteau,
> Jan Farine, Gautier Garguille
> And Gringalet and Bruscambille
> Will put some verses about her to a new tune.

And here is added Jan Farine, the farce-player whose very name means "flour," and Gringalet, who was not so well known as the big three of farce. Esternod refers several times to Gautier Garguille, to Alizon (a generic type, dating back to the sixteenth century, that played old women or nurses), and in his third satire suggests that if ever the antichrist arrives he will descend from "a Jewess, a nun, a Turlupin." It is easy to see how the libertine poets found in the *farceurs* kindred souls. There were those, however, who blasted both the free-thinking poets and the farce-players in a double salvo. The Jesuit Father Garasse in 1623 lambasted the "Turlupins" and their colleagues, and regretted that "the halls and

4. *Agnan, Arlequin, and the Milkmaid*

5. Turlupin

6. Gautier Garguille

7. Gros Guillaume

8. Guillot-Gorju

loges of the Hôtel de Bourgogne bear the marks of their depraved touch." Later in the century, in an imagined reunion between Vergil, Aeneas, and Venus, the Latin bard complains of being burlesqued by the French who have given an outhouse treatment to his verses, involving "terms of cuckoldry, of gautier garguille, and a thousand even worse." The farce-players were in the public eye, but they were not always admired.[9]

Well on into the seventeenth century, past 1630, the *farceurs* were prominent in the structure and also the management of the dramatic troupes of Paris. As signers of leases or other documents they normally used their real names. Gros Guillaume thus appeared at the end of 1598 in Benoist Petit's company as Robert Guérin — a date probably too early for him to have gained repute as the hefty two-belted Gros Guillaume. He was also mentioned as Robert Guérin in official papers of 1599 and 1600. Hugues Guéru, the notable Gautier Garguille of farcical mimicry and pantomime, signed just *Gueru* in the act of association creating Valleran le Conte's troupe of 1607. In 1608, as a part of Laporte's troupe, François Vautrel (who apparently had no specific name as a *farceur*) agreed to help Robert Guérin with the staging of the farces. Robert Guérin and Guéru (with no first name) were again with Valleran in 1610, in one of the last associations with the great actor-manager. Robert Guérin, who continued to progress in the milieu of the Paris theatre, was condemned with other actors in 1613 to thirty-six livres fine on the plea of the Confrérie. In 1615, Hugues Guéru, "called Fléchelles," his name in serious drama, was with other *comédiens du Roi* held responsible for the rent due on the Hôtel de Bourgogne, which had evidently been subleased to Claude Husson and his company. And in 1622, Hugues Guéru, "called Fléchelles," Robert Guérin, Henri Legrand — the popular Turlupin in farce — and their comrades were sentenced to a fine by the Châtelet. Leases of the Hôtel de Bourgogne in 1628 bore the names, among others, of Hugues Guéru and Henri Legrand, as did leases and condemnations in 1629, which mentioned also Guérin, "called La Fleur" (his name in tragedy). By 1632, Robert Guérin, "called La Fleur," Hugues Guéru, "called Fléchelles," and Henri Legrand, "called Belleville" (his name in serious plays), had appeared on several official documents involving the Hôtel de Bourgogne. In 1635, only Henri Legrand, "called Belleville," remained of the famous trio to join with Bellerose and other comrades in signing a new lease with the Confrérie. No official paper lists the farce-players by their stage names in farce, although this was a common practice in prose and poetry and informal commentaries of the period. Evidently the stage names in farce were not deemed sufficiently dignified to merit formal recognition, but Guérin, Guéru, and Legrand would never have been known to posterity if they had depended on their designations in serious plays.[10]

By the early 1630's, farce was giving way to drama of greater sophistication and refinement, though a few farce-players were still around and they were not without a following. The most notable of these was Julien Bedeau, destined for recognition on stage in his day, and with later writers like Scarron, Molière, and Rostand, under the farce-name Jodelet (see Figure 23). Jodelet became the archetype of valet, which was to influence Molière and receive ultimate treatment from Beaumarchais in the character of Figaro. Tallemant said that Jodelet was a good actor, though a "simple flour-face," who kept farce alive at the Marais theatre when it was dead everywhere else. He talked through his nose "because he had been badly treated when he had the smallpox" — this nasal twang, in fact, became the distinguishing feature of Jodelet's acting technique. One of Gautier Garguille's last legacies to his fellow actors in his famous will was an admonition to Jodelet to learn from the outdoor entertainers how to talk properly through the nose. In any case, Jodelet's nasality was the subject of comment well into the eighteenth century.

On one occasion the Chancellier Séguier promised him "a present" for performing at the Palais Royal. The present was understood by four lackeys to be one hundred coins, which they wanted divided into four parts for their own use. Jodelet agreed to the demand, but changed the gift from one hundred coins to one hundred lashes. Apparently there was royal interest in Jodelet's type of theatre, since in the *Gazette* of Renaudot it is mentioned that on December 10, 1634, the King transferred six actors from the Marais troupe to the Bourgogne, including Jodelet and two other *farceurs*, Alizon and Jacquemin Jadot. Nevertheless, the broad and lusty little farces of an earlier era were by this time no longer in vogue.[11]

Many of the farce-players, in the manner of François Villon, left mock wills and testaments. The *Testament* of Gautier Garguille is a diverting bit of badinage, written on "spider webs" and dated December 45, 2466. In it he paid respects to both his comrades and competitors, and assigned to Guillot-Gorju his "black coat," his "dagger," his "postures" — and his "spectacles" to keep an eagle eye on Turlupin and Bellerose when they were around his wife. Unfortunately, said Gautier Garguille, he has had quite an internal "defluxion" which has made it difficult for him to stride the boards, so he has decided to join "our old master Valleran" in the other world where he has set up a little theatrical enterprise and would be glad to have Gautier participate in it. Before leaving to help Valleran amuse the "grand Master of nature," Gautier has willed his earthly assets along with a little professional advice to the actors who have stayed behind. It is all delightfully done and shows that a gaiety of spirit was needed to the very end of the road by a player of farces.[12]

The farce-players had more than adequate competition from the street entertainers, whose theatre was the length and breadth of Paris and whose audience was anyone who passed by. All they had to do was set up a few boards on supporting trestles and, with an absolute minimum of properties, they were ready for business. The performers in the streets as well as the variety of their audience were noticed by visitors to Paris even before the seventeenth century began. Young Thomas Platter on his famous trip to Paris observed: "There are indeed many other comedians [he has already mentioned the indoor actors], artists, and musicians who exhibit continually marvelous and artistic things, and who go several times a day from one street to another. Some establish themselves in a single quarter, make their pronouncements, and pick up the money. When it appears that the quarter has well-nigh contributed its quota, they go to another spot in the city until they have filled their cashbox with a large sum. I have seen and heard that happen many times in Paris. For the Parisians are so curious they are called *badauds* ["gapers"]; and, since there are always crowds around the city, the fellow who has something extraordinary to relate proceeds to do it and the money flows in." Such was the impression made on young Platter by the activities in the streets of Paris. He observed also that there were Italian, English, and Spanish entertainers, among whom was a Spaniard "around the University" who lifted "with his teeth on to his forehead or his chest, without using his hands" a log that would normally be used to stop a carriage — and the veins in his neck almost burst. This Spaniard could also hold on his tongue a dozen naked blades without cutting himself or doing any sort of damage. The people of Paris, for further amusement, liked to go out in boats on the Seine, according to Platter, and grab for a goose attached to a rope across the water. They did this so enthusiastically that they often fell into the brown current of the river.[13]

In most cases the street performers were attached to some herb dealer or medicine man who promised to cure any and all ills. At times a single *opérateur* — the term usually applied to the street manipulators of jokes and nostrums — did the stunts and sold the medicaments, but more frequently it was a dual process. As for the matter of squeezing sous out of the public, it might be done at a fair as well as in the streets or squares of the city. Needless to say, the whole procedure had the cordial opposition of both the medical and acting professions. The doctors doubted the efficacy of most of the remedies offered for sale, while the struggling professional comedians did not like to see any sort of acting done free of charge.

The most celebrated of the street entertainers was Tabarin (see Figure 9) with his famous hat of many shapes. The name Tabarin — which came from the Italian *tabarinno*, "little coat" — had been used by a variety of operators at the end of the sixteenth century but *the* Tabarin was Antoine Girard. His earliest days are not known, though he and his brother, Philippe Girard, entertained Marie de' Medici at Blois in 1618. Philippe mounted the outdoor trestles under the name of Mondor, and he and Tabarin must have been quite a team. Tabarin's wife performed with them in the little *farces tabariniques* — which have already been compared to some of the short plays at the Hôtel de Bourgogne — in the role of Francisquine. The brothers set up their medicine show on the Pont Neuf — or, according to the engraving (see Figure 10) of Abraham Bosse, on the Place Dauphine. They could well have been in both places, since the bridge and square are adjacent to each other. They flourished in Paris from around 1618 until the death of Tabarin in 1626. One widely circulated legend had it that he retired to a fine estate near Paris before this date and that his socially conscious neighbors disliked having a former mountebank living near them. He was, therefore, shot accidentally while hunting. Sauval stated that Tabarin had a daughter who was married to Gautier Garguille, a conclusion that has been doubted in more recent years. Nevertheless, Gautier Garguille in his *Testament*, which was almost contemporary with Mondor and Tabarin, left

his robe used in the roles of kings to his "uncle, Mondor."
Whatever may have been the reality of these misty relationships, the name of Tabarin lasted a long time; as recently as
the 1940's it was used for a cabaret, the Bal Tabarin, in Mont-
martre.[14]

Tabarin and Mondor were both prime *opérateurs*, and they
attracted large crowds to their performances. Mondor played
the part of a pompous and learned master while Tabarin
acted the role of his valet. Both of the brothers were most
probably well-educated, though Tabarin took delight with his
earthy realism in deflating the Latin-flavored erudition of the
master. Whoever wrote down (there is no proof that either
Tabarin or Mondor ever took pen in hand) the little short
dialogues and interchanges between the two must have copied
the performers pretty exactly. As the collection stands at the
present time, there are in it ninety "questions," three "pre-
ambles," sixty-four "fantasies and dialogues," along with the
farces previously mentioned — to which might be added the
Farce of the Hunchbacks, where four hunchbacks are thrown
in a river only to come back and get in a fight. There is also
in the collection a wealth of contemporary material attacking
charlatans, herb dealers, and operators like Tabarin. In varying parts all of this was assembled into some twenty-four editions before 1664, which would indicate how popular the
tabarinique material was in the seventeenth century. Everybody could have seen Tabarin do his tricks without putting
out a sou, but the moneyed classes must have bought the books.
The dedication of the first edition in 1622 said that the material would appeal to all classes — "courtiers, nobles, com-
moners, merchants, knights, pastry-cooks, women." And the
women, by careful perusal of the book, would learn "what
wood made up the horns with which they ennobled their
husbands." [15]

If the copyist has done a good job of transcribing, which he
most probably did, the interchanges between Mondor and

Tabarin were fairly rough and scatological stuff. In the eighth Question, *Which is the more honorable, the posterior of a gentleman or that of a peasant*, the master naturally takes the side of the gentleman. Tabarin very bluffly brushes aside matters of neatness and perfumes and civilized adornments: he votes for the peasant because he has to stay in the open air and is never fastened up in a privy. The Master, in the process of the discussion, refers to the "partie postérieure d'un gentilhomme." Tabarin's reply to this nicety is: "Don't twist things around, I beg you, the word is *cul.*" The twenty-fourth Question is a little less concerned with anatomy and is called *In what does nobility consist.* The Master gives a learned discourse on the background and history of nobility — "nobility of the sword," "nobility of the blood," etc. Tabarin answers this quite simply and says he has nobility of the blood because his father was a butcher. Other interchanges between Mondor and Tabarin treat the medical profession, the game of court tennis, women (not very courteously), and many other subjects. The pattern is always the same, but the rough dialogue must have amused an audience that was not too squeamish or easily shocked. A fine accolade was given the material of Tabarin and Mondor by Gautier Garguille and Gros Guillaume, who welcomed it in their capacities of "Doctors and Regents in the University of the Hôtel de Bourgogne," and required all their "students" to bring a copy of it to class.[16]

There was not always cordiality between the street entertainers and the farce-players. A sharp answer was cast at the more pretentious actors of the Hôtel de Bourgogne in *The Pleasant and Delightful Fantasies of Tabarin's Hat*, which came out around 1622. The author, whoever he was, of this piece of prose argued for the street players in the following fashion: "Our French actors and comedians have taken all the pains imaginable to please with their rare plays and prologues those who have favored the theatre with their presence. But I can say . . . that Tabarin's hat, supported by the one who wears it, has caused more people to laugh in one day than the comedians have been able to make weep with their fancy sets and sad lamentations in six days, whatever comedy, tragi-comedy, pastoral, or other subject they might be playing in the Hôtel de Bourgogne or some such place." Many have enjoyed, it is true, Gautier Garguille "with his loyal assistant Guillaume aided by Dame Perrine who have performed as famous and pleasing bits as one could desire." However, there were three in this combination, while Tabarin has accomplished the equivalent in entertainment with nothing but his hat. Also, he has given relaxation to throngs of spectators without charging five sous — the cheapest entry to the Hôtel de Bourgogne around 1620 — and this has caused him to be admired by the indigent. Everybody laughed, said the writer of the treatise, at the multitude of shapes assumed by the Tabarin headgear, and chambermaids working on the Isle du Palais (the Ile de la Cité) got in trouble with their mistresses for staying out so late to see what it would look like next. A rumor had passed around that Tabarin was going to dye the hat black, so a large crowd was back the next day to see if he really had. Tabarin unquestionably blocked traffic on the Pont Neuf with his act, and it was hard for the actors paying rent on the Hôtel de Bourgogne to compete with his prices.[17]

Tabarin and other charlatans of the street corners endured the attacks of doctors, preachers, and the better established members of society in general. In *The Deceptions of Charlatans*, the sieur de Courval, *docteur en médecine*, objected to several types of charlatans who abused the true science of medicine. Among them were those who drew their audiences from crowds in the city squares and at the larger fairs. This kind of charlatan first attracted the passers-by with a pretended cure of a self-inflicted wound by the application of a special magic balm, which was only a "clever deception" and did not do any good at all. Among the worst of these fellows was one who appeared in Paris some time ago: he was

called *il signore Hieronymo*, and he "had had a stage built
in the courtyard of the Palais [de Justice], on which having
climbed in superb equipment and fine array, a heavy gold
chain around his neck . . . he let loose the best-feathered
arrows he had in the quiver of his tricks . . . to praise and
extol with a thousand lies . . . the hidden and admirable
properties of his unguents, balms, oils, extracts, quintessences,
distillations, calcinations, and other fantastic concoctions."
He did not rely solely on his own persuasive powers, but had
with him "four excellent violin players seated on the four
corners of the stage, and they did marvelous things, assisted
by a notable buffoon or funny-man from the Hôtel de Bourgogne named *Galinette la Galina*, who for his part did a
thousand mimicries, acrobatics, and clownings." * A large
crowd came up just as though they might be going to a real
theatre, and they enjoyed the antics of the clown while they
were being lulled by the "sweet harmony and harmonious
sweetness of the instruments." The audience in the beginning
had no intention of buying any of the dubious wares offered
by the charlatan, but, with their resistance broken down by
laughter and music, they ended up spending a great deal of
their hard-earned money. The charlatan added to their bewild-
erment by holding a fiery stick in his hand without burning
his palm, by stabbing himself painlessly, and by pulling out teeth
with his fingers without causing any groans or howls. The
good doctor ridiculed all these tricks and gave facile explana-
tions for them. The tooth-pulling exploit, for example, was
carried out by putting on one finger "a little bit of narcotic
powder" and on another one "a little wonderfully caustic
powder." The first deadened the patient's jaw and the second
caused the gum to open up so that the tooth "sometimes fell
out without touching it." It is to be regretted that such a
clever technique of tooth extraction has been lost to modern

* It will be noted that the engraving of Tabarin's stage resembles somewhat this description.

dental science. *The Deceptions of Charlatans* was written before 1610 and therefore preceded Tabarin's reign over the Pont Neuf and the Place Dauphine. The medicine-man under attack in the document was an Italian supported by an Italian buffoon who was evidently unable to find work at the Hôtel de Bourgogne.[18]

A more direct assault on Tabarin and a lesser-known charlatan, Desiderio de Combes, was the *Discourse on the Origin of the Fraudulent Customs and Impostures of Charlatans*, a long treatise published in 1622 and signed only with the initials J.D.P.M.O.D.R. The author — probably a member of the medical profession — was quite bitter about the street vendors of remedies and felt that it was a shame for a charlatan bedecked with robe and chain, a "prostitute" and a "procuress" by his side, and "supported by a Tabarin or a Grisigoulin," to trick the public with his doubtful products. True medicine is, in fact, a "virtue" that should not come in contact with "buffooneries," nor does it need the assistance of "clowning acrobats or Tabarins." But the medicaments of the charlatans, in the opinion of the much-initialed composer of the treatise, were ineffective and sometimes dangerous to use. This was the case with a powder recommended by the charlatans for the clearing of the body of worms: it would do no such thing and, besides, it could be bought in shops for twenty sous while the charlatans charged twenty francs for it. Other cures sold by the street operators, such as those supposed to cure deafness or cracks in a woman's bosom, were equally futile. The charlatans, then, were really a low lot but they made a great deal of money — "everybody sees what Tabarin and Mondor make in Paris, and indeed it is necessary that their profits be great to feed so many mouths, to take around with them all their equipment of violins, acrobats, roustabouts, women, children, servants, and maids." They should be banished from the city, particularly since their plays are full of "dirty words" and "crude actions," and deserve no more support than do their remedies. To patronize the charlatans in any way, therefore, is a mortal sin. Many must have stopped on the street corner to see the charlatans, nevertheless, since the treatise rather wryly conceded that Tabarin, Mondor, and De Combes have gone to their rooms at the end of the day after having filled "their coffers with our money." It was too bad that Mondor had not followed a more honorable profession, since he was well educated and had politeness and courtesy. De Combes, on the other hand, was a gross rustic who could scarcely read, write, or talk. Tabarin's qualities, rather surprisingly, were not catalogued by the doctor with all the initials.[19]

Through his ghost writer, Tabarin replied to most of the criticisms hurled by the medical profession at street vendors and entertainers, and also answered a Protestant preacher from Charenton. As for his remedies, said Tabarin in a *Response* to the doctors, he has always guaranteed them to be exactly what they purported to be, and as an indication of his integrity he would like to point to a host of completely satisfied customers. Also, he has never appeared on the streets of Paris without the permission and approval of the city authorities. He has never "mounted a stage in a public square without getting a permit from the officers of the King," or from the Civil Lieutenant, to whom he has been "infinitely obliged." On the matter of exorbitant prices for worthless merchandise, the valuable secrets of Tabarin have been sold on the Pont Neuf for as little as two farthings. Further proof of the esteem and confidence in which he has been held by his public is the fact that there has always been a terrible clamor when he has failed to appear. At times he has felt weary and tired, and would have relished a little repose "for a few days." However, his audience has been so demanding that he could not plan on even a brief vacation. So spoke Tabarin in defending his profession. It would not seem likely that an utter trickster and shyster would have had such a following.[20]

The minister from Charenton accused Tabarin of plying a trade which was nothing but "charlatanry" in the most derogatory sense of the word. Tabarin answered him with considerable skill and some display of erudition. As for the nature of his operations, Tabarin said: "I get up on my stage for two reasons: the first is to put on sale and in distribution at a very low price remedies approved for the curing of several general and common maladies; the other is to give the people free entertainment, without doing harm to anybody." In the matter of the position of drama in society Tabarin went back to the ancients and advised the preacher to remember that "comedy has been accepted among the most enlightened nations as teaching what is useful in life and what should be avoided." It would be well for the churchman to recall what "that great Roman orator" said about comedy, and that he described it as an "imitation of life, a mirror of custom, an image of truth." Here Tabarin showed his knowledge of the definition of comedy attributed to Cicero and transmitted through the Middle Ages by the grammarian Donatus. Another of the attractive features of comedy, said Tabarin, is the fact that it ends pleasantly, in which it differs from tragedy where the end is "funereal," just like the discourses of the Protestant preacher. Tabarin has made an able defense of his street programs, though he would have had difficulty in persuading Cicero that the little *farces tabariniques* of the Pont Neuf should be placed in the same category as the comedies of Greece and Rome. In any case Tabarin, with the help of the pen of his ghost-writing admirer, got into both the Christian and pagan underworlds. In one place in Hell he ran into Rabelais who was mounting a stage as the "president of the *farceurs*" and Tabarin himself was given the title of "accredited treacle-bearer of the University of the Place Dauphine." On the pagan side of the nether regions, when Gautier Garguille got to the river Styx he swam it in order to avoid paying a fare to the boatman Charon. After the argument over this economical entry was settled, the first person Gautier saw wandering around the Elysian Fields was Tabarin. They had quite a reunion. Tabarin traveled around — and he was more than just an ignorant mountebank.[21]

It was appropriate for Gautier Garguille, Tabarin, and their co-laborers to set up shop on the other side of the river Styx, since by 1630 the golden age of farce-players and street entertainers in France was ended. The farce-players had won out earlier in the century in competing for customers against Valeran le Conte and his serious repertory. They in their turn, with a progressive refinement of Parisian theatrical taste, were to give way to the more sophisticated acting of Bellerose, Montdory, and their descendants.

THE ACTOR'S PROFESSION

THE PROFESSION OF ACTING, whether it was practiced in the Hôtel de Bourgogne or in the public square, was a difficult calling in seventeenth-century France. Though conditions improved as the century advanced, they still left much to be desired. The matter of finances, for example, remained precarious and the social position of the actor was uncertain and discouraging. The questions of money and society's reaction to the professional theatre were only two of the problems that had to be faced by a man or woman who chose to make a career of the stage. Others might come under the heading of the techniques and logistics of the theatre: the training of the actor, fashions in acting, methods of transport of companies, the collection and distribution of receipts, clothes and costumes, internal structure of troupes, and similar matters. This list is far from being exhaustive, but it is sufficient to show the individual and organizational demands made upon any person who around 1600 in France wanted to spend his life as a comedian. He might well pass several decades in excitement, with occasional full pockets, and even in artistic satisfaction; but there would be many moments of frustration and emptiness of the stomach. In the famous words of Bruscambille, anyone that followed the profession of acting would find it to be "a life *sans souci* and sometimes *sans six sous*." [1]

France was slow in recognizing the legitimacy of the actor's profession, and in giving the performer on a public stage full legal and social rights. The problem was far from being resolved by the end of the seventeenth century, though progress had been made. Much of the stigma attached to the professional entertainer was traditional and went all the way back to the low estate accorded certain types of acting in ancient Rome. This general legacy of opprobrium pretty well permeated the whole of Europe and not just France alone. As for the actors, they did not always conduct themselves in such a manner as to facilitate their acceptance in the framework of society. They frequently were lax, among other delinquencies, in financial and moral responsibilities, and thus gained the hostility of the money-conscious bourgeois as well as of solid churchmen. In France during the seventeenth century even as in America today, actors as a class were condemned on the basis of the activities of some of their number. At any rate, the full privileges of citizenship were not granted to professional comedians in France until the eighteenth century. It will be recalled that Voltaire as late as 1734 criticized a society which would allow the body of the beautiful and capable actress, Adrienne Lecouvreur, who had portrayed with majesty the roles of queens on stage, to be thrown on the garbage dump when she died.[2]

A defense of the actor's profession came early in the seventeenth century from one of the comedians themselves, the rough and ribald and well-educated prologuist of the Hôtel de Bourgogne, Bruscambille. In the first place Bruscambille objects to the *comédiens* being called *bouffons*: "Shall we call buffoons those who present according to nature so many fine instructions, so many noble examples?" The *comédien* deserves high consideration and "among all the vocations that of comedy should be given first rank" because it covers everything. Bruscambille does not want the legitimate *comédien* confused with either the *bâteleur* or *bouffon*, an opinion that coincided with a later one of the Abbé d'Aubignac.* These low types of performers are ignorant and dirty and think they are devastatingly attractive to women. Such fellows, says

* See Chapter III.

Bruscambille, are beneath his consideration — "on the contrary, I mean to speak of those who represent by their actions the pure and true microcosm of nature's comedy." Terence, Seneca, Ovid, and others of the ancients are in the background of the latter concept. "The dregs of the people," Bruscambille admits, "abhor comedy and its professors like a pestilence" and "imagine it to be a precipice for the young." Persons in this class claim that the actor's life is "libertine, vagabond, useless to the public and marked by every type of infamy." Bruscambille answers that the theatrical profession, though it is not as necessary as theology, jurisprudence, and medicine, has had honor ever since the Greeks recognized their first writer and performer, Thespis. And actors like Roscius "walked on the level of the greatest noblemen of Rome," even if simple mimes and "other deliverers of treacle" did not. The theatre, too, gives good training in oral delivery to lawyers and an actor "does not make himself unworthy in the least of being connected (later) with the magistracy." This was a significant point made by Bruscambille, since there was a general belief at the time that the actor practiced an ignoble profession and had to be "rehabilitated" before going into some legitimate occupation. As for the institution of the theatre and the atmosphere around it, Bruscambille continues, it is not nearly so bad as a gambling house, a brothel, or a tavern; and in any one of these three establishments a youth will find "an infinity of debaucheries one hundred times more perilous than the theatre, and more expensive." Indeed, the theatre — particularly the serious theatre — brings "utility and profit" to a city, since it increases the knowledge of past history, makes the prosperous enjoy their prosperity, and moderates the sadness of those who are afflicted. Therefore, it is advisable for the populace to visit the "learned Théâtre Français" and forget therein both the good and bad turns of fortune. Bruscambille requests most emphatically of the general public that it be sympathetically disposed toward the actors: "Hear then our arguments with consideration, support the fair claims of the *comédiens*, see the essential rightness of their cause, do not allow them to be slandered, and they will be grateful to you forever." [3]

The process of rehabilitation was illustrated most strikingly in the case of the well-known actor, Mathieu Le Febvre, "called Laporte." In December 1619, the stain of the acting profession was removed from Le Febvre by royal action and he was entitled once more to a normal and legitimate position in society. A brief history of the affair was included in Louis XIII's *lettres patentes* dealing with it. Le Febvre was of a good family and destined for the study of "bonnes lettres." His training was interrupted in 1590 by civil strife in France. He was then just sixteen years of age, but went into military service under Henry IV. Afterward, "he had been incited and persuaded by certain persons to compose several tragedies, comedies, pastorals, and other poems both serious and amusing, which he had himself represented in public for several years." He had regarded this as a "praiseworthy" employment, though others thought it "deserved complaint." Finally, he had reached a point where he recognized that "this profession was not approved of by the most serious and grave persons" and thus "he had greatly desired to retire from it." He had done so a long time ago and he has now been living in the town of Sens with his wife and children for some ten years. In Sens, Le Febvre has conducted himself as a "bon habitant" and has accomplished a number of good works. Nevertheless, "he is afraid that people may object to him and reproach him for having been connected with the said profession of acting." Therefore, he would like to be "restored" and "rehabilitated." The King, feeling that "an error of youth" should not be perpetually hanging over Le Febvre, by the official edict of 1619 put him back into "his good fame and reputation." [4] It will be recalled that Mathieu Le Febvre, "called Laporte" was one of the better known actors in France as the seventeenth century began. He was far from being of the theatrical scum derided by Bruscambille and others. His plea for re-habilitation appeared at approximately the same moment that Bruscambille was urging a more general acceptance of come-dians. Obviously, in 1619 the actors' case was far from being won either before the King or the people of France. Other-wise, Le Febvre would not have thought he needed a legal statement to prove that he had been successfully vaccinated against the malady of the theatre and that he would no longer infect his neighbors.

Even the celebrated Valleran le Conte was used as a primary example in 1607 of one who belonged to a trivial profession in that he was called derogatorily the "buffoon of the Hôtel de Bourgogne." Some years afterward, at about the same time that Bruscambille was defending his colleagues and Laporte was being rehabilitated by Louis XIII, the satiric Claude d'Esternod said that although a *comédien* might be dressed up as a king or a queen, he was still an "homme de rien," a nobody. A little later in the century, the Gascon critic and letter-writer, Peiresc, regretted that a certain "Monsieur Valeran" had such a name — which he had borne honorably, it was con-ceded, because of his essential abilities. However, one would have shown more deference to his person "if he had changed his cognomen in order to avoid homonymic confusion with another man of the same name who had made himself famous on the stage some years ago." And Jean Chapelain, who was to become the right-hand man of Richelieu on matters of litera-ture and literary patronage, expressed regret in 1632 that the promising young writer, Jean Rotrou, was tied up with a troupe of comedians: "I am desolate that so able a young man has become involved in so shameful a servitude." Rotrou, who has a statue today erected to his honor in a square of his na-tive town of Dreux, was most likely at this time "earning his bread," as Chapelain said, by writing plays under contract for a company of actors.[5]

The profession of acting during the first part of the seventeenth century was definitely suspect — a situation that existed for such varied reasons as the loose organization of dramatic troupes, the irresponsibility of individual actors, the lack of patronage from persons in high position, and a dearth of good and clean plays. Before the middle of the century, the Abbé d'Aubignac, who was certainly concerned about the theatre and the people connected with it, said that if dramatic authors found themselves unable to compose because of the strictness of the "rules," the actors would be "reduced to taking up some honorable occupation due to the lack of new plays to put on the stage." D'Aubignac would seem to admit here that acting was not an "honnête emploi," though he drew up himself a project for the "reestablishment" of the French stage. In his plan for improvement, one of the reasons listed for the slow progress of the French theatre was the "infamy in which those are legally held who make a profession of being public comedians." Historically, D'Aubignac conceded that the first troupes of actors were made up of debauched and lost souls, and that the freedom of the actor's life attracted in a variety of ways degraded persons to it. The Kings, themselves, "marked it as infamous in order to divert from this licentious debauchery children of good families, threatening them with public shame and making them afraid of being forever incapable of associating with people of honor." Naturally, in these circumstances, the theatre did not receive the support of the best citizens, "because they thought they would be supporting vice and approving licensed dissipation." Under such conditions, plays have been poorly staged and actors have been ignorant, "scarcely knowing the French language." They have thus of necessity expressed "imperfectly what they recite, and often in a sense contrary to what it should be." It is clear that the Abbé d'Aubignac did not think highly of the earlier profession of acting in France, but hoped for a betterment of its status. That the profession of acting had not gained full recognition and acceptance by the eighteenth century is suggested in Sauval's statement concerning the plight of Turlupin's children, who were left so little of worldly goods at the death of their father that they were "reduced to becoming comedians." [6]

An occasional blow for the actors was struck by those who wrote for the theatre. The dramatist Gougenot in his play, *La Comédie des Comédiens*, which dates from around 1631, used rather effectively as a defense the device of a play-within-a-play and had such professionals as Gros Guillaume, Turlupin, Bellerose, and others appear on stage as themselves, while a comedy in verse is being prepared. A similar technique, it will be remembered, was employed later by Molière. In the introductory speech of *La Comédie des Comédiens*, as manager of the Bourgogne troupe, Bellerose talks to the audience about "calumny" and its terrible effects, and says that "our little academy" has never suffered the most scathing blasts from slanderous tongues. The reason for this is, he says, the fact that "we have always observed all the rules of virtue in order to obtain a position of honor that should free the theatre from blame and reproach." Bellerose was a trifle optimistic concerning the public recognition of the moral standards of his company, which were scarcely as high as this speech would suggest. A little farther along, in the first act of the play, Beauchâteau — a handsome young actor at the Hôtel de Bourgogne described by Gautier Garguille in his *Testament* as one "who found no feminine chastity capable of resisting him" — discusses the theatre and the problems of presenting a play. Beauchâteau also lists some of the qualities that an actor should possess: he should be "well-educated, vigorous, agreeable, humble, pleasant in conversation, sober, modest, and above all a hard worker; which is quite far from the opinion of a number of people who believe that a comedian's life is nothing but libertinism, and a license for vice, impurity, laziness, and lack of control." Georges de Scudéry's

La Comédie des Comédiens of 1632 (with the same title as Gougenot's play) has in it contemporary actors thinly disguised under other names and who give considerable information on the theatrical situation of the time. In the second act one Blandimare * says that comedians are not to be esteemed *en masse*: some are good and some are bad, and critical taste should be applied to them even as to "poetry, melons, and friends." Later in the century, Chappuzeau, who loved the theatre and everything connected with it, stated that he wanted a comedian to live "in moral correctness" and be catalogued among the "honorable people" of the world. A little before 1700, one of the historians of the city of Paris, Germain Brice, made a rather intriguing statement: "In the earlier centuries, actors were regarded as infamous fellows and as persons worthy of excommunication, with whom it was not permitted to have any relations; but all that is changed at present, and there is not much difference between a comedian and any other man, except when the irregular conduct of some ones of them distinguishes them from *honnêtes gens*." Many "honorable people," especially those connected with the Church, were not in agreement with Brice.[7]

If the social position of the early professional actors in France was a matter for discussion, that of the first actresses on the public stage was even more so. The most glowing account of the charms and virtue of an actress is the story of the unknown beauty who performed with Valleran le Conte in Bordeaux during the early 1590's. According to the chronicler Gaufreteau, she was "a very beautiful creature of a woman, who, contrary to all the ordinary rules of this profession [of acting], was refined in manners and conversation, and anyone who had not known about it would not have believed that she was an actress. Several young men of Bordeaux fell in love with her, as much for her gentle and refined conversa-

---

* He is really Montdory, whose fame at the Marais theatre had already begun.

tion as for her beauty." She was courted both by pretty speeches and by gifts, but she never responded to any of these attentions. She was evidently of good birth, probably the daughter of some lawyer in Paris, and had married a comedian who, in his "debauched attitude," dragged her over the country to participate in his profession. She never stooped to the low roles of farces, however, but "played marvelously" the parts of princesses or queens — "for, by her manner, her words, and her gestures you would have taken her for one." When she received young gentlemen in her lodgings after the theatrical performance was finished, she enjoyed polite and serious conversation — even about the "science of history" — and she upbraided "frankly and openly those young men who addressed to her too freely words suitable for a carnival, and said that when she was away from the theatre she was not a *comédienne*." After the death of her husband she returned to Paris where she lived "correctly and honorably." [8]

There were other commentaries on actresses from those who were much closer to the theatre than the infatuated young man from Bordeaux. Gautier Garguille, with behind-the-scenes realism, did not forget "our actresses" in his mock legacy: to them he left their "laudable jealousies" of one another, their right to receive presents from stage-door suitors after the show, and an admonition to pay no attention to the "stupid opinions of the people." Scudéry has La Beausoleil, one of the actresses in his *La Comédie des Comédiens*, speak out in defense of those of her sex whom many consider in private life to be the counterpart of any crude role they may perform on the public stage: "But it is an error into which almost all people fall in regard to the women of our profession; for these persons think that the farce is the image of our personalities, and that we only act out in the theatre what we are in real life. They believe that the wife of any one of the actors unquestionably belongs to the whole troupe; and, imagining that we are communal property, like the sun or the elements, every man feels that he has the right to make us suffer the importunity of his demands." Men consider that they have free entry to actresses' rooms, and for a few men who are *honnêtes* there are a thousand who are not. Their conversation is boring, their criticism of poetry is pedantic, and their amorous advances unwelcome. Such men show that they are as "deficient in judgment on matters of verses as they are in knowledge of the qualities of virtue in women." The story of the beautiful and chaste actress of Bordeaux and the long speech of La Beausoleil have one feature in common: they both would indicate that there was a steady stream of masculine visitors into an actress' dressing room.[9]

The conclusion was fairly general that the early professional actresses were not too strict in their morals. Paul Scarron, who gave a sympathetic picture in his novel, *Le Roman comique*, of the trials and tribulations of a wandering band of comedians during the first half of the seventeenth century, makes a particular point of the "virtue" of La Caverne and her daughter, two actresses in the troupe. In all the groups of performers going around the country, there would not be found two *comédiennes* whose standards of conduct were higher — and "this does not mean that all professional actresses are lacking in virtue; but in the opinion of society as a whole, which could be wrong, they are less weighed down with it than with old embroidery and grease-paint." A more emphatic conclusion, certainly, toward both men and women on the early public stage was that expressed by Tallemant des Réaux. Tallemant thought that the men who acted at this time were "almost all scoundrels." As for the feminine assistants who shared the boards as well as the beds of the actors, these "wives lived with the greatest license in the world; they were women used by the whole company, even by actors who were in a different troupe." That this estimate of professional actresses had not changed too much a little later in the century is evidenced in Tallemant's story concerning Boisrobert,

Richelieu's secretary and something of a man of letters besides. To a rehearsal of *Mirame*, a play written at Richelieu's behest by Desmarets de Saint Sorlin, one of the composers under his patronage, Boisrobert invited a young girl, a "mignonne" who had acted for a time in the troupe of Montdory. This preparation for a private performance in the Cardinal's palace was an occasion of considerable social importance, attended by Louis XIII and his household as well as by the King's brother, Gaston d'Orléans. The royal audience was much irritated to find an actress among the guests. Boisrobert, who probably had fallen victim to the demoiselle's charms, explained that she had been asked to the affair not as a social equal of the lofty assemblage but as a *comédienne* — and, said Boisrobert, "I consider them all strumpets, and I do not think that any one of them has ever been anything different." Boisrobert's explanation of the presence of one of society's rejects at such a function was thought to be rather lame and, according to Tallemant, because of the episode Boisrobert fell into disgrace.[10]

The rather pathetic situation of the professional actress was signalized in 1620 by Tristan l'Hermite, who was later to gain fame for his vigorous tragedy, *Mariamne*. Tristan wrote a letter at this time to a "belle comédienne" (who has remained unidentified), in which he sympathized with her difficult social status and the ravages that would be made upon her charms because of her unprotected position in the world. Tristan began his epistle in a tone of melancholy: "None of France will grow tired of admiring you, but for my part I can only pity you and mix secret tears in with the applause that you receive from the crowds." The young Tristan most likely was enamored of the unknown young actress. A further commentary on the position of any woman connected with the professional theatre was made much later by the historian of plays and players, Lemazurier. In describing the career of Gautier Garguille, Lemazurier mentioned the fact that the

wife of the farce-player married again after his death. Though
Lemazurier with possible inaccuracy made her the daughter
of Tabarin, his analysis of her remarriage is of interest: "The
daughter of a mountebank and the widow of a *farceur*, she
had no reason to expect to enter into a distinguished marriage;
either the man who married her had to be very poor, or he had
to have dulled sensibilities." The wives of actors, whether or
not they performed in public with their husbands, suffered
along with the actresses the stigma of the professional theatre.
Some of this stigma disappeared by the middle of the seventeenth century, after the theatre had become more fashionable
and young ladies of wealthy bourgeois families could become
"fond of comedy," as did Alcidon's visionary daughter, Sestiane, in Desmarets de Saint Sorlin's play, *Les Visionnaires*.
Sestiane's love for the theatre, however, was in the nature of
a social patronage of an institution that was by 1640 something
of the mode. She would definitely have lost caste if she had
joined any troupe as a professional *comédienne*. The situation
created a strange paradox: after the early 1630's actresses became more and more necessary to the success of a play and
their personalities through the years came to be better and
better known — culminating, possibly, in a figure like that
of "la divine" Sarah Bernhardt; yet they remained for many
of the French a group of *déclassées*. It might be legitimate to
say that the gifted actress was and is detached from society's
standard methods of compartmentalization — or, in the words
of the contemporary critic, Léopold Lacour, "hors classe." [11]

With or without the approval of the world outside the
theatre, the early professional actor in France went on working
at his job. After 1600, his numbers increased and the records in
Parisian and provincial archives continue to yield evidence of
his wanderings all over the nation. As a generality, the actors
would be formed into a company of from eight to twelve
persons, with the most able and experienced member as the
chief of the troupe. The little traveling band described by

Scarron in his *Roman comique* was limited in its productions because it had in it only seven or eight men and women when it was at "full strength." This would have been a large enough number to produce a play if they had all been ready for duty, which they were not. Even in Paris at the Hôtel de Bourgogne the royal comedians could be reduced by circumstances to no more than seven or eight. Some of Valleran le Conte's agreements contain eight names or fewer, but this is deceptive evidence since the actresses did not always sign official papers. The preferred complement for the Parisian troupes would be nearer a dozen, which would allow for a greater variety of repertory. Also, there was the question of the individual competence of an actor; in theory, a *farceur* could perform in serious drama as well as in farce, but this was seldom the case in reality. All of which made important an actor's histrionic background and his technical training. Many of the tricks of the trade were passed down in an acting family from the parents to the children. The actress La Caverne in Scarron's novel said she was the "daughter of a comedian" and had always heard that in her father's household there had been no other profession than that of acting. Such a system of dramatic coaching was apparently followed by the Béjart family of actors, into which Molière married. It was a bit too ingrowing to offer a balanced knowledge of the demands of the stage.[12]

Youngsters destined for a career in the theatre could come as apprentices under the tutelage of the more experienced members of an acting company. One of Valleran le Conte's major contributions to his profession was his taking of teenagers under his wing to train them for the stage and its mysteries. These adoptions on the part of Valleran began before 1600 and he evidently expected the fledgling thespian to do all sorts of jobs in connection with the staging of plays. In 1599, one Marye Lescuier put her fifteen-year-old son, Nicolas Gasteau, under the guidance of Valleran to learn "the science of comedy" and to become proficient in "playing on the spinet, the viol, and in singing music." The training seemed to have paid off because Nicolas Gasteau in 1607 was one of eight actors who signed a paper forming a dramatic company under the direction of Valleran. The same system must have been employed in the early years of the actor, Estienne de Ruffin, since in a contract of 1606 Valleran and his wife, Jehanne de Wancourt, agreed to "feed, nourish, look after, house, and keep the said Ruffin during the said time as they have done before and are now doing." If Ruffin should get sick Valleran promised to take care of him "just like a good father." All of which would suggest that Ruffin had formerly been apprenticed to Valleran; unfortunately, Valleran was unable to carry out the financial commitments he made to Ruffin in the 1606 contract. Later in 1606, a "schoolboy" named Alexandre du Mesnil, of the parish of Saint Etienne du Mont in Paris, signed up with Valleran for one year, and was to perform any theatrical service that would be demanded. For this he would be given a small portion — one eighth of a share — of the receipts from the productions, even though he might be ill and not able to take part in the show. In 1609, a fifteen-year-old boy named Sidrac Petit-Jehan was put in the service of Valleran to learn to be a comedian. Young Sidrac was to stay with Valleran for three years, during which time Valleran was to be responsible for feeding, clothing, and lodging the boy. Sidrac would receive money for his services only when he showed that he "knew how to act." This experiment also must have turned out successfully, for some two and one half years later Sidrac Petit-Jehan was signing official documents as a member of Valleran's company. Petit-Jehan was thus one of the comedians of the King when he was seventeen or, at most, barely eighteen years of age.[13]

The most illustrious of Valleran's apprentices was Pierre le Messier, later to become famous under the stage name of Bellerose, and Valleran's successor as *chef de troupe* at the

Hôtel de Bourgogne. Jacques le Messier, the father of Pierre and a royal functionary in the town of Senlis, put his son in the service of Valleran for two years by an act that was signed April 8, 1609. Valleran promised to furnish the usual food, lodging, heat, clothes (including shoes), and other things needed by the boy. The master also agreed to take the young Pierre and "show, teach, and instruct him in the science and industry of representing all tragicomedies, comedies, pastorals, and other plays." During this period the youngster was to be under the complete control of Valleran. A slightly sour note was struck in the following specification: in case young Pierre should not care for Valleran's guardianship and run away, the father promised to "search in the city and suburbs of Paris and if possible bring him back to the said master." In any event, the agreement must have worked out satisfactorily, since the young Le Messier stayed with the profession of acting in which he was to gain notable distinction. Too, Jacques le Messier undoubtedly thought Valleran was doing right by his son because on December 9, 1609, the daughter of the Le Messier, Judicq, was apprenticed to Le Conte "to learn to act in comedies and play the spinet." Earlier in 1609, on October 26, another girl was put under the guidance of Valleran and his wife: this was Jehanne Crevé who on this day was entrusted to Valleran "in order to learn the science of comedy." On January 15, 1610, Symon Diye from Brittany put his daughter, Elezabel, in Valleran's charge for seven years to learn how to "read, write, and play the spinet," and "to represent on the stage and in public all comedies, tragicomedies, and pastorals." It was important for later developments in the French theatre that future actresses were being given training so early in the century, although as yet there were few legitimate roles for them to play.[14]

There was the question of an actor's training in the techniques of his trade and there was also the question of his general education. Much comment was made during the cen-

tury, some of which has already been noted, on the comedian
who was too ignorant to understand or interpret his lines. One
of Valleran's apprentices just mentioned above was to be
taught how to read and write — which would seem fairly
basic to any profession. However, too pedantic or specialized
a learning was no help to the actor. Gougenot has a provocative commentary in his *Comédie des Comédiens* on the matter
of the need for versatility in a performer on the public stage.
In a gathering of several of the players, the Capitaine (the
standard descendant of Plautus' *Miles Gloriosus*) contends
that the role of a soldier is all that he will play; anything else
is beneath him. Bellerose — this is Gougenot's imagined Bellerose but the picture probably is pretty accurate — disagrees
with such an attitude. He illustrates his arguments by pointing
to Gautier Garguille, who is creating quite effectively in the
play the character of a lawyer. Gautier, obviously, has had no
legal training; but if he had had and could represent lawyers
only, he would be less valuable to the troupe than a man
without a doctorate in law but with enough versatility to play
other roles. Bellerose phrases the idea as follows: "It is true
that one cannot be a good actor without understanding clearly
what one is reciting; but this comprehension comes through
experience to some who do not have it through training in
letters." [15]

If the theatre were relieved of its infamy, according to one
theory, persons of greater capabilities would take up acting
as a profession. The reverse side of the picture was that, if
actors conducted themselves honorably and without debauchery, the stage would not continue to have the official
condemnation with which it had earlier been marked. To
insure progress in the excellence of the institution of the
theatre, one suggestion was that there be appointed a Director, Overseer, or Grand Master of Theatres and Public Games
in France, who would watch over the actions of the comedians and render an account of them to the King. One method

of making sure that the proprieties were observed would be not to allow girls to act in public unless they had a father or mother in the troupe. All widows in a company of actors would be required to remarry within six months after their year of grief, if they expected to continue their careers on the boards. The Director of Theatres and Public Games would be expected to keep an eye out for promising actors in the colleges and in the provincial troupes, and oblige them to "study the representation of spectacles as well as declamations and expressions of sentiment." Those who came to be attached to the royal troupe would have a *Brevet du Roi*, and a "certificate of capacity and probity." All of which is in anticipation of the present-day Conservatoire in Paris, which strives to assure the national theatres of a constant flow of promising young men and women to fill out the corps of singers and actors as the need arises.[16]

The proposed Director of Theatres would have discovered his ideal trouper in an earlier picture of what an actor should be. In Scudéry's *La Comédie des Comédiens*, Blandimare listed the desired qualities for a comedian: "It is necessary first that nature make her contribution by giving him a fine facial expression, because that is what strikes the spectators first; then he must have an impressive bearing, free and unconstrained movement, a clear and strong voice; his speech must be exempt from the bad pronunciations and crude accents of the provinces, and always reflect the purity of the French language; he must have the mind and judgment for the understanding of verses, and the force of memory to learn them quickly and to retain them a long time afterward; he must not be ignorant of history and fable, for otherwise he will mix things up and recite them often with the wrong sense or tone." Further, he should not indulge in extravagant postures, and should have a modest confidence that is not too bold nor too timid. All types of emotion should be reflected on his face at the appropriate moment — tears, laughter, love, hate, indifference, disdain, jealousy, anger, or ambition. Incidentally, a comedian with all these qualifications would be just about as "rare as the phoenix," Blandimare concluded. One of the group of players to whom Blandimare was talking admitted that Blandimare had set up quite an "idea of perfection," but the troupe at hand, in the mind of this actor, was "not too far from it." [17]

The deviation from the broad and crude histrionic methods of the farce-players, begun with Valleran le Conte, continued with Bellerose and Montdory. The young Pierre le Messier, famous under his stage name of Bellerose, was the most apt pupil in Valleran's training school for budding actors and actresses. Born probably in 1592, he was put in Valleran's hands when around seventeen years of age. Shortly thereafter Bellerose was acting at the Hôtel de Bourgogne in a company formed by Valleran and Laporte, by the agreement of January 28, 1610, which was supposed to operate for three years. A little more than nine months after Bellerose started as an apprentice he was a full-fledged member of a dramatic troupe under his master. A tribute to his abilities may well be noted in the fact that Valleran, when he signed the contract, asked for two shares of the profits of the company for himself and "the said Pierre (le) Messier." On the other hand it was agreed that the sister of Pierre le Messier, Judicq, was not to be taken into the company until a year later and then on the basis of her demonstrated progress in acquiring acting skills. In the meantime, she was to learn techniques and to perform free when needed. Bellerose and Valleran in a subsequent agreement during 1610 were still to have two shares of the profits; the closeness of their association is confirmed by the fact that in these papers Valleran signed for both himself and Le Messier. The two were most likely together in troupes traveling during the next few years over France and Holland. After the death of Valleran, Bellerose may have become im-

mediately * *chef de troupe* at the age of twenty-one or twenty-two. This was a big job for a youngster, but it was one
that he was destined to hold for more than thirty years. The
company, with inevitable changes in personnel, was with
Bellerose in Marseille in 1620. After considerable journeying
over foreign and domestic terrain, he was back in Paris in
1622 — the moment that for a long time was thought to be
the beginning of his career in the French capital city.[18]

Bellerose and his companions, despite many difficulties and
momentary invasions from other troupes, remained the prime
occupants of the Hôtel de Bourgogne after 1625 and guarded
zealously their title of *comédiens du roi*. The great trio of
farceurs, Gros Guillaume, Gautier Garguille, and Turlupin
— with whom Bellerose was associated — were ending their
activities as dramatic tastes were beginning to change. In
1630, Bellerose married the widow of an actor, Nicole Gas-
saud, who had recently arrived from the provinces. She was
the sister of one of Molière's later comedians, the plump Du
Croisy. In any case, Bellerose and his wife performed together
in the company for nearly two decades. She remained active
after his retirement which occurred in 1647 when Bellerose
turned over his large theatrical wardrobe, his titles of *chef* and
orateur de troupe, and a lot of administrative headaches to the
good actor, Floridor. Bellerose was far from poverty-stricken,
and had most likely been able, as was said of some of the
members of the royal company, to "amass money to buy
houses both in the country and the town." [19]

The technique of Bellerose on the stage was quite different
from that of the farce-players. He sought to remove from the
boards the rough gaudiness and exaggerated slapstick of both
his French and Italian predecessors. He preferred a more
natural style to masks and flour and stuffed torsoes. Gautier

* This is the opinion of Madame Deierkauf-Holsboer; but it seems pretty
fast.

9. *Tabarin and his famous hat*

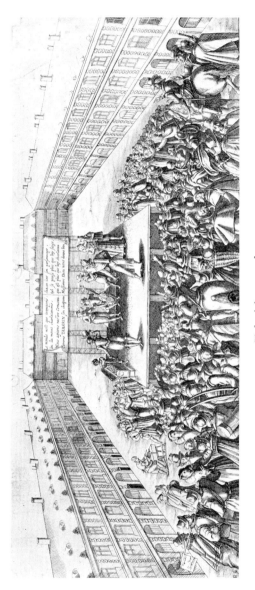

10. *Tabarin's street show*

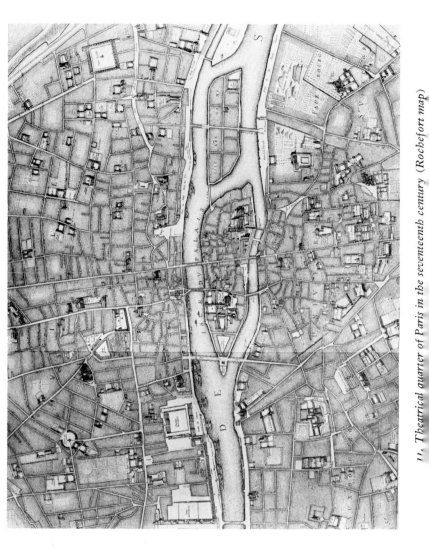

11. *Theatrical quarter of Paris in the seventeenth century* (*Rochefort map*)

Garguille, who knew him well, paid him a bit of homage when in Gautier's *Testament* Bellerose is asked to preserve his "gentleness in amorous episodes, his theatrical delicacies which are almost unknown except to him." Chappuzeau called Bellerose, along with Montdory, an "accomplished comedian," but La Rancune in Scarron's *Roman comique* said Bellerose was "too affected." Tallemant des Réaux, as he looked back on the actors of the earlier part of the century, was not too complimentary of Bellerose, who was "a painted-up comedian always watching where he was throwing his hat for fear that he might spoil its plumes." In continuing analysis, Tallemant added on Bellerose: "It is not that he did not do well certain long recitals and tender speeches, but he did not understand what he was saying." As for La Bellerose, Tallemant said she was "the best *comédienne* in Paris," but "so fat that she was like a turret." Lemazurier in a later century admitted that he knew little about the wife of Bellerose but he had "heard that she had beauty." The Frères Parfaict in a slightly earlier period maintained that they had no information on Madame Bellerose, but praised Bellerose as being "one of the first and most excellent actors in the tragic genre" under Louis XIII. There was no other such "perfect comedian" in the royal troupe as Bellerose. In his capacity of *orateur* of the company, he "made announcements gracefully, talked easily, and his little discourses were always a pleasure to hear." The Frères Parfaict cushioned their praise of Bellerose with the story concerning madame de Montbazon, who in the latter part of the seventeenth century asserted that she could not really care for monsieur de La Rochefoucauld, the famous writer of maxims, because he resembled Bellerose too much and was therefore "too insipid." Bellerose's stage manners and reforms were evidently considered prim and old-fashioned before his death in 1670.[20]

The contemporary of Bellerose during the formative period

of the French classic theatre, and in many ways his competitor, was Montdory.* He, too, was in essence a protégé of Valleran le Conte since Montdory's first certain theatrical connection was in an association of actors formed by Valleran on March 31, 1612. It will be remembered that in this company one Gilleberts, "called Mondaury," was given half a share of the profits, after all expenses of operation had been deducted. Guillaume des Gilleberts, who took the stage name of Montdory, was born in the town of Thiers in Auvergne in 1594. According to the somewhat romantic biography of the actor done by Elie Cottier, Montdory was sent to Paris around 1609 to avoid an epidemic raging on his native soil. There he saw the lusty theatrical life of the capital city, with its farce-players and charlatans and entertainers in the streets. It is possible that the stage name of Montdory could have been inspired by the famous *opérateur* and companion of Tabarin, Mondor. Tallemant, in his long discourse on Montdory, said that he was sent to Paris to visit a *procureur*, and went to see plays on festival days and Sundays because the *procureur* thought the youngster "would spend less money and become less debauched in the theatre than anywhere else." Montdory was so fascinated by things dramatic that "he became a comedian himself — and, although he was only sixteen years old, they gave him the principal roles, and he gradually became the leader of a troupe composed of Le Noir and his wife, which had formerly been with the Prince of Orange." † In his admiration for Montdory Tallemant has become overly enthusiastic: it is most unlikely that a sixteen-year-old would have been given leading roles in Charles le Noir's company — with which group, however, Montdory was later associated. When he was eighteen, according to the above contract with Valleran, Montdory was getting only half a share in the profits of the troupe. All of which would

---

* This is the way the actor signed his own name, rather than *Mondory*.
† Maurice of Nassau, Prince of Orange (1567–1625).

intimate that he was not yet a fully established actor, as was Bellerose at the same age. The young Montdory could well have been infatuated with Madame le Noir, who was supposed to be a pretty thing and the favorite of the patron of authors and actors, the comte de Belin. Montdory was also smitten with another actress, La Villiers, who played opposite him on occasions; but the gossips had it that she did not care particularly for him.[21]

Montdory and Bellerose were probably both with Valleran le Conte on the trip that took him into Holland in 1613. During this year the Prince of Orange entertained the Count of the Palatinate, Frederick V, and his young wife, Elizabeth Stuart, the only daughter of James I — and Valleran and his troupe furnished the "comedy." For the next few years the trail of French actors traveling in and out of France is blurred. They continued to be popular in Holland, since on April 17, 1618, the Prince of Orange assured safe passage for a company to reënter France on their way to Nantes in Brittany, where they gave a series of performances. Of this company and the reception given it in Nantes, mademoiselle de Rohan wrote to the sister of the Prince of Orange, the Duchess of La Trémoille, on December 10, 1618: "We have seen some excellent comedians, who say they are attached to your brother. They are very circumspect, and careful of their language, not only in front of us but also in the city, according to reports." The make-up of this troupe is not known but Montdory was possibly a member of it, since later events proved that he had won the patronage of the Prince of Orange. On July 14, 1622, the Prince's players rented the Hôtel de Bourgogne to present a repertory for a month, "even as they have done before." This statement would suggest that they had performed earlier in the dirty and dilapidated Hôtel de Bourgogne. In any case, Charles le Noir was in the company and so was Montdory, "likewise a comedian of the Prince of Orange." On April 14, 1624, Montdory and the actor, Claude Husson, signed a contract for two years, an association that took Montdory away from the Prince of Orange's troupe. The Prince's comedians, after his death in 1625, continued to exist under his name and under the direction of Charles le Noir and others, until 1629. By this year, neither Montdory nor Charles le Noir was a part of the Prince of Orange's company, but had formed one of their own, destined to be the future Théâtre du Marais with which the royal comedians at the Hôtel de Bourgogne were to be in competition for several decades. Montdory and Le Noir avoided the theatrical complications of Paris as their new organization was getting under way. Little is known of this period of two or three years in the provinces. The historian of the theatre of Rouen, E. Gosselin, states that it is "almost certain" that Montdory and his troupe were in Rouen in 1628. He must have been close by because he picked up Pierre Corneille's play, *Mélite*, along the way and thus introduced a new author and a new company to Paris. Corneille said later in his *Examen* of the play: "The success of it was surprising. It established a new troupe of comedians in Paris, in spite of the merit of the one (the *comédiens royaux*) which was in the position of considering itself unique; it equaled the finest thing that had been done up to that time, and made me known at the Court." The signal success of *Mélite* and Montdory's company took place in the latter part of 1629, or possibly during the first weeks of 1630.[22]

After occupying several other places in the Marais quarter, Montdory and company went in 1634 to the transformed hall on the rue Vieille du Temple which has since been thought of as the Théâtre du Marais. There he was to make the reputation that has come down to later generations. Despite problems of keeping his company up to full acting strength, he staged toward the end of 1634 Mairet's *Sophonisbe*, a good tragedy dealing with the love of a Carthaginian lady for a Roman soldier. In 1636, he triumphed in Tristan l'Hermite's

Mariamne, with a vigorous portrayal of the role of Herod. Montdory's success with Corneille's *Le Cid*, late in 1636 or early in 1637, made of it one of the great dates in the history of the French theatre. Sometime later in 1637, during a revival of his triumphant characterization of Herod in *Mariamne*, Montdory was seized with an attack of apoplexy that resulted in a paralysis of the tongue, an affliction from which he never fully recovered. On November 13, 1637, he wrote a touching letter to Boisrobert in which he said he wished he could mount the boards again and that Their Majesties' theatre would for him most happily be his "tomb." Despite a long rest and the treatment of curative waters, his career was ended. Montdory, who bridged the gap in the French theatre between experiments in tragedy and the majestic periods of Corneille, died in 1654.[23]

Others had been good but Montdory was the first great actor to come out of the early public theatre. The comments of those who knew him or knew about him were generally favorable and made of him the Roscius of the French stage. Gautier Garguille, who was in the rival troupe at the Hôtel de Bourgogne, called Montdory the "cock of the (Marais) parish" and advised him never to forget that he was "always the boss" and that the "troupe could not subsist without him." On a practical level, Gautier therefore suggested that Montdory should take twice as much of the profits from operations as any one else in the organization of the Théâtre du Marais. Balzac in a letter to Boisrobert said that Montdory added graces to "ordinary poets," and "the sound of his voice supported by the dignities of his gestures ennobles the most commonplace and banal conceptions." Scudéry in his *Apology for the Theatre* in 1639 said that "the famous actor Montdory has had few equals, certainly, in past centuries or in our own." Tristan l'Hermite thought Montdory was an "illustrious performer," and Corneille felt that in Montdory's rendition of Herod "the excellence of the actor," as much as the quality

of Tristan's verses, "elevated the personage." Tallemant des
Réaux was high in his praise of Montdory and left out the
vinegar with which he usually seasoned even his honeyed
remarks. As for the actor's appearance, he was "neither tall
nor well set-up," but "carried himself well." He never played
in farce, and his wife never played at all. His abilities at any
rate were remarkable: when he lost several of his actors by
royal order to the Hôtel de Bourgogne, he reorganized the
Marais troupe and made it stronger than before, "because he
alone was better than a whole company." Any critic of Montdory, said Tallemant, should see his Herod four times to be
convinced of the actor's art. It was too bad that Montdory
had not been given the authority to train other comedians,
particularly those who thought that they knew "as much as
he." In the concept of Tallemant, Montdory was "perhaps the
most notable performer that has existed since Roscius."
Michel de Marolles in his *Mémoires* confirmed this point
when he said he had enjoyed seeing "the rare Montdory, who
has not left any successor and who might well have been
compared, without any flattery, to the Roscius of the Ancients"; Montdory was clearly "the most perfect actor of his
time." Chappuzeau, in his exuberant fashion, described Montdory as an "excellent comedian" and fine *orateur de troupe*,
in an association that was filled with "good actors and actresses." Later centuries were a tiny bit critical of Montdory.
Lemazurier did not consider him a "perfect actor," in spite
of his reputation. His manner of acting was "forced," and his
delivery exaggerated — but this was a "general fault" of the
period. He was of moderate stature, and "talked gracefully."
The Frères Parfaict blamed the fashion of overacting, current
in the seventeenth century, on the silly plays which were performed before 1630. Even these sounded fine in Montdory's
delivery, which was "supported by a pleasing manner, much
feeling, and a quality of voice that went to the heart." He
was really a "very excellent comedian"; and as *orateur* he

made quite neatly "announcements and little speeches." He was of "moderate height, proud in manner, and with an expressive face." He had his "hair cut short and he even played the role of heroes without ever wanting to put on a wig." The Frères Parfaict do not reveal the sources of their information on actors they could not have known, but they do say that their estimate is more accurate than that of others who have written on the theatre during their time.[24]

Montdory's skill in his profession was praised by one who had seen him in action. The Abbé d'Aubignac in his analysis of theatrical techniques said that an actor should come on stage very calm, or very excited, or midway between these two states (in a "demi-passion"). The third condition is very difficult to depict; therefore a play should have a few tranquil words for the performer to work up to a "demi-passion." The portrayal of the mid-emotional state depends very much on the skill of the performer: "This problem can be solved in a way that I have seen practiced by the premier actor of our time, I mean Montdory: before speaking on these occasions, he would walk around some moments on the stage as though dreaming, working himself up a bit, shaking his head, raising and lowering his eyes, and taking different postures according to the sentiment that he wished to express — which he did, in my opinion, in order to animate himself a little and get himself in the proper condition to represent a demi-passion." All of this would make the shift more natural from inertness to greater violence of feeling. But, once he had lifted himself into a frenzied emotional state the actor, including Montdory as well as lesser lights, was likely to give way to ranting and shouting — a malady that has come down into the twentieth century at the Comédie Française. Molière satirized such bombast when he said in Les Précieuses ridicules that the comédiens royaux were the ones who knew how "to swell out the words." A delightful series of jibes at overacting is to be noted in Guéret's popular Parnasse réformé, which had five editions in France by 1674. By using the device of having ancient and modern literary and dramatic figures appear together in the same place, Guéret has everybody from all ages talk to and about everybody else. Montfleury — a comedian popular after the middle of the seventeenth century and called "illustrious" in all roles by Chappuzeau — sounds off at the exhausting requirements made of actors in serious plays. Tristan, in creating the demanding role of Herod in *Mariamne*, would have been willing, says Montfleury, for a Montdory to "die every day in the week" in the playwright's service. If Montdory had not strained himself over the grand tragic passions, he would still be alive today. As for himself, Montfleury explains: "Whoever will be curious to know what I died of, let him not ask whether it was of fever, or dropsy, or the gout: I can tell him it was from *Andromaque*." * Apollo, as moderator of the discussion, listens to a number of complaints and then draws up a new list of regulations. Among them, "fustian" is forbidden to mount the boards and those are condemned to shame who would create on stage "hubbub mal à propos." By implication proper hubbub would be legitimate.[25]

Montdory's popularity was further indicated in Scarron's *Roman comique*, where the little traveling company of "comédiens de profession" put on Tristan's *Mariamne* with the young leading man, Destin, playing the violent part of Herod and "reciting in the tones of Montdory." Some general ideas on the manner of declaiming poetry, always a difficult problem in the theatre, were given by one of the older actors in Scarron's story: "One must observe the patterns of speech, and not make it seem like poetry, but pronounce the periods as though they were prose; they should not be chanted, nor should one stop in the middle or at the end of a verse, as the rabble would do, which is very lacking in grace; one must

---

* Racine's famous tragedy of 1667, in which Montfleury played the role of Oreste.

handle the lines with confidence; in a word, they must be given animation by action." All of which is rather sound advice, and Montdory could well have been the model for it.[26]

As the public theatre was gaining acceptance in France, competition among the actors and their companies was vigorous if not always aboveboard. The Confrérie de la Passion, it has been noted, interfered with the actors' freedom of renting halls and limited the places in which they could perform. The comedians also interfered with the activities of one another, individually and in groups. Charles le Noir and his charming *comédienne* of a wife were advised at one time not to let their troupe be disturbed by newly arrived members in it: if the newcomers could not fit harmoniously into the company, they should go "back to the country." Charles le Noir himself participated in a bit of inter-company strife in 1625 when he rented the Hôtel de Bourgogne from under the nose of Bellerose and the royal comedians. Le Noir was then chief of the Prince of Orange's troupe. The *comédiens du Roi* were very much irked at this move and proceeded to give performances in front of the Hôtel de Bourgogne in the open air — which, as can be imagined, led to considerable confusion. On August 14, 1625, the civil authorities of Paris upheld the lease of the Hôtel de Bourgogne by the Prince of Orange's comedians and forbade Bellerose's troupe "to trouble them or to play any place around the *maison et hôtel* de Bourgogne," or in that general area on the rue Saint Antoine. The Prince of Orange's company added further insult to the royal players by grabbing off one of their number, Louis Galian. Some time earlier a group of actors from the country were forbidden by the authorities "to hurl any insults into the said Hôtel de Bourgogne while performances are being given, or to throw stones, powders, or anything else which may cause the people to riot." [27]

In 1611, five of the King's "comédiens ordinaires" allowed

one Fleury Jacob and his wife, Colombe Venier, to join their company while touring the provinces. Jacob was very much of a good-for-nothing but his wife continued with the group, as best she could, the "profession of *comédienne*" in which she had been brought up. Jacob got an edict from the Parlement of Toulouse against the above five on the ground that they had taken off his wife and kept her: these actors, including such well-known figures as Hugues Guéru and Estienne de Ruffin, were to be banished from France. Jacob later admitted that he had lied, the King in 1613 annulled the decree of banishment, and the actors' property was not confiscated; but Fleury Jacob should certainly have lost any standing he might have had with his fellow entertainers. From a notary's act of 1633 in the town of Le Mans there comes the evidence that "Nicolas Devis, sieur des Oeillets, comédien du Roi" was relieved of his furniture, baggage, and other equipment by another actor, Claude Nolleau, of the same company. Des Oeillets was the husband of the actress destined to gain fame under this name later in the century; nothing is known of Claude Nolleau. In any case, such easy pilfering of a colleague's possessions was more likely to happen in the provincial dramatic companies than in the Parisian troupes. However, since most of the early actors had spent a good deal of time traveling around before settling in Paris, many of the relaxed habits of the country may have carried over to the city.[28]

The most thorough job of raiding of one troupe by another was done under the sanction of the King himself. According to Théophraste Renaudot's *Gazette* of 1634, "His Majesty wished to take and join to the troupe of Bellerose" six actors from the Marais organization. These were Charles le Noir and his wife (she of the "sweet little ways," in the words of Gautier Garguille), Jodelet, l'Espy, Jacquemin Jadot, and Alizon (the player of old nurses). With such reinforcement, the royal comedians were able to pack the Hôtel de Bour-

gogne on December 10, 1634, for a play of Scudéry. Montdory's outfit was pretty well decimated by this royal transfer,
but he did not "despair of the safety of his little republic"
and sought to "repair the damage." It was true that the
comédiens royaux were in rather difficult straits at the time
on account of the recent deaths of Gros Guillaume and
Gautier Garguille. And Louis XIII, in his concern for the
general dramatic welfare of his realm, could well have used
his powers to strengthen any company that needed it. The
Renaudot *Gazette* of January 6, 1635, said that the "kindness
of the King" was such that he wanted to support *three* dramatic companies in his capital — that of Bellerose, Montdory's,
and another in the faubourg Saint Germain. Little is known
of this last group, except that they apparently had poor success in the tough theatrical league of Paris. Madame Deierkauf-Holsboer has contended recently, with considerable
plausibility, that two of the actors, Jacquemin Jadot and Alizon, transferred by Louis XIII to the Hôtel de Bourgogne
came from the Saint Germain group. This would have meant
that Montdory lost four rather than six performers, and thus
his problem of reconstruction would have been slightly less
grave. Tallemant said that Louis XIII took the actors — only
Charles le Noir and his wife are named — away from the
Marais organization "to spite the Cardinal de Richelieu,"
but that Montdory picked up the good trouper, Baron, and
carried on. Unquestionably, there was a great deal of hop-
ping around from one company to another, and a contract
was not eternally binding. Jodelet, for example, despite his
official transfer to the King's own comedians, was a few years
later back with the Marais troupe.[29]

The actors, whether they were in strong or weak associations, faced severe punishments if they broke too many official
regulations. They could be fined or sentenced to terms in
prison. On October 4, 1624, by a decree of the civil chamber
of the Châtelet, the comedians of the Hôtel de Bourgogne

were to be "brought in as prisoners into the prisons of the Court." Their crime was that they had advertised a play — the sentence does not say that it was actually performed — called the *Grand Buffoonery of the Porters, Wine Peddlers, Bourgeoisie, the Commissioner (Commissaire), and the Tavern Keeper.* This satiric play was considered by the Châtelet authorities to be "greatly prejudicial to the public, and derisory of the powers of justice and scornful of the royal officers and of the duties of the said commissioners." The farce, which it must have been, had evidently been read by a committee of censorship at the Châtelet. How long the comedians were incarcerated — or whether they were pardoned by the King, as Henry IV had done in a similar case earlier in the century — is not known. As a generality, all comedians were threatened with fines if they put on any shows at "unseemly hours"; on Sundays and festival days it was improper to start the performance before three o'clock in the afternoon. Also, "insolences" in front of the Hôtel de Bourgogne to disturb a company of rival players carried the promise of punishment.[30]

The most usual type of fine was that administered for the benefit of the Confrérie de la Passion against any comedians who might have performed in some spot other than the Hôtel de Bourgogne. The standard amount of this assessment early in the century was sixty sous a day, and it was applied with hearty impartiality to any and all comers: to Claude Husson, Laporte, Robert Guérin, and the *comédiens du Roi*, or to an unknown like Mathieu de Roger. In 1619, the daily sixty sous were levied against a certain Claude Advet for the time he and his companions had "played, leaped around on a rope, and represented several facetious matters" outside the Hôtel de Bourgogne. A little later on, in 1627, a few wandering comedians, "Greek in nationality," ran afoul of the Confrérie's privilege and were condemned to fines. A Spanish troupe came into Paris briefly in 1625 and somewhat earlier a group of actors who called themselves the "Loyal and Brave Ones": nothing much is recorded about these actors, but the sixty sous a day threat must have shortened their sojourn in the capital. One of the larger fines was that requested in 1631 by the Confrérie and confirmed in 1632 by the authorities of the Châtelet: this was a levy of a crown a day (which was three livres or sixty sous) against Charles le Noir and his company for playing 135 days in a *jeu de paume* and not in the Hôtel de Bourgogne.[31]

The rights and privileges of an actor inside a troupe became better clarified as his profession gained in public recognition. He was paid if the company made any money, and the profits of operation were divided into shares. For illustration, if a company consisted of twelve members there would theoretically be twelve *parts* or shares. The *chef de troupe*, however, would most likely have at least two shares or their equivalent and a *débutant* no more than half a share. An apprentice could be assigned an even smaller fraction or, for a time, nothing but his bed and board. This system has already been noted in some of the company contracts drawn up and signed by groups of actors; it continued throughout the century and is basically intact at the state theatres of France today. Some elements of royal subvention came in before 1700 and such underwriting is still carried on by the French government at the present time. It was the general practice during the seventeenth century for the actors to divide up the proceeds at the end of the day, after the expenses of the performance had been deducted. Such a plan worked well when a play was popular and the bills could be paid on the spot; it was not so good when the audience was sparse and the candle furnisher or scene painter was waiting outside for his money. The Théâtre du Marais, as it became more prosperous and credit conditions improved, paid off its operating expenses only once a month. But even at the Marais the actors, who usually could find a place for a little ready cash, got their stipend immediately after they had removed the grease paint and stopped work for the day.

The manager of a troupe got extra shares but he deserved them because of the many things he had to buy. In the 1598 contract between Valleran le Conte and his troupe and Adrien Talmy and his company, Valleran was supposed to get one fourth of the receipts. In return for this large percentage, he had to furnish the players with "clothes, masks, beards, crowns, scepters, and other things." The combined association was to perform both in Paris and in the provinces, and Valleran was responsible for the transport and "the playing of the viols." When on the road, the two halves of the group might well travel separately, but Valleran still had to supply the "conveyance and the carriages." A similar contract was signed by Valleran in 1607, though it was probably not a type of arrangement under which he became too opulent. As for the cost of transport, some idea of that can be gained from the agreement made by one Jehan Brilloit in 1610 with Valleran, Laporte, and their companions. Brilloit contracted to take the comedians any place they wanted to go, with their "trunks, clothes, and baggage in his *charrette* and with his horses." It would cost thirty livres of Tours for twenty leagues. If the actors wanted to travel by water, all their stuff would be put in "boats and barques." By March 7, 1611, Valleran had accumulated a variety of debts, in spite of his allotment of one fourth of the profits from the productions of the combined companies; among other persons to whom he owed money was Jehan Brilloit: 149 livres of Tours for "having carried their baggage into several and diverse cities during a period of several years." In a later contract of 1612, Valleran had just two shares but no mention was made in it of his handling the matter of carriages and boats and other expenses. This is the same association in which Montdory received half a share and Judicq Messier along with another girl (named "Jehanne" and nothing else) a full share between them. Both these demoiselles most likely got married before they signed another agreement to do more play-acting.[32]

It was important, in any case, for an actor to have a full share, or even half a share, in a company and not be just a dramatic day-laborer. A shareholding position gave him a bit of standing with his fellows and something of a voice in the making of policy. This situation was rather amusingly illustrated in Gougenot's *La Comédie des Comédiens*, where Gros Guillaume and Turlupin say that they are tired of being treated as valets by the rest of the troupe on account of their being paid wages for their services. Bellerose agrees to allow them to be shareholders, and the other actors are willing for these two to be accepted fully into the company. The two farce-players then feel better about their status and stop grumbling. The audience must have laughed over this scene, especially those who remembered that Gros Guillaume had been *chef de troupe* on several occasions at the Hôtel de Bourgogne.[33]

One important item of the actor's expense was his clothes and costumes. Early in the development of the public theatre they were quite modest, but progressively they became more elaborate. In the words of Tallemant des Réaux, "in those [early] times, the actors rented their garments from the old-clothes dealer; they were dressed disgracefully and they did not know what they were doing." Tallemant here is rather harsh, but the sellers of frippery were near to the Hôtel de Bourgogne in Les Halles and must have had many of the comedians as their customers. For the wandering players clothes and costumes were an extra tribulation. With the baggage and an actress or two piled high on an overloaded cart, the men of the company would trudge along with the horses in the dust and mud that covered the winding roads of France. Occasionally, as happened in Scarron's story, some generous soul would give a tattered band of comedians a collection of "half worn-out clothes." But some of the costumes in Valleran le Conte's company were highly ornate; even if they did come from a second-hand shop, it was the best of its kind. On June 28, 1598, Valleran settled a debt of two hundred crowns to a "master old-clothes dealer" for seven *robes*, "five of silver and gold cloth and one of damask and one of changing taffeta, of which five were for the use of women and two for the use of men." These garments had evidently come into the dealer's hands from some noble's household, either legitimately or through the scheming machinations of a profit-minded valet. It is to be noted, in any event, that Valleran was at this early date providing equipment for actresses, prospective or already existent, in his troupe. Could the beautiful and chaste *comédienne* of Bordeaux have returned with him to Paris? Valleran continued to provide in 1599 "habits" for the combined personnel of his and Benoit Petit's companies, along with "music and the playing of viols." Valleran had increased his holdings of fancy costumes by 1606, because in May of this year he signed the whole collection of more than a dozen articles over to Estienne de Ruffin in payment of a debt, along with "five specimens of viols ornamented with mother of pearl" and a handsomely decorated scimitar. Among the costumes were two "robes in gold cloth made in Turkish fashion and garnished with buttons on tails." By 1611, when things had become pretty bad for Valleran, he conceded that among his debts was an item of 368 livres of Tours for "habits to be used in comedies." Even in Valleran's time, though it might throw him into bankruptcy, an actor had to be well dressed when he paraded before an audience. It is incorrect, therefore, to assume that on the early public stage in Paris the performers customarily appeared in dirty, dull, and bedraggled regalia.[34]

That splendor of costuming continued to be important in the theatre is proved by the inventory of the wardrobe of Charles le Noir, along with that of his wife, on August 18, 1637, made just after the actor's death. The estimated value of the collection — and the estimate was on the conservative side — would come to more than eight thousand dollars today. There were in the wardrobe twenty-one complete costumes for men, or enough for a whole troupe. One of them was valued by the examiner at the equivalent of over four hundred dollars. It will be observed that by this time the individual actor owned his own costumes and they were not the property of the company, as would seem to have been the case earlier when Valleran le Conte assumed responsibility for them. Charles le Noir, fortunately for him, lived to see a more prosperous era in the professional theatre. In addition to sumptuous raiment, he and his wife were able to buy in 1637 an expensive house in Paris, which he enjoyed only very briefly. Bellerose had also accumulated a handsome wardrobe during his long career on the boards. When he retired from the Hôtel de Bourgogne, he sold his stage finery — according to one report, to his successor, Floridor — for twenty thousand livres. Comedians, in the opinion of Chappuzeau, just naturally spent a great deal of money on clothes, whether "inside or outside the theatre." Possibly the actors put most of their earnings on their own backs, since Madame Boniface, the wife of a comedian, complains in the Gougenot play about the fact that her husband will buy her no fine clothes, especially no ornate costumes "to appear on stage in sufficiently splendid garb to represent the personages." [35]

Though there was no Actors' Equity Association in the seventeenth century, the players had a few protective clauses in their contracts to help out in case of unforeseen misfortunes. Apprentices, as has been seen, were to be fed and clothed and to be cared for when they were ill. There was also a rather standard provision by which an actor was supposed to receive his share of the proceeds when he was sick and therefore unable to appear before the public. Other members of the company carried his roles during the period of his indisposition. Such a contract was that of March 29, 1610

— which included such well known figures as Valleran, Gros Guillaume, Gautier Garguille, Laporte and his wife (Marie Venier), and the young Bellerose. In accordance with the terms of the contract, all members of the association would be expected to be on hand at the precise hours of rehearsal and performances and "to furnish the costume that will be required." However, in case any one of the company should happen to be ill, "nevertheless he will have and will draw his share just the same as if he were in good health." The actors were by this time evidently already feeling a protective interest in the welfare of their own.[36]

The life of a professional actor in the early seventeenth century in France was a hard but not altogether unhappy one. Fortunately, it was not a completely miserable and difficult existence, since so many managed to stay in it. By so doing, they assisted the public stage in reaching before 1700 a level of artistry that was possibly the highest that France has ever known.

V

THE THEATRICAL
QUARTER OF PARIS

THE THEATRES AND OTHER AMUSEMENT SPOTS OF PARIS,
as Henry IV and Louis XIII sought to improve the mechanics of living in their city along the Seine, were in a fairly
concentrated area, in easy reach of both prince and pauper.
On either side of the river, as well as on the Pont Neuf or the
Ile du Palais (now the Ile de la Cité) in between, a man could
find a little relaxation from the demands of commerce or the
responsibilities of government. The pages and guardsmen in
the Louvre, or a royal entourage with attendant ladies and
gentlemen, could go out the north gate of the palace and
turn north-northeast for a performance at the Hôtel de
Bourgogne some eight hundred meters away. If it were a
Sunday this procession could stop en route, by veering a
block to the east, to murmur a few prayers for its collective
soul at the splendid new church of Saint Eustache, a possibility that was foreseen in the numerous edicts keeping the
theatres closed on the Sabbath until three o'clock in the afternoon. Five or six hundred meters due east from the Hôtel de
Bourgogne was the Jeu de Paume de La Fontaine and in the
same block other *jeux de paume* that had been at times turned
into provisional theatres. Some three or four hundred meters
farther to the east was the Théâtre du Marais (see Chapter
VII) which was sitting on top of a sewer on the rue Vieille
du Temple and at "an extremity of Paris." The critics of the
seventeenth and eighteenth centuries who wondered how

Montdory and company could make a success of a theatrical enterprise so far out in the country — and it is true that in the maps of seventeenth-century Paris vacant land is visible a few hundred meters on east of the Théâtre du Marais — forgot that the Marais was not too much removed from some of the favorite cruising grounds of royalty and accompanying segments of polite society. The Place Royale (nowadays the Place des Vosges) was even farther east than the Marais, though closer to the river than the theatre by some four hundred meters. And the Place Royale, the popularity of which was signalized by Corneille in a play of the same name, was in the time of Louis XIII the scene of many glamorous spectacles. Immediately south of the famous square was the Arsenal with its complexity of buildings, gardens, and mall — the home of Henry IV's dour finance minister, Sully, and later the setting for a number of fancy parties.[1]

If a courtier or street-peddler headed west from the Arsenal, he would come along the river to the Place de la Grève (the present-day terrain of the Hôtel de Ville and its square), near which was the old Hôtel d'Argent, a home in its time for a few passing theatrical companies. A little more than two hundred meters west of the Place de la Grève was the rue Saint Denis, and a wanderer curious about the dramatic history of Paris could stroll north on it several long blocks until he reached the Hôpital de la Trinité, where the Confrérie de la Passion had its first home and in which had been the oblong hall destined to be the model for theatrical interiors in France for over three centuries. The stroller, however, might have turned off the rue Saint Denis through the Cemetery of the Innocents to Les Halles; or he could have a little farther north picked up a capon in the poultry market across the street from the Hôtel de Bourgogne. If a play were about to begin, he most likely took the fowl under his arm into the *parterre* as a non-paying and squawking guest. The courtier who had left a dance or musicale at the Arsenal, on the other hand, probably continued west along the Seine until he reached the Louvre with its gardens on the south side. In any case, if he were one of those who left the north gate of the Louvre earlier in the day, he had by now made a circular, or elliptical, tour of the amusement possibilities on the Right Bank * of Paris — and he had seen a cross section of the many types of inhabitants that made up the capital city. (A visualization of the trip that he took may be gained from Figure 11.)

Good prospects for diversion awaited the king or lackey who went out the south gate of the Louvre and looked across the river to the Left Bank * of the city. He should first have gone east along the banks of the stream some several meters until he reached the Pont Neuf, where there was always something going on when the seventeenth century was young. The charlatans on the bridge were gay even as they were on the Place Dauphine, which filled out the western end of the Ile du Palais and bumped squarely, as has been seen, into the Pont Neuf. After listening to the rough skits and smooth sales talk of the *opérateurs* on the Place Dauphine, a man might resume his way over the Pont Neuf to the Quai des Augustins on the south side of the river and he would now be coming into the faubourg Saint Germain district, with its many *jeux de paume*. As he stepped off the bridge, he would be only some three hundred meters to the east of the Hôtel de Guénégaud, which was to be used by Molière's group and other theatrical companies later in the century. But in the early 1600's a royal guardsman with a free afternoon or a student playing hooky from the adjacent Collège des Quatre Nations would not have stopped at the Guénégaud establish-

* The Right Bank is north of the Seine, and the Left Bank south. If an observer stood on the Pont Neuf and looked at the current of the river flowing west, the northern part of the city would be at the right and the southern at the left. Also, many sixteenth- and seventeenth-century maps of Paris put North where East would be today, and thus turned all points of the compass clockwise ninety degrees. This system may have had something to do with the designations of Right Bank and Left Bank.

ment, since it was not yet creating enough noise with its plays for the academicians at the Collège des Quatre Nations to ask that the place be closed down, a request they made nearer the end of the century. At this time the seeker of amusement would have continued on straight south for around five hundred meters, with a little twisting around for angular street intersections, until he ran into that area of infinitely varied diversions, the Foire Saint Germain. If the fair of Saint Germain had not yet opened, he might well find the theatrical troupe that operated sporadically, if not too success-fully, in the faubourg Saint Germain with the permission of Louis XIII. There still was a chance to see a play in progress by zigzagging a few hundred meters east of the Foire Saint Germain to the Hôtel de Cluny, though this pile of stone was occupied only infrequently by purveyors of drama. Besides, the Hôtel de Cluny was too near the Sorbonne and other in-stitutions of learning to offer a completely relaxed atmosphere for gaiety and good fun. It was advisable for a man with a determination to be amused to go on back to the other side of the river.

In a general way, the section of the Right Bank east of Les Halles to the ramparts and fields, and south of the old fortress known as the Temple (the seat of the Knights Templar in France), was called the Quartier du Marais or "Quarter of the Marsh." There were no exact lines of demarcation be-tween it and the quarter of Saint Eustache, or Saint Denis, or Saint Martin, or others that might overlap. Nevertheless, ideologically the Marais quarter was more inclusive than were the others of an area, of a point of view, and of a varied mix-ture of the citizens of Paris. In it, and on immediately con-tiguous terrain, were the first public theatres of the capital; and in close proximity to the theatres lived the actors who put on the grease paint and produced the plays. Under the con-tinuing improvements of Richelieu and Louis XIII its vege-table gardens became building lots and it was turned into a fashionable section of the city, with "fine town houses inhabited by a number of the nobility and illustrious personages." As the bourgeois became wealthy they, too, built dwellings in the Marais quarter and sought to ape the seigneurs in manners and mode of living. It was important to have a porte-cochere on a house: the inhabitants of the rue Michelle-Comte, it will be noted in their 1633 complaint against the actors in the Jeu de Paume de La Fontaine, spoke very proudly of their large collection of portes-cocheres. Everybody in the Marais liked to get out on a Sunday afternoon and promenade, a predilection that made Sunday a good day for the theatre. The Marais quarter's problems of dehydration were remembered later in the seventeenth century when the historian, Henri Sauval, said the rue Vieille du Temple "ran along a great marsh." [2]

Marguerite de France, the quite frustrated first wife of Henry IV, lived in the Marais sector in the Hôtel de Sens. After her lover, Saint-Julien, had been slain before her eyes she moved across the river on the Left Bank. The comte de Belin, the patron of the Théâtre du Marais and admirer of actresses — he was called by Chapelain the supporter of the "little comedians" — occupied a house in the Marais quarter whenever he was in Paris. Cinq-Mars, the favorite of Louis XIII during the King's later years, liked to slip away from the somber society of King to do a little celebrating with other "gentlemen of the Marais." The Marais area was unquestionably à la mode during the first decades of the seventeenth century. In this lively section of Paris there flourished — along with the halls given over to drama — cabarets, gambling halls, and brothels. It harbored the great courtesan, Ninon de l'Enclos, and the free-thinking Théophile de Viau stayed at the edge of the quarter on the rue des Deux-Portes. The brother of Louis XIII, Gaston d'Orléans, in a mood for mild amusement or more serious debauchery, frequented the Marais and found it satisfying and versatile in its offerings.

High society both lived in the district and passed through it in search of diversion.[3]

Actors and writers also made their habitat in the Quartier du Marais. The brilliant young dramatist, Jean Rotrou, resided on the rue François, not far from the Théâtre du Marais; and not far from the spirited and capable actress, Madeleine Béjart, who dwelt on the Impasse Thorigny and who probably had an amorous interest in Rotrou before she became the sister-in-law of Molière. Rotrou, according to Henri Chardon, was "the object of the glances of all the beauties of the Marais." Valleran le Conte early in his Paris career lived close to the Hôtel de Bourgogne on the rue Montorgueil, and later on the rue Peronet near Saint Eustache. In the year 1625, the dramatist Alexandre Hardy was making his domicile "in the Marais du Temple." Paul Scarron, the author of the story about comedians, *Le Roman comique*, was another frequenter of the Marais. There must have been some actors' and authors' boardinghouses in the quarter along with the impressive residences that were entered through the portes-cocheres.[4]

Whatever the over-all housing situation was in the Quartier du Marais, the district managed to incorporate a quantity of ladies of easy virtue. There was a general order against their staying in private houses and, from time to time, an edict was issued demanding their exit from Paris within twenty-four hours; neither of these estimable requirements was very strictly obeyed, even though the *lieutenant criminel* lived close at hand in a splendid house only a few blocks west of the Théâtre du Marais, just off the rue du Temple. The prostitutes, as a matter of good business policy, liked to be around the Hôtel de Bourgogne and the Marais theatre on the rue Vieille du Temple. One of the most famous houses of ill fame during the period was the Huleu (from *hurleur*, "howler") on the rue du Temple, not too far from the Hôtel de Bourgogne or the *lieutenant criminel*. As for the Théâtre du

Marais, it seems to have been well provided with theatrical camp followers. From the time of Henry IV, according to Sauval, "a colony of immodest women carried on with impunity their traffic in the rue de la Perle, at the end of the rue Vieille du Temple." The rue de la Perle formed the south side of the block in which was located the Théâtre du Marais. The seventeenth-century maps of Paris show no building of any kind on this one-block length of the rue de la Perle, but it is understandable that such a structure might well have been omitted by a royal draftsman. As for the general subject of feminine virtue in the neighborhood, the farce-player Jodelet was given credit for an amusing quip about it. A play had recently been presented wherein the goddess Juno renewed lost virginity by means of a magic fountain. Jodelet's comment on this device was: "If a fountain like that existed in the Marais quarter, its basin would have to be oversize." [5]

From a 1622 document comes a story concerning the rue Vieille du Temple before it became the final home of the Théâtre du Marais. Sitting in the window of a house on the street destined to become famous in the theatrical history of Paris was a very curious and observant parrot. It made regular and sometimes caustic comments on those who passed underneath the window along the rue Vieille du Temple below. One *gentilhomme* as he went by was always called a *maquereau* (or "procurer"). The gentleman protested to the owner of the bird to no avail; every day the parrot gave forth the same standard greeting. The parrot and its owner, therefore, were brought up for trial before the civil court of the Châtelet. After a full accusation was made by the gentleman, the judge asked him just what was his position in the Quartier du Marais. The plaintiff was quite vague about it, and could not show that he had any profession or any fixed income or habitat in the community. In view of these circumstances, the parrot was acquitted and the gentleman judged by every law of logic to be a *maquereau*; the bird was "reputed to have told the truth" and was permitted to return to its perch in the window. There was no doubt that the Marais was an intense and lively quarter, and it offered a varied clientele for the operations of the theatre.[6]

When the weather was passably good and a person yearned to get outdoors after many weeks of cold and wet weather, the place to go was across the river to the Foire Saint Germain. It had something to amuse and interest everybody, including long covered stalls for protection against the rains. The 1609 Quesnel map of Paris (see Figure 13) shows the Saint Germain fair plainly marked with two roofed-over areas and plenty of open space all around; the Rochefort plan of the city later in the century depicts a more complicated roof structure, but there is still adequate room for circulation around the stalls. The Foire Saint Germain was about two hundred meters southeast of the Abbaye de Saint Germain, under the general jurisdiction of which the fair began. The Foire Saint Germain, like the famous Foire Saint Laurent, started in the Middle Ages.

One of the many seventeenth-century historians of the city of Paris, Claude Malingre, said before 1640 that the Foire Saint Germain was held "under two great halls joined together and covered over, in which there are several streets." This description would seem to conform to the representation of the fair depicted on the Quesnel map. The sieur Dechuyes in a guidebook to Paris published a few years afterward, in 1656, said: "The square of the Foire Saint Germain des Prés, in the faubourg Saint Germain, is closed by four gates, one on the rue de Tournon, another on the rue des Boucheries, the third on the rue du Four, and the fourth on the rue Guisarde; in the said square is the enclosure where takes place every year the Foire Saint Germain, opened on the third of February, in an extensive covered area." Germain Brice stated toward the end of the century that the fair began on February 2 and that it had a large number of "covered passages, arranged in a square." [7]

The historian Sauval, who had evidently seen a great deal of it during the seventeenth century, gave a complete description of the Foire Saint Germain. During the internal strife of the Ligue it was rarely held, but in 1595 Henry IV had it continue for three weeks when "it had never lasted more than one." By 1630 it was of six weeks duration, "and in our days it has begun to run for two months." The length of the session depended on the will of the King, and both Henry IV and Louis XIII enjoyed participating in the diversified entertainment offered by the fair. Sauval has provided several details on the fair's dimensions and general construction. It was composed of "two halls one hundred thirty paces long and one hundred paces wide, made up of twenty-two sections, and covered with a very elevated framework." This latter structure caused much admiration and was probably the "largest covered area that there is in the world." The whole expanse was divided by nine streets into twenty-four "islands." In the various stalls were sold cloth, glassware, porcelain, and pottery — and, more importantly, gold products, linen and fabrics, and paintings, "all these vain ornaments of luxury and voluptuousness" brought in from China and India and other parts of the globe at great risk of life. On the rue de l'Orfèvrerie, for example, there was a rich collection of mirrors, crystal chandeliers, jewels set in silver and gold, and an "infinity of precious stones." Much of Sauval's descriptive picture of the Foire Saint Germain is confirmed by the famous engraving (done during the century) of the fair with its roof off (see Figure 12) — though the number of stall and street divisions do not correspond exactly to Sauval's count. The incredible number of commodities offered for sale can be judged by the signs on the various stalls in the drawing; and, for amusement, there is a good stage at the left with four or five players underneath a sign marked "opérateur." Also, close by is a smaller platform with a performer or two and a musician; farther down on the right-hand side of the picture is a stall given over to marionnettes and in front of it is one advertising "double beer" and "Spanish wine" — a neat juxtaposing of dramatic and bibulous diversions. In the space in front of the stalls may be seen a cross section of the people of Paris: ladies and gentlemen (with sedan chairs and handsome carriages), bourgeois and children, and peddlers and dogs. Everybody had a good time at the Foire Saint Germain.[8]

The terrain of the fair was so popular that it was frequented both night and day. According to Sauval there were really two fairs: "In the daytime one would say that it is open only for the people, who come there in crowds; and at night for persons of quality, for the great ladies, and for the King himself. The rich streets are magnificent in the light of chandeliers and torches, especially the streets where there is the glitter of gold; and they all come there to gamble and to be amused, so that the place at this time is less a fair than an enchanted palace where all the beau monde is assembled as though for a party." Sauval's colorful word picture is scarcely borne out by the detailed engraving of the Foire Saint Germain, which would suggest that it was big enough to contain all classes at the same time. Nevertheless, it is most likely that on occasions the King with his ladies and gentlemen — or an important nobleman with his cohorts — might take the whole thing over as they did the Hôtel de Bourgogne. Anyway, the Foire Saint Germain in the early decades of the seventeenth century was no mere hog-and-heifer exhibit blended in with sweet pickles and homemade pies. A man could find there a recently published book, or a pamphlet insinuating the latest political or amorous intrigue on the King's side of the river. There was an adequate number of games of chance to catch unwary sous, and sufficient emplacements for "comedians, clowns, wheel-spinners, jugglers,

manipulators of marionnettes, rope dancers, and charlatans."
Such a variety of entertainers presented a real threat of competition to the Hôtel de Bourgogne and the other theatres in
the Marais sector. The actors on the Right Bank were quite
satisfied to have the Foire Saint Germain function for only a
limited number of weeks in the year.[9]

The evidence from contemporary commentators on the
popularity of the Foire Saint Germain during the reigns of
Henry IV and Louis XIII is rather compelling. The serious
Pierre de l'Estoile, who in his lugubrious way saw most of
everything that was going on, had some words to say about
the fair of 1605: "During the Foire Saint Germain of this
year, where the King went regularly to take a promenade,
murders and an infinity of excesses were committed in Paris."
It was, in fact, the worst fair that had ever been seen —
lackeys cut off the ears of a student, and everything in general
was out of control. In 1607, the fair lasted "three entire
weeks" and did not close until February 23. The King pro-
longed it because the Queen "liked to stroll around at the
fair and the King liked to gamble." There had never been,
according to L'Estoile, a worse fair than that of 1607, especially for gambling. In spite of his pessimistic chronicling of
events at some of the fairs, L'Estoile, after a good description
of the assassination of Henry IV in 1610, concluded his long
story of sixteenth- and seventeenth-century France with a sonnet praising the Foire Saint Germain. The first quatrain of *Les
merveilleux effets que la Foire Saint Germain produit* pays
tribute to both the two- and four-legged animals at the fair:

> It is a pleasure when the fair begins:
> One-eyed fellows, hunchbacks, and scaly beggars are admired;
> Blockheads, gapers, and calves are esteemed,
> And, even as to the Saints, one pays them a bow.[10]

No fair was staged in 1611 on the Saint Germain terrain
because of the sad death the previous May of Henry IV, one

of the prime supporters of the institution. Foreign merchants who had come to Paris in the February of 1611 for the fair were allowed to show their wares in the halls around the Tuileries. The fair opened up again in the time of Louis XIII, who enjoyed it but was not the ardent patron of it that his father was. Louis XIII was taken to it, at any rate, as early as 1609 and thus became acquainted with the spectacle when he was a small boy. The courtiers and their ladies continued during his reign to cross the river for the colorful mixture in February of men, beasts, commodities, and diversions. That gay blade, the Maréchal de Bassompierre, said that the 1617 Foire Saint Germain was "amusing," and that the 1622 fair, flavored with several beautiful ladies, had been mighty fine. The Abbé de Marolles admired both Les Halles, where everything was sold "for the delights of the mouth"; and the Foire Saint Germain, which is a "complete and entire city" under one roof and in which "in a certain season is found an infinity of things for the delectation of the curious." A gentleman who was curious about the whereabouts of a lady with whom he was smitten might find her at times enjoying the attractions of the fair. Tallemant des Réaux tells the story of a monsieur d'Avaux who one evening ran into his beloved by chance "masked at the fair where she was gambling." * This lady, a certain madame Saintot, "had all the style in the world, and a keen wit which she liked to show off." The feminine patrons of the fair, even as those of the Hôtel de Bourgogne or of the Théâtre du Marais, were on all rungs of the social ladder. Esternod, one of the sharper satiric poets during the period, has a frank recital of a "story that occurred recently at the Foire Saint Germain between a nobleman and one of the most notable and renowned courtesans of Paris." And there was also a bit of satire in verse,

---

* The lady was probably playing tricktrack, or backgammon, which was a favorite gambling game of the period. Large sums were won and lost at it during the seventeenth century. Dice, too, were a popular (and quick) way to get rid of money.

printed in 1609, about the "petite bourgeoise" of the channel town of Dieppe whose stupid husband let her go to all the country fairs; as soon as "the following year begins to extend a hand [toward February]," she was expected to show up at the Foire Saint Germain.[11]

The professional comedians, with their repertory that went from farce all the way to tragedy, were never able to set up any firm installations in or around the Foire Saint Germain. One of the reasons for this situation was, naturally, the Confrérie de la Passion's monopolistic control of dramatic operations in Paris during the first decades of the seventeenth century. Another was — and this one was equally important — the carnivalistic spirit overhanging the crowds that came into the territory occupied by the fair. This heterogeneous assemblage was seeking amusement and relaxation, but it was not intent on seeing a play with complications of plot or characterization. The few customers who might have relished such a performance were outnumbered by the gapers and strollers wandering aimlessly about. Concentration on even a simple dramatic story would have been well-nigh impossible.

Nevertheless, the more legitimate players of plays did make an effort to draw some patronage from the multitudes that came to the Foire Saint Germain. An ambulant troupe was permitted to present secular mysteries (if they were clean) at the Foire Saint Germain in 1595 — but for the duration of the fair only, which at this date would have been three weeks or less. For their brief stay the provincial company had to pay a fee to the Confrérie, a proviso that cut down on the profits; and there was bad feeling between the Saint Germain group and the actors occupying the Hôtel de Bourgogne at the time. The provincials apparently thought that the contest was unequal: their repertory was outmoded, they owed money to the Confrérie, and their supposed colleagues in the Bourgogne did not want them to stay in town;

so they left and nothing more was heard of them in the capital city. Several years later, the religious authorities of the Abbaye de Saint Germain allowed one André Soleil and one Isabel Legendre, "comedians," to "restrict and enclose" a piece of terrain "behind the pillory" and to "erect a scaffold stage" on it. They were permitted to present "decent amusement to the people for the duration of the fair of the present year" — which was 1618 since the date of the document is January 20, 1618, or about two weeks before the opening of the fair. The comedians were forbidden to represent any "improper or scandalous plays," nor were they allowed to put on any kind of play, scandalous or otherwise, during church services. According to agreement, these two performers were allowed to shut off a portion of space behind the pillory for their showings; which would have enabled them to charge admission and would have prevented just any idler from stepping up in range of their stage, as could have been done for the *opérateurs* in the Foire Saint Germain engraving. The Quesnel map of 1609 depicts an object inside the fair grounds that might be a pillory, though it looks a bit more like a gallows. "Behind the pillory" may have been in a corner of the walled-in terrain of the fair and therefore reduced by half the fencing problems of André Soleil and Isabel Legendre, who probably were a complete company offering nothing but Harlequin and Columbine skits. In any event, nothing further was heard about them or their organization.[12]

A few years later, according to the *Gazette* of Théophraste Renaudot of January 6, 1635, a full-fledged dramatic company was functioning in the faubourg Saint Germain through the "kindness of His Majesty." This troupe was not connected with nor limited by the Foire Saint Germain, but occupied rather some one of the numerous *jeux de paume* in the neighborhood. There was, too, until well past the middle of the seventeenth century a "jeu de longue paume" only some fifty meters or so from the east side of the Abbaye de Saint Ger-

12. *The Foire Saint Germain around 1650*

14. *The Hôtel de Bourgogne* (*Bullet map*)

15. *The Hôtel de Bourgogne* (*Gomboust map*)

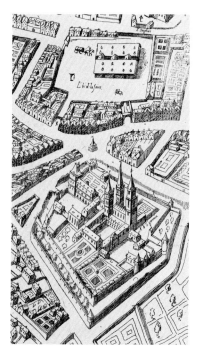

13. *The Abbaye and Foire Saint Germain* (*Quesne*

main. The "game of the long palm" came to be the least popular of the bat-and-ball games, so it is to be wondered why such an elongated piece of terrain would have been retained so long near the abbey. It was not much more than one hundred meters north of the Foire Saint Germain, and must have been rented out to performers who were willing to take a chance on an uncovered stage. Renaudot's 1635 company before this date may well have set up some scaffolding there as an experiment. However that may have been, no troupe in the Saint Germain area was, as has been noted, successful in its competition with the royal comedians at the Hôtel de Bourgogne or with Montdory's actors in the Thèâtre du Marais.[13]

The popularity of the Saint Germain fair, as well as the desire of the comedians across the river to make a little profit from its vogue, was indicated in La Pinelière's play of 1634, *La Foire de Saint Germain*. Though the play is now lost, the stage-decorator Mahelot left in his *Mémoire* a complete listing for the properties needed in staging it; other contemporary comment shows that the royal comedians at the Hôtel de Bourgogne performed in it. Mahelot's memoir specifies, among other things, the shops of a jeweler, a painter, and a candy maker — and a table on which dice may be thrown. Guillot-Gorju's daughter presided over the exhibit of paintings, and Gros Guillaume was in charge of the jeweler's shop, his mouth watering like that of a thirsty Tantalus when other people were eating candy and he had none. The play, with all the detail of setting outlined by Mahelot, must have been an accurate picture of the prime center of amusement and relaxation over on the Left Bank. In that respect it resembled Corneille's description of the activities around the Place Royale.[14]

The theatrical quarter of Paris, during the first decades of the seventeenth century, was in regard to the nature of its offerings pretty well divided by the river. The legitimate

theatre held on to its hard-won gains, and plays and performers on the Right Bank in the Bourgogne and Marais
became progressively more finished. The Left Bank during
this period was given over for the most part, in catering to
the tastes of the customers of the Foire Saint Germain, to
rope dancers and manipulators of marionnettes. The Pont
Neuf and the Place Dauphine, naturally, had a little of everything in the way of dramatic hors d'oeuvres. When the fair
was not in session, the Left-Bank operators drifted in their
turn down toward the river with their attractions. One of
the best marionnette agitators during the first half of the
century was Pierre Datelin who taught his art to his son,
François. Datelin normally installed his little shows on the
rue Guénégaud if there was no fair to draw the crowds. He
also had a very well-trained monkey, which lost its life at the
Foire Saint Germain when Cyrano de Bergerac ran his sword
through it thinking it was a man. As for the theatres at the
Foire Saint Germain, the first one of any permanence was
not built until 1678. By the eighteenth century there were
several of them and they were a real threat to the Comédie
Française in audience appeal. At this moment the Comédie
Française was itself on the Left Bank, and more strategically
located to compete closer at hand with the attractions of the
all-inclusive Foire Saint Germain.

The theatrical amusement area of Paris in the early 1600's
was not so extensive as to wear a man out if he wanted to
sample three or four types of diversion on a day of leisure.
Unless he had a horse he would get his feet pretty dirty from
the mud and animal droppings that covered the streets of the
city. If he did not want to walk and relished a semisedentary
relaxation, he could drift down the Seine in a boat and, with
no humane society to prevent it, grab at a fowl hanging
over the river on a cord. But this might involve an unexpected
dip in the brown and sewer-fed waters below.

THE HÔTEL DE BOURGOGNE

THE "HOUSE COMMONLY CALLED THE HÔTEL DE BOUR-
GOGNE" had an influence on matters theatrical in Paris for over
one hundred fifty years.[1] It is rather unusual for a physical
structure and the control thereof to play so dominant a part
in the artistic life of a nation. For many decades the development of the professional theatre in the French capital was
inevitably linked to the Hôtel de Bourgogne. It was the only
building in Paris at the beginning of the seventeenth century
given over solely to the representation of plays; and, most regrettably as far as the progress of drama in the city was concerned, any troupe of actors coming in was forced to use it
and not allowed to equip another hall without paying a fee
to the Confrérie de la Passion, the legal administrators of the
Hôtel de Bourgogne. The Confrérie's monopolistic dominion
over the production of their mystery plays went back to
royal privilege granted in 1402 by Charles VI. By extension,
after they had constructed the Hôtel de Bourgogne around
the middle of the sixteenth century, the Confrérie de la Passion argued that their monopoly included *all* dramatic activity
in the city of Paris. Their position lacked logic but succeeding monarchs tended to reaffirm it by decree far into the
seventeenth century. It was a frustrating situation for the
actors — but there was no denying that the Confrérie had
built the Hôtel de Bourgogne.

The Hôtel de Bourgogne during the seventeenth century
was put down in the prose and poetry of a number of authors
and was mentioned in many an official record. However, no

complete drawing or engraving of its exterior has been discovered for present generations to see. An engraving (Figure
20) at the Bibliothèque Nationale of an early seventeenth-
century theatre audience may have been inspired by its
interior. Visual evidence does exist concerning the appearance
of the areas used by Richelieu and Louis XIII for private
dramatic activities. The artists of the Court, understandably,
would have paid attention to these splendorous enclosures.
It is unfortunate that the only public theatre of the period
found no artist to draw its clear picture. In any case, a pretty
good idea of what it looked like on the outside can be derived
from seventeenth-century maps of Paris; and some concept of
its interior * is to be deduced from contemporary leases and
other commentaries. One detail about the main hall of the
Hôtel de Bourgogne is fairly certain: there could scarcely
have been a worse spot in which to watch a play.

The theatre of the Hôtel de Bourgogne was rectangular in
shape and approximately three times as long as it was wide.
The oblong design was certainly not in imitation of curved
Greek or Roman amphitheatres which were copied by the
Italians. Some *jeu de paume* may have given the model for the
Hôtel de Bourgogne, since the three-to-one ratio of length
to breadth was standard for the court tennis establishments.
An even more likely influence on the construction of the
Bourgogne was the great hall of the Hôpital de la Trinité
which had been used by the Confrérie for their plays until
this large building on the rue Saint Denis was turned into a
refuge in 1539. The *grande salle* of the Hôpital de la Trinité
was, according to the seventeenth-century historian of Paris,
Claude Malingre, 136 by 38 feet † with arcades backed by
crosses and the whole edifice solidly made of building stone.
The Confrérie gave both sacred and profanes plays here

---

* Some of the engravings of the *farceurs* may give a stylized version of
the stage at the Hôtel de Bourgogne.

† These dimensions, as well as others in this chapter, are derived by
counting the old medieval measurement of a *toise* as six feet four inches.

and they were seen by "persons of diverse quality, for the most part artisans who often left divine services to take their recreation at the said mystery play." It must have been difficult to take one's dramatic recreation in such a hall, which was longer and relatively narrower than the Hôtel de Bourgogne. Even worse was the salle du Petit-Bourbon in the Louvre — used for royal spectacles and later by Molière's company — which was said to be something like 221 by 45 feet. It was also very high and a person at the end away from the stage could scarcely have seen or heard anything. The hall of the Hôtel de Bourgogne was, in the opinion of Bapst, less than half this long and thus the interior dimensions of the Bourgogne *salle* would have been around 102 by 36 feet. If these dimensions cannot be absolutely certain, they are relatively so on the basis of the Gomboust, Rochefort, and Bullet maps, which show the shape clearly of the Hôtel de Bourgogne.* More exact information on the theatrical construction of a slightly later era has been unearthed by Madame Deierkauf, who has discovered the architect's plans for the renovation of the Marais theatre in 1644, after a fire. The new *salle* was 34.43 by 11.70 meters and 16 meters high.† These dimensions made the new Marais a little larger than the old one, and a trifle more spacious than was its competitor, the Hôtel de Bourgogne.[2]

The ground floor, or *parterre*, of the Hôtel de Bourgogne contained no regular seats and would thus accommodate several hundred — probably nine or ten — standing, milling, and noisy customers. Stools and benches could be put in the parterre on occasions, and there may have been long benches along each side wall of the hall, as there were in the Marais — a thoughtful detail that enabled as many as eighty weary standees to sit down periodically for a few moments' rest.

* See Figures 12, 14, and 15. There is further evidence later in this chapter on the size of the Bourgogne.

† Which would have made the new Marais something like 114 by 39 feet, and 53 feet high.

A clause in a rental contract of the Hôtel de Bourgogne in 1621 specified that a certain widow Dellin would be allowed to put "up to a dozen stools wherever she could" in the parterre and "sell macaroons, bread, wine, and other things in the said parterre." This commercial operation was not to prevent the comedians, for their part, from locating benches and stools in the parterre "wherever they wished." A portion of the audience in the parterre being seated forms a picture a trifle different from that usually imagined at the Hôtel de Bourgogne. A patron on a stool would have had a hard time seeing anything on the stage, so when the place was crowded for a good show everybody must have stood up, including a few optimistic souls who tried to stand on the stools. The floor was perfectly flat and it took a considerable craning of the neck for even a standing customer to keep an eye on the actors. The benches and stools, therefore, were most likely used only when the audience was of modest size. The matter was taken up again in a lease of the Hôtel de Bourgogne in 1622 which contained a clause preventing the comedians from "putting or permitting to be put by anybody at all a bench or stool in the parterre of the said place." This would have eliminated both sitters who were watching the play and those sitters who were chatting in the back of the hall over a cookie and a drink. The standees were five or six feet lower than the level of the stage, though they could go up to its very edge since there was no orchestral pit at the Bourgogne during this period. The stage of the Hôtel de Bourgogne has been estimated to be around twenty-three feet wide and sixteen and one-half feet deep, which would have made it smaller than that of the new Marais. It is remarkable that any dramatic illusion could have been created in such a cramped enclosure.[3]

Above the parterre and running around the walls of the main hall of the Hôtel de Bourgogne were galleries and loges. How this space was divided is still something of a moot question. From statements in leases drawn up by the Confrérie of their establishment — and the Brotherhood usually made clear what parts of the Hôtel de Bourgogne they were renting — some idea of the shape of the upper area may be determined. In one document the Confrérie allowed the actors to use "the great hall, loges, stage, and galleries of the said Hôtel de Bourgogne." On the basis of this and similar terminology it has been assumed that there were two galleries at the Hôtel de Bourgogne, one over the other, running around the three walls of the hall. Much of this space, probably most of the lower gallery, was divided into loges. There certainly was a large number, since the actors were forced to give so many away to an assorted group of claimants. The upper gallery may have had fewer loges and been equipped with rows of chairs. And, above this area, there might have been another partial gallery called the *Paradis*, since this was reserved at one time for the Confrérie and was over "the loge of the ancient masters." In a lease of 1606 to Valleran le Conte, on the other hand, it was agreed that the actor-manager and his company would have the use of the "upper gallery called the Paradis." A Paradis existed in the new Marais: it was something of a third gallery, on the two sides of the hall, fitted out with benches. There is doubt that the second gallery at the Hôtel de Bourgogne extended around the end of the hall farthest from the stage. It did not do so in the second Marais theatre and there is reason to suppose that the general assumption that such was the case at the Bourgogne is wrong. The Marais had a sort of steep balcony called the *amphithéâtre* at the end of the hall from the stage, on the floor level of the first gallery. That the same sort of installation was in the Hôtel de Bourgogne is indicated in a 1626 lease to the *comédiens du Roi*, which stipulates that the previously mentioned widow Dellin will have control of "two little stalls underneath the amphithéâtre." These were most certainly for her macaroons and wine as well for other things to eat and drink. Since the new Marais, which had formerly been a renovated *jeu de paume*, would have wanted to imitate the traditional theatre — dilapidated as the Hôtel de Bourgogne had been — it might well have copied an amphithéâtre in the Confrérie's old building. The back part of *salle* of the Bourgogne was unquestionably dark, and an amphithéâtre sitting one story above the parterre for something like the last twenty feet of the hall would have made it darker. At least two documents show that the stairways — there was a minimum of two — leading up to the galleries needed illumination: the Italian company under Fritellino was required by the Confrérie in 1609 to pay twenty-five sous a performance to the concierge of the Bourgogne for "lighting the candles [or 'greases'] above the steps on the days when it will be necessary"; and the French actors in 1619 were expected to give the concierge twenty-five sous a performance for "furnishing and putting greases on the steps leading to the said galleries from each side." [4]

As for the galleries at the Bourgogne, some idea of them before 1600 was given by young Thomas Platter. The youthful student from Bâle pointed out first that a person could get into the Hôtel de Bourgogne for half price, "on condition that he remain standing." On the other hand, "the spectators paying full price may go up into the galleries, where they can sit down, stand up or lean on a rail in order to see much better." No loges were enumerated by Platter, but they must have been in the Bourgogne at this time, since some were built into it when it was constructed. The *rampe*, or rail, he mentioned would hardly fit into the architecture of loges. It may have been on the two sides of the upper gallery only, or around a portion of the lower gallery. It is strange, however, that Platter who was so keen in his observations catalogued no loges at all. The Confrérie from the beginning had reserved for its officers one or two (two, according to Beauchamps) "for themselves and their friends" and "distinguished by grills" at the entries. If these loges were anything like the size of those in the new Marais, which probably was the case, they were a little less than six feet by five and might contain six persons seated in sardine-like fashion.[5]

Other details on the interior of the Hôtel de Bourgogne — such as lighting of the salle, corridors around it, windows and doors, and heating — might be put aside momentarily for a glance at the outside of the building. It was judged by seventeenth-century cartographers of the city of Paris to be sufficiently important to be designated on several maps of the capital. It is usually in these drawings the only building outlined in an area of several blocks, which would suggest that several less significant structures had been omitted from the plan. The basic structure of the Hôtel de Bourgogne may be seen in the Rochefort map of Paris where the old theatre's long rectangular design is clearly visible. A large part of its construction must have been done in stone, like the great hall of the Hôpital de la Trinité which it imitated, since it had by this time gone through a rigorous existence of over a century. The Gomboust map (Figure 15) shows the same general oblong silhouette of the Bourgogne facing on the rue Mauconseil but with appendages going out from the back of the building toward the rue Française. These could have been storage rooms or possibly shops mentioned in some of the leases and not included by the Confrérie in their contracts with the actors. The Hôtel de Bourgogne, with its attachments, on the Gomboust plan of Paris is the only building in the whole block bounded by the rue Mauconseil, the rue Française, the rue Pavée, and the rue Montorgueil. The other houses in this square of city terrain were obviously too insignificant to be marked by the engraver's tool. A like situation apparently existed later in the century when the Bullet map (Figure 14) of Paris was made, for the Hôtel de Bourgogne, more sharply drawn, appears on it in the same general manner as it was fashioned by Gomboust. This must have been the way it looked externally, then, in the

seventeenth century and the Rochefort drawing has left off
the side structures, keeping only the main body of the theatre.
The departure of the Italian company from the Hôtel de
Bourgogne, in 1697 — ordered by the King — was depicted
in a drawing that shows the actors getting their belongings
together in a little square facing the locked-up theatre. The
artist gives several details on this end of the old Bourgogne but
has made the edifice only a little more than one story in height,
when in reality from the floor of the parterre to the peak of
its roof the distance was at least forty feet. Four fairly large
windows are pictured here with three smaller ones nearer the
roof. The façade is definitely made of building stone, although
a lower shed has been added to the very center at ground
level; this must have been used as something like an entrance
foyer, which the building in its earlier form could well have
lacked. Two doors (one partially obscured by a ladder) are
discernible in the drawing, at each side of the shed, and these
are more in keeping with the original plan of the building and
an entrance to it shown in the engraving accompanying
Georges de Scudéry's play, *La Comédie des Comédiens*,
printed in 1635 (Figure 16). Here a drummer with his drum,
the porter who collected the entrance money (in theory), and
a Harlequin are all seen standing outside the door at the
righthand side of the Bourgogne as a customer would enter
it.[6]

The old Hôtel de Bourgogne ended its life as a theatre during the eighteenth century and the entrance on the rue Mauconseil in 1783 led into a hall given over to the sale of grain
and leathers. This market was demolished later in the nineteenth century to allow the prolongation of the rue aux Ours
bisecting the rue Etienne Marcel. All that remains today
of the ancient structures around the Hôtel de Bourgogne is
the tower of John the Fearless in a courtyard off the rue
Française with a plaque and its legend: "This tower erected
around 1410 by John the Fearless was attached to the Hôtel

d'Artois, residence of the Dukes of Burgundy, and formed a
part of the wall of Philip Augustus."

The main door of the Hôtel de Bourgogne, according to a
number of commentators, had over it in stone a symbolic
image of the Mystery of the Passion. Chappuzeau said in 1673
that "one still sees over the *grand portail* of this Hôtel [de
Bourgogne] a stone on which are done in relief the Instruments of the Passion." The Abbé d'Aubignac stated earlier
that the Confrérie de la Passion sought to purify the theatre
of "public and mordant satires" and that "over the door" of
the Hôtel de Bourgogne could still be seen the "marks of this
ancient brotherhood." And the Frères Parfaict said that the
Confrérie "set over the door of their Hôtel a stone, where in
relief was shown the Mystery of the Passion." There can be
little doubt, therefore, that such a stone existed but over which
opening of the Bourgogne was it put? Probably over a door
on the rue Mauconseil, if the assumption is correct that this
was the main entrance at the time the Confrérie was performing its mysteries. Yet there is some doubt that such was
the situation in the seventeenth century. François Colletet, one
of the historians of the city of Paris during the period, spoke
of the Hôtel de Bourgogne in 1677 as the place "where they
play the comedies, on the rue Pavée toward the rue Montorgueil." The rue Mauconseil and the rue Française were not
mentioned by Colletet. A twentieth-century chronicler of
the history of Paris, the Marquis de Rochegude, is of the same
opinion as Colletet and said that the Hôtel de Bourgogne was
to the left of the present street number of 44 rue Etienne
Marcel and that the principal entry to the building was on
the rue Pavée-Saint Sauveur. If this were the case there would
have been more room for the courtyard and carriages as depicted in the 1697 picture of the Italians' departure from the
theatre, and a porte-cochere might have allowed patrons to
drive into the inner area. On the basis of the evidence in the
maps already considered, there was no room for a courtyard

in front of the rue Mauconseil entrance to the Bourgogne. This side of the building opened directly on to the street. On the other hand, traditional information from the Confrérie's own records would suggest that the Hôtel de Bourgogne could be entered from the rue Française or the rue Mauconseil. Historians of the city of Paris, and its theatres, on into the eighteenth century took this same point of view. Michel Félibien said that the Confrérie's Hôtel de Bourgogne sat "on the newly constructed rue de Saint François (the rue Française) which runs into the rue de Mauconseil." And Antoine de Léris stated around the middle of the eighteenth century apropos of the Hôtel de Bourgogne: "This building is still in existence on the rue Française, and over the door there are still visible the Instruments of the Passion." A contemporary historian, Marcel Poète, in his three-volume study of the life of Paris says, with Félibien, that the Hôtel de Bourgogne was "contiguous to the rue Neuve-Saint-François, today the rue Française, which had been recently cut through at the site of the Hôtel and came out on the rue Mauconseil." The Gomboust and Bullet maps both indicate that there might have been a porte-cochere on the rue Française with an interior courtyard at the side of the main building. Such a disposition of space would have necessitated a primary entrance to the salle on this side of the Hôtel — which would have been perfectly possible, although opposed to the Scudéry engraving and the 1697 drawing. Through the more than two centuries of its existence, the Hôtel de Bourgogne may have varied its system of entrances and exits. If the evidence along the way is at times conflicting as to how the spectators got in and out of the building, one detail can be fairly certain: they did not do it quietly.[7]

The long and incredible domination by the Confrérie de la Passion of the theatrical world of Paris can be better understood when a look is taken at the system by which they constructed and controlled the Hôtel de Bourgogne. Much was written in the seventeenth and eighteenth centuries, with the support of little documentation, on the Confrérie and their astute manipulation of the theatre they built. Chappuzeau said that his information came from "a few theatrical pieces in Gothic characters left us by a Doctor of the Sorbonne." Beauchamps a little later asserted that the history of the Hôtel de Bourgogne was to be found in "a brochure, in quarto, of seventy-one pages printed in Paris in 1632." The Frères Parfaict were somewhat more helpful in their long history of the theatre in that they, at least, copied down a few official papers having to do with the Confrérie and the actors' conflicts with them. The Frères Parfaict, incidentally, were most sympathetic with the comedians who had to deal with the Confrérie and designated the Brotherhood as a group of "vile artisans." In any event, the story of the Confrérie de la Passion and their vise-like authority over the Hôtel de Bourgogne was told several times but with the minimum of bother about sources.[8]

The best recital of the struggles between the actors and the Confrérie was assembled by the Confrérie itself and is contained in that famous "brochure of seventy-one pages" referred to by Beauchamps. A copy of this little document, chewed by worms and blurred by moisture, is still in existence at the Bibliothèque Nationale; it has been cited by scholars but not fully analyzed. Even its lengthy title gives a wealth of information on the relations between the companies of actors and the Confrérie: *A Collection of the Principal Papers concerning the Acquisition Made by the Dean, Masters, and Governors of the Confrérie de la Passion of the Ruin and Plot Where Was Built the House Commonly Called the Hôtel de Bourgogne, Located in This City of Paris, on the Rue de Mauconseil and the Rue Neuve Saint François . . . Charters and Confirmations from the Very-Christian Kings Charles VI, Francis I, Henry II, Francis II, Charles IX, Henry III, Henry IV and Louis XIII the Just . . . to Show that the Said*

Dean, Masters, and Governors ... Are ... True and Legitimate Owners, Proprietors, and Possessors of the Said Hôtel de Bourgogne, and to Justify Their Innocence in Regard to the Insults and Theatrical Calumnies of Robert Guérin Called Lafleur, Hugues Guéru Called Fléchelles, Henri Legrand Called Belleville, Pierre Meissier Called Bellerose, and Other Comedians Their Associates, So-Called Comedians of the King by Royal Choice, Who Have Accused Very Falsely (Subject to Correction) the Said Dean, Masters, and Governors, and Confrères, of Being Usurpers of This Hôtel de Bourgogne (Paris, 1632). This is a slight abbreviation of the original title, which is, essentially, a series of accusations and defenses. In addition, it indicates immediately that around 1630 the "owners, proprietors, and possessors" of the Hôtel de Bourgogne considered that it faced on the rue Mauconseil and the rue Française. It could most probably, then, be entered from either of these streets — which was suggested also by several maps of seventeenth-century Paris.[9]

Much of the history of the property formerly owned in Paris by the Dukes of Burgundy, as well as the background of the struggle between the actors and the Confrérie, can be dug out of this fascinating *Collection of Principal Papers*. On October 11, 1543, Francis I issued an edict declaring that the Hôtel de Bourgogne, the Hôtel d'Artois, and other dilapidated town houses would be put up for sale. The houses were in a state of "ruin and decadence," but the property was considered suitable for the erection of "fine dwellings." Notices were posted on the doors and, later, royal commissioners assembled in "the halls of the said Hôtels de Bourgogne and d'Artois" along with a large crowd interested in the sale. The old house of the Dukes of Burgundy thus had a door or two as well as a reception hall still standing. At the 1543 auction one Jean Rouvet, a "bourgeois merchant," obtained a part of the Hôtel de Bourgogne land on which he promised to "build and erect livable and manageable houses." On August 30,

1548, Jean Rouvet sold — his own building operations had evidently progressed very slowly — a little more than half of his purchase to "honorable men Jacques le Roy and Jean le Roy, master masons, Hermant Iambefort, master paver, and Nicolas Gendreville, driver of our Sire the King's artillery chariot," all of whom were "bourgeois of Paris and at present Masters and Governors of the Brotherhood of the Passion and Resurrection of Our Saviour and Redeemer Jesus Christ." The size of the tract delivered by Rouvet to the representatives of the Confrérie was 17 *toises* * by 16, or about 108 by 102 feet, and it was covered with a "hovel." The Confrérie agreed to pay Rouvet and his heirs 225 livres of Tours in "annual and perpetual rent" along with a yearly tax to the King. They also promised to have constructed a "completely new great hall and other edifices" within two years, and "in the *grande salle* there will be several loges of which the said Rouvet will have one of his choice, for himself, his children, and friends as long as they live, without paying anything and without anything being taken off the rent." Rouvet claimed that he had already spent a good deal of money on the development of the terrain — on "walls, foundations, and other construction." The Confrérie could have in the beginning bought the whole installation for 4500 livres of Tours, but apparently were unable to raise this much money in one lump. With the expenses of erecting their new theatre and the constantly overhanging annual rent, they had to derive a revenue from their own productions or from the rental of the hall.[10]

The Confrérie received an unexpected blow when the Parlement of Paris issued an edict on November 17, 1548, forbidding the performance of "sacred mysteries" in "the said new hall" — which would imply that some sort of construction

---

* A *toise* was 1.95 meters or around 6 feet 4 inches, according to standard estimates. Cotgrave in his 1611 *Dictionarie* gives variants from five feet to more than seven feet.

had gone on in a hurry. The prohibition of the Mystery of the Passion was probably less damaging than the Confrérie thought it to be, since such plays were beginning to fall of their own cumbersome weight, and both the Catholics and the Protestants were opposing their excesses. Although "sacred mysteries" were eliminated, Parlement allowed the Confrérie to produce "secular mysteries" if they were "honorable and legitimate." Exactly what type of play fitted into this category would be hard to say. The most significant clause for the Confrérie in the 1548 edict of Parlement was the one that forbade the performance of "any play or mystery, whether in the city, faubourgs, or suburbs of Paris, unless under the name of the said Confrérie, and for the profit of that organization." And here was the basis of the Confrérie's monopolistic control over dramatic productions in the French capital for something like a century. In 1554, a royal edict confirmed the rights of the Confrérie to present "mysteries" (but not *sacred* mysteries) and other "honorable and relaxing plays, without offending anyone, in their hall of the Passion called the Hôtel de Bourgogne, or in any other legitimate place, if they want to, that seems more convenient for them." This concession would seem to be the foundation for the Confrérie's claim that an acting company had to pay the Brotherhood a fee for performing outside the Hôtel de Bourgogne as well as rent for producing plays inside the hall on the rue Mauconseil. All these privileges granted to the Confrérie were reaffirmed by Francis II in 1559. They were not important to the organization in this pre-professional era, but they were to be a solid source of revenue in later decades. All the above rights and privileges of the Confrérie were renewed by Henry III in 1575. They were further solidified in the royal edict of Henry IV in April 1597, which spelled out in most certain terms the actors' subjugation to the Confrérie: "And it is forbidden to all players, comedians, or anybody else, to perform or represent in the city, faubourgs, or

suburbs of Paris any play other than in the said * hall of the
Passion called the Hôtel de Bourgogne, and for the profit of
the said Confrérie and in its name, following and in conform-
ity with the decree of our said Court of Parlement of the seventeenth of November 1548." In this same and exact language Louis XIII restated the Confrérie's authority over the
dramatic world of Paris, in December 1612. The continuity
of the Confrérie's royal privilege ran into the seventeenth
century, therefore, on a series of edicts the legality of which
could not be questioned. For the budding companies of actors
it was a strange and frustrating situation.[11]

As for the original tract of land, 17 toises by 16, obtained
by the Confrérie for their new theatre, there is evidence that
a portion of it was sold. By an official paper of January 1566,
the Confrérie was given a reduction in the sixteen livres of
Paris (the livre of Paris was a trifle more valuable than the
livre of Tours) due the King in annual taxes on the Bourgogne
property. The lessening of the impost was logical because one
Henri Guyot had the "beginning of an edifice" on the plot,
and a certain Jean du Bois had "a segment, with construction
begun, 8 toises long and 3 toises wide" on the rue Mauconseil.
Also, a man named Jean du Verger had another slice of the
frontage on the rue Mauconseil on which he had put up a
"town house, courtyard, well, and appurtenances." All of
this terrain must have fronted on the rue Mauconseil — as is
certain for two of the lots — and had a depth of something
like fifty feet toward the rue Pavée. This would appear to be
a quite limited area — something like sixty by fifty feet if
the three plots were each three toises wide — on which three
men could create edifices, town houses, and courtyards. In
the burgeoning and compressing Paris these terms were relative and thus the edifices, town houses, and courtyards were
necessarily on a small scale and jammed tightly together, a

* This page is worm-eaten, but the words here must be *dans ladicte*,
"in the said."

situation that would have been necessary in order for about forty feet to be left on the rue Mauconseil for one end of the Hôtel de Bourgogne. The width of the inside of the salle at the Bourgogne, on the basis of this reconstruction, would have been under forty feet — allowing for the possibility of a narrow alley running along its side off the rue Mauconseil. Such a little avenue was frequently used with buildings of similar size and shape, the *jeux de paume* (see Figure 22). The three lots that were sold off the property had to be shallow in order for the ell-shaped extension to be possible from the main building of the Hôtel toward the rue Française, all of which is visible on the plans of Paris previously cited. Therefore, from its original piece of ground the Confrérie must have retained a back strip, if the rue Mauconseil was the front, running into the rue Française. The over-all measurements of the salle of the Hôtel de Bourgogne can, then, with certainty be said to have been something like 108 by 38 feet. These dimensions would not allow for corridors down each side of the salle, which have been imaginatively assumed by some critics, nor for much of a foyer at the rue Mauconseil entrance. Elaborate devices for the circulation of the customers were not considered necessary even by the seventeenth century, since the new Marais theatre in 1644 had no corridors along the sides of the salle. However, at the Bourgogne, as was the case at the Marais, there may have been a small entrance foyer formed by an interior wall, one story high, across the whole width of the building. The overhang of the first gallery with its loges provided the darkened outlines of passages along each side of the hall, and the supporting floor of the amphithéâtre — which probably existed at the Bourgogne, one story above the parterre — made a murky recess at the end of the hall for buffets with cakes and wine. Though these areas were not cut off by interior walls * running around

---

* Except the low wall cutting off the cramped entrance foyer, if there was one.

the salle, they were dimly enough lit to permit the picking of a pocket or a spirited bit of amorous byplay.[12]

The *Collection of Principal Papers* contains the story of one of the major quarrels between the Confrérie and the comedians over the Hôtel de Bourgogne. The documents on both sides of the controversy between the Masters and Governors of the Confrérie and the "so-called comedians of the King" are included in the famous little brochure. On October 12, 1629, Robert Guérin, Hugues Guéru, Henry Legrand, Pierre le Meissier, and their associates, "all comedians of Your Majesty," presented to Louis XIII a request that the Confrérie's control over the dramatic life of Paris be broken. The actors mentioned first that they had been retained by both Henry IV and Louis XIII "to represent for their Majesties and for the public, *la comédie.*" Several individuals calling themselves the Masters of the Brotherhood of the Passion have claimed that the Hôtel de Bourgogne belonged to them and that it was the only place in which "histories and comedies" could be presented. They have prevented the royal players and "other foreign actors" from putting on their shows elsewhere in the city, and have thus made a profit "as much through the said rental of the said house as through reserving for themselves several loges which are in it." In this way, "the pretended Masters derive gain from the work of the said comedians, who quite often have found themselves without any profit after all expenses have been catalogued and paid." At times the Bourgogne has been rented to "Italian comedians and other foreigners," who have paid the Confrérie "large sums." Under these conditions the French company has sought to find another hall for its activities; but when it did so it has been forced to pay the Confrérie "a crown a day" for the period that the players produced outside the Hôtel de Bourgogne. In addition to forcing the *comédiens du Roi* to pay them double, the Confrérie has also on many occasions failed to adhere to the terms under which it leased the Hôtel de Bourgogne. The Brotherhood's primary aim has been to make money, which it has managed to accomplish "under the pretext of doing pious works." The Confrérie's monopoly over theatrical activity is "pure usurpation" and should be broken, the actors said to the King. It should be remembered that up to this time the Confrérie, by tradition and royal decree, had every legal right to do exactly what it was doing — aside, naturally, from breaking leases or not living up to the terms of a contract. In any case, the King decided that the Confrérie would be presented with the charges listed against them by the actors is the *troupe du Roi*.[13]

In an *acte* of October 26, 1629, the Masters of the Confrérie answered the complaints proferred against them by the "so-called comedians." Unfortunately the two pages of the document as it appears in the *Collection of Principal Papers* are badly blurred and spotted from dampness, but the gist of the Confrérie's reply is clear enough. The actors had no right to enquire into the Brotherhood's "titles and contracts" by which it has operated the Hôtel de Bourgogne, since the Confrérie had "legitimately acquired the land on which the said house is built." In this paper Hugues Guéru and Henry Legrand were both listed as "living on the rue Pavée," which would put them practically in the back yard of the Hôtel de Bourgogne. The Confrérie received one of its first royal rebuffs from the King's Privy Council on November 7, 1629. In the decree of the Council on this date the actors were designated as "the comedians in ordinary to His Majesty" and the Brotherhood as "the so-called Masters of the Confrérie," under which claim and "other specious titles they have seized the house located in Paris commonly called the Hôtel de Bourgogne." The Confrérie was ordered, on the strength of the request of the comedians, to show within eight days "the titles and justifying documents for their pretended authority over the Hôtel de Bourgogne." A shift here from earlier official attitudes toward the Brotherhood is to be noted. On November 8, 1629, the royal bailiff took Louis XIII's order to the Confrérie and left it "in the house of Nicolas Réveillon, one of the said pretended Masters, their so-called Dean . . . on the rue de la Tannerie." The Dean of the Brotherhood thus lived in the district of Les Halles and may have tanned leather or butchered beeves when he was not managing the Hôtel de Bourgogne. The comedians in the 1629 edict were required to pay the contracted rental on the Hôtel de Bourgogne, but they were to have the use of "the totality of that house, without the reservation of any loge" for the Confrérie. Nor would the Confrérie be privileged to have one of its members stand at the entrance doors of the Bourgogne, on the days that plays were being presented, for the purpose of picking up a few coins from the paying public. The penalty for such an endeavor was "five hundred livres fine against each of the pretended masters" or a possible term in prison. The rigor of the proposed punishment is a trifle surprising. The Confrérie had probably been selling at the door space in the several loges over which it had control, since it was stated in this same edict that the Masters had been accustomed to reserving "the better part of the loges and galleries around the house." The 1629 decree is one of the first royal pronouncements favoring the actors and limiting the powers of the Confrérie.[14]

The question of the free loges had long been a sore point. As will be remembered, before the Confrérie had built their new theatre, the first owner of the land, Jean Rouvet, reserved one of the best loges in the house for his family and friends as long as any of them should be alive. By the early years of the seventeenth century the Confrérie had solidified the policy, despite the objection of the acting companies, of reserving for the free use of the Brotherhood six loges in the Hôtel de Bourgogne. At times there was an argument in the Confrérie itself as to the division of these boxes among the "for-

mer masters" and the "functioning dean and masters." The
1612 lease of the Bourgogne by Robert Guérin and his companions specified nine loges reserved for a variety of claimants: five for the Dean and Masters of the Confrérie, one for
the former Masters, one for the Prince of Fools (the President of the old medieval dramatic society, the Enfants sans
Souci), one for the Civil Lieutenant, and one for Jacques de
Fonteny, "so-called controller of comedians." The Confrérie
had arguments with Fonteny over his position, but later in the
century listed as one of their group "Maistre Iacques de Fonteny, an accomplished man versed in the best literatures."
Anyway, in the *Collection of Principal Papers* the Confrérie
defended its holding of the free and reserved loges. In the first
place, the Confrérie maintained rather arrogantly that their
Dean was officially the "controller of French and foreign
actors," and as such lent dignity and responsibility to the
theatre. Their loges were reached "by their large door" at
which they received "all those who do them the honor of
entering by their aid" — and the number who came into the
Bourgogne this way reached the "number of one hundred
fifty or approximately so." These details might explain why
the Confrérie collected money outside the door, though it
would have been impossible for them to stuff one hundred
fifty persons in their six loges. Their *grande porte* would con-
firm the fact that there were at least two entrances to the
Hôtel de Bourgogne.* In further approval of the use of "their
side," the Confrérie stated: "It is indeed certain that magistrates, financiers, and other qualified persons — ladies, young
ladies, and bourgeoises — for the greater part consider the
side of the said Dean, Masters, and Governors better protected and less exposed to insults." The Confrérie, so they
said, had taken the responsibility at the Bourgogne of "the
protection of everybody" and of "looking out about fire and

---

* The Confrérie undoubtedly considered "their door" to be the one that
entered the loges on the east side of the Bourgogne.

other accidents." All of which were laudable exploits, if carried out, but the actors did not think they were getting value received from the free passes issued to the Confrérie. And there is little doubt that the comedians were right.[15]

In answer to the attack made by the *comédiens du Roi* in 1629, the Confrérie staunchly defended their organization. They argued that all their officials were respectable "bourgeois of Paris, merchants, or of honorable vocations" and that they could "carry on under the law all of their activities active or passive." They were not "infamous" in any of their relations with other citizens, and they could hold any job without need of "benefit of rehabilitation." At least one hundred fifty of their number could be put in the highly respectable category of deans, masters, or governors — which would have much more than filled up the Confrérie's loges if the whole group had decided to attend a play at the Hôtel de Bourgogne on the same day. The Confrérie then listed eleven points of argument against the claims of the actors, including all the previous royal grants and concessions insuring their rights to "the land and relic of a house where they have had built with their very own funds, on the terrain commonly called the Hôtel de Bourgogne, the grande salle, loges, and edifices which are there." The Confrérie were therefore well-accredited property owners, with the freedom to rent their holdings to any prospective occupant they considered acceptable. The rentor, for his part, had no reason or right to complain over the fact than a rental fee was charged. The Confrérie were, according to their own contentions, in no sense of the word "usurpers." But the "so-called comedians of the King" might well be classified as "imposters, slanderers, and false accusers deserving to be punished in exemplary fashion." The Confrérie's argument had weight with the authorities, and as of 1630 the conflict between the Brotherhood and the acting companies was far from being resolved. And the whole dramatic life of the city of Paris suffered from it. A parting blast at this time from the Confrérie against the comedians was to the effect that "the theatre encourages impudence and a facility in lying." The comedians, contended the Confrérie rather speciously, would have people believe that all the holders of the old tract belonging to the Dukes of Burgundy were usurpers. This would involve an area some sixty toises by sixty toises in size, where there were buildings more than ten of which could be described as "very fine town houses." The Confrérie has given a rather interesting piece of evidence here showing that the original grant to the Dukes of Burgundy in Paris was a square of land almost 384 feet by 384, of which the Confrérie de la Passion utilized less than one tenth for their Hôtel de Bourgogne.[16]

The threat that the Confrérie held over the actors for playing outside the Bourgogne was not an empty one. In the *Collection of the Principal Papers* there is a sentence of March 13, 1610, by the Prévot de Paris against Mathieu le Febvre, called Laporte, Marie Venier, his wife, and their companion comedians for playing in the Hôtel d'Argent, "the Hôtel de Bourgogne being then occupied by other comedians." Laporte and company were sentenced to pay to the Dean, Masters, and Governors of the Confrérie three livres of Tours for each day that they played in the Hôtel d'Argent — and they also were charged with the "expenses of executing the said sentence." The same type of fine was levied on February 16, 1622, against Etienne Ruffin, called La Fontaine, Hugues Guéru, called Fléchelles, Robert Guérin, called Lafleur, Henri Legrand, called Belleville, and "other of their companion comedians" for playing in the Hôtel d'Argent instead of the Hôtel de Bourgogne. The Confrérie was able also to make it difficult for the actors to rent any halls in the city when the price of the Hôtel de Bourgogne seemed high or some foreign company was in it. As early as April 1599, an official notice was issued to one Léon Fournier, carpenter, and all other bourgeois prohibiting them from renting courtyards or other such places to "French or foreign comedians" for their plays. Much later, on October 13, 1621, a certain Estienne Robin, keeper of a jeu de paume on the rue du Bourg-l'Abbé, was forbidden to rent his establishment to any and all actors; in case he did, the stage and all dramatic installations would be torn out. The edict was made more inclusive on March 4, 1622, when Robin and "all other keepers of jeux de paume" were prohibited from renting their indoor courts to acting companies. The Confrérie had no intention of leaving even a small loophole for dramatic productions outside the Hôtel de Bourgogne.[17]

The comedians fought back vigorously against the Confrérie's strangling monopoly, but to little avail during the first part of the seventeenth century. Various *Remonstrances* were sent to the King, and it was requested by the actors that the Confrérie de la Passion be abolished as "useless, prejudicial, and scandalous to religion, to the state, and to private citizens." All the property of the organization should be sold for the benefit of the poor, with the "exception nevertheless of the Hôtel de Bourgogne which will be attached in perpetuity to your troupe of comedians." The Confrérie, said the actors, were a spendthrift lot who were not really interested either in their religion or their families, and were undeserving of the "title of bourgeoisie." The actors agreed, if they were given operational command of the Hôtel de Bourgogne, to keep it in good repair and to pay into the royal exchequer whatever was decided to be a legitimate rental. These are the highlights of the *Remonstrance* of early 1615. According to Bapst and Fournel, the actors requested Louis XIII in 1613 to rebuild the Hôtel de Bourgogne, "with more elegance and convenience and with all necessary measures taken for genteel people to be able to come there without being mixed in too bad company." Most of the pleas sent forth by the King's comedians went unheeded, even though the theatre as an institution continued to gain favor with the people of Paris. The Abbé d'Aubignac said as late as 1647, in speaking of the Hôtel de Bourgogne, that "the *comédiens du Roy* have been there for a long time in consideration of a rather sizable sum that they pay every year to these Brothers of the Passion who have continued to be proprietors of the house." [18]

And thus did the old and dark and drafty Hôtel de Bourgogne, struggled over by the comedians and the Confrérie, play its part in the establishment of the professional theatre in France. It was so uncomfortable and ill-adapted to the presentation of plays that the occupants of even the expensive seats, if they were to participate in the offerings of the actors, needed to have "perfect senses of seeing and hearing." By any sort of modern standards, the place must have been miserably cold in winter. On February 14, 1609, young Louis, the future King of France, was "taken to the Hôtel de Bourgogne at four o'clock; brought back at eight o'clock completely congealed with cold." Thus the good doctor Héroard described quite laconically what was probably the second trip of the Dauphin to the public theatre — and this, in view of the unusual hours, must have been a special performance for the royal household. Young Louis had gone earlier to the Bourgogne on February 6, 1609, but on this occasion he had stayed only one hour and a half. In the opinion of Chappuzeau, who was very much of an optimist concerning things theatrical, conditions were better in the halls of Thespis later in the century: "In the wintertime, they [the actors and their companies] keep a great fire going all around, which was not the situation in former days." For the hot weather, Chappuzeau wished somebody would invent air conditioning for the theatre: "All that would be needed is to find a system of giving it a little coolness in summer, which is not easy because everything is closed up and the air cannot get in." [19]

The old Bourgogne forgot some of its earlier somber years

when the Italians took it over later in the century. They occupied it peacefully "for several years," said Germain Brice, and
their incomparable Arlequin corrected customs by means of
laughter — or at least such was the case if one could "believe
the sign that was over the stage, the body of which was the
mask of Arlequin himself with these words: *castigat ridendo
mores.*" The life of seventeenth-century Paris was rather
thoroughly bound up with "a house commonly called the
Hôtel de Bourgogne." [20]

A JEU DE PAUME
CAN BECOME A THEATRE

THE *jeu de paume* or "GAME OF THE PALM," the sport of kings and the king of sports in France from the Middle Ages into the seventeenth century, made its indirect contribution to the early public theatre. In the beginning, as the name suggests, a ball was simply batted with the palm of the hand against a wall, either on the inside or outside of a building. The first refinement came with the addition of a glove to protect the naked hand from too much battering. When a racquet was added the game developed more complications: more rules were needed and also more walls. A racquet with a short handle, the *courte paume*, rather than the long-handled variety (the *longue paume*), became the favorite implement of the player. This type of racquet is also most likely responsible for the designation of the game as "court tennis" in England and America. At any rate, the short-handled racquet allowed the sport to be practiced in a more restricted space, and special halls of limited dimensions to be constructed for it. These might or might not have a roof over them, but a covered court offered better protection for both players and equipment. The halls themselves came to be called *jeux de paume* or sometimes *tripots*. The term *tripot* has rather lost caste today and is likely to mean a gambling house or a low tavern; but, at the end of the sixteenth century a place might be spoken of as either a jeu de paume or tripot "because from the beginning these halls were common to players of the

game of the palm and to entertainers who danced on a cord."
If this was true, the jeux de paume always had around them
certain theatrical associations. After 1600 the "royal game of
the palm" began to lose some of its popularity — too much
gambling and wine connected with it was one of the reasons
— and a number of its halls were turned into theatres.[1]

There were many jeux de paume all over the land of
France and, without too many difficulties, they could be set
up for dramatic productions. The estimate varied as to how
many were in Paris as the sixteenth century came to its end,
but there were certainly several hundred. The young Thomas
Platter did not fail to observe the jeux de paume: "There
are also in Paris numerous jeux de paume, especially in the
faubourgs; when any person tears down a house, he often
puts up a jeu de paume in its place. More profit is thus derived than from the reconstruction of the house, for as much
can be borrowed on these tennis courts as on a dwelling.
Some claim that Paris contains around eleven hundred jeux
de paume; if it is conceded that there are only half that many,
the number is still considerable. According to my own observations, there is a large group of those who play the game."
Undoubtedly, many persons in Paris were indulging in the
diversion of court tennis at this time and many halls had
been constructed for it. Probably they were fewer than fourteen to eighteen hundred, as some visiting Italian and Dutch
ambassadors counted them, but still there were enough to give
relaxation to many Parisians. A contemporary student and
lover of the sport, Albert de Luze of Bordeaux, has estimated
more modestly that Paris harbored something like two hundred fifty jeux de paume at the end of the sixteenth century. Luze has from various sources located over one hundred
of these, of which a considerable quantity was on the Left
Bank of the Seine and several more across the river in the
Marais quarter. Both areas became important theatrical and
entertainment districts during the seventeenth century. The

concentration that could be made of jeux de paume on a given piece of land can be noted from the Vellefaux drawing (see Figure 22), done in 1615, and based on a section of the Quesnel map of Paris, which dates from 1609. Vellefaux, a royal civil engineer and draftsman, enlarged a portion of the Quesnel plan involving a segment of the rue de Vaugirard and the present terrain around the Palais du Luxembourg. The drawing was done on a piece of parchment, which is still well preserved at the Archives Nationales today, though it did get lost and was rediscovered in 1957 only by accident. The roofs of the jeux de paume on the Vellefaux enlargement were colored in a beautiful soft red which, unfortunately, could not be reproduced in a photograph. But one of the buildings shown on the plate, the Jeu de Paume de Becquet, was later to be the home of the early opera.[2]

Royalty during the sixteenth century was more ardent in its support of the game of the palm than of the theatre. Francis I was a good player and his son, Henry II, was a better one. Charles VIII earlier had died at the château of Amboise from having bumped his head against the top of a doorway into a gallery where he had gone to watch a match of jeu de paume. The Valois monarchs were so fond of the game that a fine and quite large court was constructed in the Louvre; it was said in the seventeenth century that the only entrance to the Louvre was "in the pinnacle of a jeu de paume." Charles IX enjoyed playing, but the real devotee and master of the game among the Kings of France was the first of the Bourbons, the lusty Henry IV. He played it to the hilt, the way he did everything, and all over Paris. It was said of him that "the exercise of *la paume* put oil on the springs of the soldier king." Outside Paris in March 1590, Henry IV played with some bakers in a hall in the town of Mantes. In Paris, he spent a great deal of time in the Jeu de Paume de la Sphère in the Marais quarter. On September 16, 1594, he passed the whole afternoon at the Sphère, and on September 24, 1594, he chased so many low volleys or sliced services that he tore his shirt. On October 27, 1594, the King had a good day at the Sphère because he won four hundred crowns, which were stacked up in the center of the court under the net. He had the marker pick up the coins and put them in a hat, with the statement: "I am keeping these and they will not be stolen from me, for they will not pass through the hands of my treasurers." In May 1597, Henry IV was again at the Sphère, playing before an audience that included several ladies. His smashes or placements evidently were not under control since he lost all his money; whereupon he went over to the spectators' gallery and borrowed some from madame de Monsseaux — "whom he caressed rather thoroughly." In June 1598, the King had a workout "in his tripot in the Louvre, with many ladies and foreign visitors for his audience." The game was stopped long enough for Henry to go over to the duchesse de Beaufort and have her remove her mask — it was still the fashion for ladies at Court to wear them at this time — so that "the Spaniards could have their fill of looking at her." [3]

The King's frequenting of a particular jeu de paume, together with ladies and gentlemen of his Court to cheer him on, could not have failed to give the chosen establishment an enormous amount of free publicity. The Jeu de Paume de la Sphère must have gained largely in customers and revenue from Henry IV's presence in it. Some years later, after his death and with interest in the game declining, the Sphère was made into a theatre by Montdory and his troupe. Several other jeux de paume in same neighborhood of the Marais quarter were also in their turn fitted out for theatrical productions. The lingering stories of the Vert Galant's breaking a few racquets in the Sphère — an easy thing to do because the ball was pretty hard — must have added to its drawing power after it became a theatre. In any event, Henry IV was the last of the French kings to be really an expert at court tennis. Henry began playing *à la paume* with his son when the young Dauphin was six years old, but the future Louis XIII did not have the coordination or quickness of reaction to become good. Even as young Louis, the sons of wealthy bourgeois were taught jeu de paume in the early seventeenth century, along with dancing and the use of weapons, to make them seem more genteel. In any time or place the game of the palm was an expensive diversion.* It is understandable in view of the money involved (both for equipment as well as for wagering) that many of the courts in France were changed into theatres.[4]

The game must have been exciting if a man could afford to play; and there was once a famous woman named Margot who was agile enough to win even against masculine competition. Many rules were written down for the sport and there was also tradition to be followed. In 1599 a certain Forbet, a "master in this exercise," drew up a little treatise, reprinted in 1632, in which he spelled out some twenty-four rules for the sport. His regulations are rather hard to follow in matters of technical exposition but they do show some of the social features attached to the performance. Two markers were needed to keep score, and in case of dispute the spectators should be consulted. A match might well on occasions be called because of darkness or rain. The game was supposed to give delight to both the mind and the body, but "without swearing or blaspheming the name of God." The floor of the hall should be made of tile. If the ball should go into the galleries, or any other place, and strike a spectator it was still in play. That a thing like this could happen was shown by the incident of February 1602, when a young man was struck with a ball "right in the temple" and killed, in a "wretched

* Today in the United States there are only some six courts, and the champions through the years have been men of wealth. It is noteworthy that the present two courts of the Racquet and Tennis Club in New York are almost identical in measurements with those of a standard jeu de paume in Paris of around 1600. Also, terms like *grille*, *tambour*, and *dedans* — which go far back in the history of the game to designate certain areas of the court — are still being used in the jeux de paume on Park Avenue.

17. *Interior of a jeu de paume, early seventeenth century*

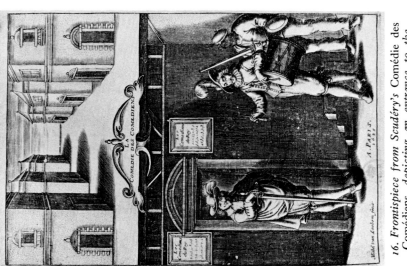

16. *Frontispiece from Scudéry's* Comédie des Comédiens, *depicting an entrance to the Hôtel de Bourgogne*

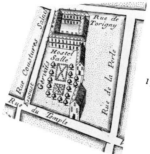

19. Detail, showing Théâtre du Mar

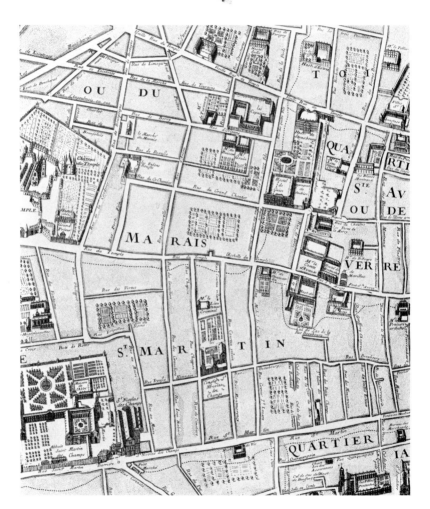

18. Marais quarter and Théâtre du Marais (Bullet map)

little jeu de paume, near the Cordeliers." Disputes, too, could occur for one reason or another, since in the same year of 1602 "two French gentlemen" killed each other at the dueling ground of Pré-aux-Clercs "because of a quarrel they had had the day before in the Jeu de Paume." But there could also be tournaments with fine prizes: a "bouquet and hat of flowers," or "gloves and *aiguillettes* of silk," a "silver racquet," or a "silver ball." Quite clearly in the early seventeenth century many persons frequented the jeux de paume as performers, spectators, drinkers, and gamblers. Some of them might win a prize — which was not likely to happen, it was said, later in the century: "The game of the palm or *Sphoeromachie* no longer has its former position or its ancient glory. It is so much changed that it is not now recognizable, and there being no more crowns or palms for its victors, it has become an occasional amusement." Possibly a slight added reason for the decline in France of this long popular diversion with a bat and ball was the edict of 1613 that put a tax on racquet strings, and thus increased the operational requirements of a sport that was already using up a lot of francs. Fortunately, the habit that people had acquired of going to the jeux de paume carried over when the halls became a part of the early public theatre.[5]

A jeu de paume, even if it had a pretty red roof, was no architectural thing of beauty nor any satisfaction to a city planner. The Parlement of Paris expressed its feelings on the matter when on July 16, 1602, it opposed the project of one Anthoine Loys to put up another such edifice in the city. The official decree made two strong points against the jeux de paume: there were already so many of them that they brought about the "debauching of youth"; and they added in no respect to the "ornament and decoration" of the capital. The decision of the legal body was supported, naturally, by the *maîtres paumiers*, the "masters of the game of the palm," who did not want any further competition in their business of exercise and entertainment. The Vellefaux drawing is the best known visual evidence as to what a jeu de paume in the early seventeenth century looked like externally, and what its relation was to other buildings adjacent to it. Though this district around the present Palais du Luxembourg was not the primary area of the early public theatre, there were theatrical ventures in the vicinity. As far as these jeux de paume are concerned, they most probably represent a general plan of construction that was standard all over the city.[6]

The Vellefaux piece of parchment indicates quite clearly the large number of jeux de paume that could be concentrated on a limited piece of terrain, and the easy availability of a tennis court to a company of actors that might want to rent it. That the dramatic troupes were doing this fairly early is proven by the sentence against Estienne Robin, *maître paumier*, for signing over his establishment to a group of comedians. Robin apparently was not too much scared by this edict, nor were other proprietors who found it profitable to open up their gaming halls to actors. Therefore, the director of a troupe of performers could locate readily a manager of a jeu de paume who was willing to take a chance on renting it. On the Vellefaux map, which depicts an arc (or, more exactly, half a hexagon) formed by the rue d'Enfer, the rue des Francs-Bourgeois, and the rue de Vaugirard, six jeux de paume of various types are visible. Three are covered with handsome red roofs, and two of these three are marked by the artist as "jeux de paumes couverts." Two of them are not covered and are designated as "tripots." They would have been open to the weather, except for the galleries running around the walls, and thus less satisfactory as theatres — although this lack of protection would not have ruled them out completely, since Valleran le Conte on one occasion rented an open courtyard in order to compete with the Confrérie's monopoly of the Hôtel de Bourgogne. The sixth jeu de paume is still in the process of construction, and therefore not yet ready for volleys either from racquets or from actors' tongues. At any rate, in an area on three streets with a combined front footage of no more than two hundred yards, there existed six edifices in seventeenth-century Paris that could be used for theatres — and it has been noted that at least one of them, the Jeu de Paume de Becquet, was.[7]

The Vellefaux plan shows that a jeu de paume might well sit in back of another house — a dwelling or a shop or probably both — that fronted directly on the street. Such a location would help to explain the large number of tennis courts in the city; they were put up rather cheaply in the rear of more attractive edifices and on the less expensive portions of building lots. They were reached by doors or gateways that did not require, in general, entrance into the houses at the front; exterior walkways ran the length of the jeu de paume, on one or both sides of it. Between the front structure and the building for the tennis players there was frequently a little courtyard, which would have assisted in easing traffic jams at the gates or along the walkways. Many of these points may be seen in the Vellefaux drawing. An immediate reaction from the more insulated and soundproofed twentieth century is one of amazement that the inhabitants of the front buildings could have stood either the banging of the balls or the ranting of the actors in their back yards.

A companion document to the Vellefaux drawing gives considerable information on the dimensions and general setting of the jeux de paume in the hexagonal arc just examined. This document is another bit of parchment in the Archives Nationales and is included in a group of deeds or land transfers of the Fief du Clos au Bourgeois (the Luxembourg area) during the sixteenth and seventeenth centuries. It is a blueprint of some of the lots and buildings of the district, done to scale and measured in toises. Since the executor of the plan has put down his scale on it, the size of the jeux de paume and some of their surroundings can be pretty well determined. The outer walkways along the buildings are six to eight feet

wide, and the little courtyards around twelve by twenty feet
— which would not have allowed much circulation for a
theatrical crowd. One of the jeux is exactly ninety by thirty
feet — if a standard toise is assumed to be around six feet;
and another, the "jeu de paume du Mont Gaillard, belonging
to Monsieur Picart," is about ninety-five by twenty-eight
feet. The names of several owners are given, as was done
for the houses in the Vellefaux drawing. The blueprint and
the Vellefaux plan belong to approximately the same time —
the blueprint possibly a trifle earlier — since the Vellefaux
buildings fit the linear plot so exactly. The line drawing would
suggest that along the walkway side of a jeu de paume were
two entrance doors, each one about thirty feet from an end
of the structure. Very few of the jeux de paume of this portion of Paris were still in existence a little more than a century
later, though Mont Gaillard was on the census taker's report
of 1757.[8]

Jeux de paume toward the end of the sixteenth century were
built in profusion from the Luxembourg area through Saint
Germain des Prés on to the river. One of these, the Jeu de
Paume des Mestayers — built in 1595 on the present rue de
Seine through to the rue Mazarine — was the one occupied by
Molière, in his early venture into the professional theatre. It
is not known whether another house sat in front of the entrance, but some years ago the Mestayers' dimensions were
reconstructed from documentary evidence and they conform
very closely to those of the jeux de paume in the Clos aux
Bourgeois. The interior of the Mestayers was around ninety
feet by thirty — the preferred size — and would hold, after
a stage and other theatrical installations were put in, an audience of about eleven hundred if it was tightly packed. The
floor was as hard as tile, or the polished stone of Caen, could
make it, and more stone was used at the entrance doors to
keep the prospective spectators from getting their feet muddy.
The only light came from the open space around the upper

walls below the roof, which was supported by wooden pillars — and a blowing rain could drench the parterre. The
Mestayers's floor was some thirty-four feet from its roof line;
and the last fourteen feet going up offered nothing to stop the
dampness or the winter's blasts.[9]

The best concept of what a jeu de paume looked like on
the inside can be gained from the engraving (Figure 17) accompanying the Charles Hulpeau publication of the rules
of the game in 1632. The general dimensions of the building
are quite obvious from the excellent perspective of the artist's
drawing; more specific details are also visible: the hard and
smooth floor, the wooden pillars and beams, and the open
space below the roof line. This was normally covered with
netting, some of which can be seen in the engraving, to prevent a wild smash from flying out of the place into the street
or the river. The open area around the top would not seem to
be as large as that estimated in the Mestayers, but the artist
probably was not drawing from actual measurements. The
door at the extremity of the building was in all likelihood
quite usual; however, there are no side doors as suggested in
the Clos aux Bourgeois blueprint. With or without several of
these variations, it would still not have been too difficult to
turn a jeu de paume quickly into a reasonable facsimile of
the Hôtel de Bourgogne. The spectators' gallery for the game
could with relative ease become a series of ground-floor loges,
and another gallery could be put on top if the sloping roof —
the *pente* used in putting the service ball in play — were torn
away and a floor substituted. A similar construction, when the
season was good and the agents of the Châtelet not too close
at hand, might be attached to the other side of the building.
Then, with a bit of scaffolding to make a stage at least twenty-
five feet wide and maybe fifteen feet deep, and five or six feet
above the level of the parterre, a hardy little dramatic company was ready to compete with the Hôtel de Bourgogne.

In the provinces, when a traveling company of actors was

allowed only a very limited stay in a town, the most temporary of installations would turn a local jeu de paume into a theatre. In Paris, too, the same sort of thing could be done; but, as the seventeenth century progressed the Parisian troupes were more hopeful of longevity and therefore risked more permanent equipment in a transformed tennis court. While the game of the palm was still popular in France, a jeu de paume might be full of racquet wielders and their cohorts early in the day, and of actors and playgoers later in the afternoon. An enterprising proprietor of a jeu de paume could thus increase the profits on his establishment. The temporary seats and scaffoldings of the actors would be stored after the performance back of the *grille* at the end of the hall or outside if the weather was not too threatening.

A vivid picture of an active provincial jeu de paume and a traveling dramatic company's association with it is to be found in Scarron's *Roman comique*. The story opens with the arrival of a small troupe into the town of Le Mans, their packages and trunks loaded on a cart pulled by four oxen and a mare with a colt. The actors went past the tripot called La Biche, where the proprietress, who "loved a play better than a sermon or an evening prayer," gave hay to the oxen and the mare. The little company in appreciation put on a show — outside the jeu de paume since a match was going on in it. The place was also full of loafers and hangers-on. A brawl started, with much smashing of heads with racquets, when two of the athletes discovered that their clothes had been stolen for the use of the actors. The players of tennis had come out in their shorts, and without having been "rubbed down," because they wanted to "hear the comedy." Order was finally restored and later in the week the actors gave a performance inside the jeu de paume, "and those of the audience who had often seen plays in Paris maintained that the King's own comedians never did anything better." As for the factual history of the jeux de paume in Le Mans, the city council in 1612 limited their number to ten. This was done because their construction was for the most part of wood and they thus created quite a fire hazard. Also, they were rather flimsily built and easy victims to the winds and the rains.[10]

Most of the towns in the provinces had one or more jeux de paume that were convertible on demand into theatrical halls. The court built in Metz in 1578 was used both for tennis and plays. It had walls painted black on the inside — a standard procedure to insure contrast with the white ball — and end walls solid all the way to the roof. At one extremity of the hall was a gallery with seats in it for spectators, which was convenient either for the observers of a tennis match or for patrons of the drama. Not all the jeux de paume were so well equipped, though there were usually benches around for players and spectators and sippers of good red wine. Among the several jeux de paume in Rouen around 1600, the two most favored for dramatic purposes were *les Braques* on the rue du Vieux Palais and *les Deux-Maures* on the rue des Charrettes. The attitude of the town council toward actors and acting, as well as the epidemics that struck the city of Rouen on into the 1620's, caused these halls to see only limited service. There was objection, naturally, from competing operators to one specific jeu de paume's having the monopoly of rental to dramatic troupes passing through a town. The city fathers of Dijon on one occasion refused to give to a gentleman named Annequin, even if he paid a fee, the right to set up his "tripot de la Grande Salamandre" as the only jeu de paume in the area available to traveling comedians. Some nice profits must have been derived from renting to a troupe that managed to entertain the bourgeois for more than two or three days, without shocking the local churchmen or incurring the wrath of municipal officialdom. The Italian company in Avignon in 1598 leased a jeu de paume for "several weeks" even though the hall was "very expensive." A stage was put up in it and everybody had a fine time.[11]

The most significant influence of the jeux de paume on the
early public stage occurred, quite understandably, in the city
of Paris; a whole series of them in the Marais quarter was used
by Montdory and his company, and they formed the collective
basis for the Théâtre du Marais. The eighteenth-century historians of the theatre spoke rather vaguely of comedians
coming into the Marais district around 1600 to the Hôtel
d'Argent, "near la Grève." Later they "transferred their
theatre to a Jeu de Paume at the upper end of the Vieille rue
du Temple, above the sewer." This would scarcely have
seemed to be the most advantageous location in which a
dramatic company might set up shop, but the Marais quarter
was being cleaned up at this time and was becoming a popular
section of Paris. A prospective audience would scarcely have
been deterred by the nearness of the sewer, since the whole
city was pretty well permeated with odors, many of them
bad. In any case, the anonymous jeu de paume sitting on top
of a drain had a name — several names, in fact, because the
Théâtre du Marais in its formation was located in more than
one jeu de paume.[12]

When Montdory and Charles le Noir came to Paris with
their company to offer steady competition to the royal comedians at the Hôtel de Bourgogne, the invading troupe occupied successively four jeux de paume. All of them were in the
Marais district within an area of four or five city blocks. The
first one was the Jeu de Paume de Berthault, on the Impasse
Berthault, and it was there in all probability that Corneille's
Mélite was given in 1629. Operations were so successful that
the actors were assessed the well-publicized fine of one hundred thirty-five crowns for having performed that number
of days outside the Hôtel de Bourgogne. Montdory and companions then moved to the Jeu de Paume de la Sphère, after
the termination of a lease of some twenty-four months at the
Berthault. The rental of the Sphère, famous in an earlier era
for the mighty racquet wielding of Henry IV, began around

the middle of December 1631. The comedians stayed in the Sphère for only three months since they had to pay the rather high figure of twelve livres of Tours a day for it. For this sum, however, they were permitted to use a room adjacent to the jeu de paume to "dress and undress." The company was privileged to install a "stage, galleries, and other necessary things" in the Sphère, but at the expiration of their lease the place had to be turned back into a tennis court. Montdory and his companions went in 1632 to the Jeu de Paume de la Fontaine, rue Michel-le-Comte, and signed a lease with the proprietor, Jacques Avenet, for two years — all of which was done with the permission of the Civil Lieutenant of Paris. The Frères Parfaict said that this happened "toward the end of 1632," though it might have taken place in March 1632, immediately after the expiration of the contract on the Sphère. Whatever was the exact moment of Montdory's beginning activities at la Fontaine, it was a successful period in the life of the troupe: the audiences were large and the neighbors complained about the noise. In 1634, Charles le Noir and Montdory took their company to the hall from which they would move no more, "the large covered jeu de paume standing on the Vieille rue du Temple and on which hangs the sign les Maretz." This was the spot that would come to be known as the Théâtre du Marais.[13]

The tennis court that became the Théâtre du Marais was indicated on many plans of Paris of the period. The representation most frequently reproduced is that of the Gomboust map, which shows the Marais as a detached building with a garden and trees behind it. A more exact idea of the structure and its surroundings may be gained from the Bullet map, which is very clear and gives more details. The whole area of the four jeux de paume used by Montdory and his companions is visible in Figure 18; the little square containing the Théâtre du Marais itself and the buildings around it has been magnified in Figure 19. It will be noted that the theatre itself faces the rue Vieille du Temple and opens directly on it.* Behind the theatre can be seen a smaller jeu de paume, trees and a garden, and a larger building that is probably the Hôtel Saint-Gervais. All these buildings and others were described in a deed of sale of the property which dates from October 26, 1633. There is little doubt, then, that the large jeu de paume which became the Marais theatre looked externally very much like the drawings on both the Gomboust and Bullet maps; but the Bullet plan gives a more exact concept of the constructions around the theatrical hall. Where did the actors assemble and keep their growing and expensive wardrobes? Evidently in an adjacent smaller house, not depicted on the map, even as they had done according to the earlier arrangement at the Jeu de Paume de la Sphère. An interesting confirmation from the Bullet map is the famous *esgout*, or "sewer," marked in at the corner of the Vieille rue du Temple and the rue Coustures Saint-Gervais. The eighteenth-century chroniclers were not wrong in saying that drama and drainage were in close proximity at the Théâtre du Marais.[14]

Montdory and Charles le Noir must have had in 1634 great confidence in themselves, their company, and the future of the theatre in Paris. In that year they leased the Jeu de Paume du Marais from its proprietors for five years; it was an audaciously long contract and one that demanded three thousand livres of Tours in annual rent. Such an extensive agreement would have made feasible quite permanent theatrical installations and not the sort of scaffolding that could be put up or down in a couple of days. It also meant that the tripot of the Marais had ended its career as a haven for batters of balls and

---

* The Marais jeu de paume apparently had no houses in front of it, as was the case with the tennis courts in the Clos aux Bourgeois — possibly because land values were not so high in this recently reclaimed area and therefore a jeu de paume could sit on the best part of a lot. The site of the old Théâtre du Marais is marked today by a building bearing the number 90, rue Vieille du Temple — or Vieille rue du Temple, as it was called in the seventeenth century.

smashers of racquets. Henceforth it would echo the miseries of Tristan l'Hermite's Herod or resound with the couplets of Pierre Corneille as his heroes balanced duty against love. There is some question as to whether Montdory and Charles le Noir with their players went into the Marais theatre in March of 1634 or later in the year. Whatever the exact moment of their arrival into their new home, it was the beginning of the golden age in the history of the troupe. Despite the ravages made on the personnel of the company in December 1634, by royal edict, Montdory's group was destined to be for more than a decade the very genuine and successful rival of the Hôtel de Bourgogne. Some have felt that because of the collaboration of Corneille and Montdory the Marais was the leading troupe of Paris during the period. In any event, it all took place in a theatre on the rue Vieille du Temple, the most famous transformed jeu de paume in French dramatic history.[15]

On January 15, 1644, after almost ten years of prosperous occupancy by the company under the leadership of Montdory, Charles le Noir, and then Floridor, the Théâtre du Marais burned down. It must have created quite a blaze, since it was said to have been visible "from all over Paris." Only the heroic efforts of the monks from the convent adjacent to the theatre kept all the buildings in the block from becoming dust and ashes. That the monks were close at hand is confirmed by the 1633 deed of sale of the Marais jeu de paume: in this document were listed, along with the Marais tennis court, a hospital, a convent, three other jeux de paume, several smaller dwellings and wells of water — all in the plot bounded by the rue Vieille du Temple, the rue Coustures Saint-Gervais, the rue de Thorigny, and the rue de la Perle. It would have been hard to find a more catholic community. Anyway, the dry and combustible wood in the Théâtre du Marais flamed like tinder, and it is remarkable that no one lost his life. A contemporary engraving (Figure 23) shows the actor, Jodelet, getting out of the conflagration with the fire licking at his coattails. Underneath the picture is a bit of doggeral which has the famous farce-player saying he has lost everything and asking a little assistance from those gamblers who are luckier than he:

I am getting out of the fire more wretched than a church-mouse,
If you do not help me I shall be down to my undershirt,
All my possessions are burned up with our tripot,
Put me back by your gifts into my normal feeling of good humor.[16]

Neither Jodelet nor the company as a whole could have been in too dire financial straits on account of the burning, since a contract was signed almost immediately to rebuild the Théâtre du Marais. It was reconstructed according to the same general plan — though a trifle larger and more elaborate as to accessories — of the old one. By June 3, 1644, the new building was ready for interior installations, and the contract was let for the stage, loges, and other internal necessities: it came to 3000 livres of Tours, a very lofty sum for the decoration of a jeu de paume, in this case one that had never been used for the bat and ball game. The comedians paid all told for their new building 10,500 livres of Tours, which was a very powerful indication of their prosperity. The renovated Théâtre du Marais was most likely constructed with outer walls enclosing those of the old jeu de paume and thus the interior dimensions of the new building were the same as the exterior measurements of the hall that had burned. The latter, according to an architect's record in 1678, were 34.43 meters by 11.70 meters; therefore, the salle of the new theatre would have been this size, which would have made it quite capacious. There were probably two windows in the façade — the Bullet map would suggest that there were three — of the building and two entrance doors. As for further fenestration, two windows were in each long side of the structure. The stage * was built on two levels; the first was 1.95 meters (about six

* For more details on the stage, see Chapter VIII.

feet higher than the ground floor and extended across the whole width of the building. It had an over-all depth of 12.67 meters, but not all of this space was available for a stage set, since there were corridors, a stairway, and compartments for the actors in back of the stage, all hidden from the view of the audience by an inner wall. The floor of the first stage was about a foot higher at the back than at the front edge, and this slope enabled the actors to be seen more easily by those standing on the flat floor of the parterre.[17]

The new Théâtre du Marais had two ranks of loges along each of its sides, one row on top of the other. The first row was about seven feet above the level of the parterre; there were nine loges in each row, or thirty-six loges altogether at the sides of the hall. Four more were at the end opposite the stage and at approximately the same height as the stage. Each loge was 1.95 meters wide and 1.30 meters deep, and furnished with chairs. Above the two ranks of loges on each side was a third gallery called the paradis. The two paradis were not divided into loges, but were equipped with long benches. Behind the four loges in back, and on the same level, was the amphithéâtre, a steep series of bleacher-like rows of benches. The amphithéâtre as well as the loges could be reached from stairways in the entrance foyer; there were also steps leading from the level of the amphithéâtre to the paradis. Most probably, two entrance doors admitted the audience into the foyer, which extended the whole width of the building. The Gomboust map suggests two entrance doors, and there is other evidence to this effect — though the Bullet plan indicates only a single outside entry. Once inside, a customer might be rather cramped if the show was a sellout, since the foyer was only some fifteen feet deep. Many modern theatres, however, have no more space than this before entering into the orchestra. At the Marais, a door on each side of the foyer's inner wall permitted a prospective standee to go into the parterre. The renovated Théâtre du Marais was some six-

teen meters in over-all height, and it would contain around
fifteen hundred customers, seated and standing. When it was
completed and ready for business in October 1644, it was
better equipped than the Hôtel de Bourgogne and was, therefore, the most modern public theatre in Paris.[18]

A builder's list of specifications and measurements, as the
rehabilitated Théâtre du Marais shows, can be most enlighten-
ing concerning the interior arrangement of a building, even
if no drawing of it exists. No such collection of information
has come to light for the Hôtel de Bourgogne, but it is safe
to assume that the Marais company, when they rebuilt the
Jeu de Paume du Marais, copied some of the features of the
hall that had been originally constructed to be a theatre. The
Hôtel de Bourgogne, then, must have had the same general
appearance on the inside and the same interior design as the
reconditioned Marais. There has been much theorizing and discussion as to what, among other things, the terms amphithéâtre and paradis meant in various leases and documents involving the Hôtel de Bourgogne. The two words probably
had the same specialized meanings as in the new Marais: the
amphithéâtre was a steep balcony at the end of the hall away
from the stage, and the paradis was the uppermost gallery on
either side of the theatre. In any event, the new and shining
Marais forced the management of the Hôtel de Bourgogne
to do a pretty complete job of refurbishing their establishment
in 1647.

A jeu de paume could unquestionably become a theatre
but not a very good one. Its form and shape were quite well
adapted to the game of the palm, but scarcely appropriate to
theatrical representations. Neither was the Hôtel de Bourgogne, for that matter, which had about the same shape and
dimensions of a jeu de paume. It is to be wondered whether
some builder of jeux de paume created the salle of the Hôtel
de Bourgogne for the Confrérie de la Passion in 1548 and

thus started a tradition of theatrical design in France that could not be broken for more than a century. The greater likelihood is that the Confrérie imitated the long oblong space that they had occupied earlier in the Hôpital de la Trinité. The same sort of square or oblong construction was used, too, in royal ceremonial halls, some of which were employed for public and private dramatic productions — the salle du Petit-Bourbon, for example, in the Louvre and the salle des Etats in the royal château of Blois.

It is somewhat surprising to find evidence that actors in the early part of the seventeenth century had enough money to indulge in the pasttime of jeu de paume. Such would seem to be the case, if the remarks addressed by a colleague to the handsome young actor, Beauchâteau, can be believed: Beauchâteau, a devastating man about town, was advised always to drink his wine straight, and "never to come out of a jeu de paume without having himself dried and rubbed down." A bath in this era was, naturally, not necessary — and it might have brought on a cold. Anyway, Beauchâteau must have been one of the rare actors who performed in a jeu de paume both as an athlete and as a thespian. At the end of the seventeenth century there were still some famous players of jeu de paume in Paris, but they were mostly professionals who advertised their exhibitions with posters, "just like comedians." The King was pleased with some ball-batters in the tennis court of Fontainebleau in 1687. Nevertheless, the game of the palm had very much declined by this time, and "now they play publicly in the jeux de paume nothing but billiards." The awkward and drafty halls were no longer needed for theatres, but in an earlier epoch, when an acting company wanted to stand up to the Hôtel de Bourgogne, they had been rather handy spaces to have around.[19]

THE STAGE IS SET

THE GREAT SPECTACLES OF THE MIDDLE AGES IN FRANCE, the mystery plays, were usually put on outdoors and on enormous stages; such productions were for the most part community projects and no time or money was spared to make them elaborate and complicated. When plays and players moved inside later in the sixteenth century, whether into the Hôtel de Bourgogne or a drafty jeu de paume, compression and simplification were necessary in order to keep activities within the limits of four walls. It is true that from the early fifteenth century the Confrérie de la Passion in Paris had a covered hall for its home base at a time when drama was not protected from the wind, sun, and rain. On the other hand, well on into the seventeenth century drug salesmen and performers at fairs did their skits in the open air, with a stage set up on trestles, a few benches or stools in front of a piece of canvas for a backdrop, and a box full of miraculous remedies. Nevertheless, as a generality it can be said that before the end of the sixteenth century the theater as it developed into public entertainment had moved indoors. The early professional companies would occasionally produce in an open courtyard on an improvised stage, but this was not normal or to be preferred. The troupes both lost and gained when they got a roof over their heads, though the profit was greater than the loss. An outdoor production was more relaxed and informal, but less finished and more subject to interruption. Interior operations gave a company a greater feeling of permanence and solidity, and permitted the outlining of a more

definite schedule. However, the movements of an actor indoors were more cramped and restricted as he went through
his paces when the stage was set.

The stage at the Hôtel de Bourgogne, or in an improvised
jeu de paume of approximately the same dimensions, was
neither very wide nor very deep. It extended across the whole
of one end of the Bourgogne, and thus would have had an
over-all opening of around thirty-four or thirty-five feet.
Unfortunately, this space was cut off on each side by the
line of first loges at the same level as the stage. It can be assumed that each loge and the corridor behind giving access
to it took up a minimum of six feet. Therefore the width of
the stage, as far as the job of acting was concerned, was reduced to about twenty-two or twenty-three feet. The space
at the sides, though murky and poorly lit, would have certainly been needed for the circulation of the actors and the
movement of properties. As for the depth of the stage at the
Hôtel de Bourgogne, that is a rather difficult matter to de-
termine. E. M. Laumann more than half a century ago, in a
study on theatrical machinery since the Greeks, said that the
Bourgogne stage was seven meters wide and five meters plus
a few centimeters deep; no authority was given for these measurements, though the width of seven meters was pretty close
to correct for the scenic opening. A depth of a little more
than five meters, or around seventeen feet, would have been
rather shallow for the stage sets described by the decorator,
Laurent Mahelot, who has left a memoir with drawings of
some of his designs for the Hôtel de Bourgogne in 1633 and
1634. Mahelot's sketches, as may be seen in the several re-
productions of them included in H. C. Lancaster's critical
edition of the record, show that the scene designer visualized
considerable depth in a number of his settings. The illusion
of distance, it is true, could have been maintained by a backdrop painted in disappearing perspective — as is obvious, for
instance, in Mahelot's drawing for the set of Alexandre

Hardy's *Cornélie*. The very example used by Laumann in his unsubstantiated list of dimensions of the Bourgogne scene is taken from another Hardy play, *La Folie de Clidamant*, lost today but described by Mahelot as to the requirements for its setting and pictured in one of his drawings. Laumann, who evidently had not seen the Mahelot sketch (Figure 24), thought that everything would be so crowded that the ship from which the heroine was supposed to jump in the play would have been the size of a "box for dominoes." [1]

It might be well to look at the equipment that Mahelot planned to put on stage for the setting of *La Folie de Clida-mant*: "In the middle of the stage will be needed a fine palace; and, at one side a sea on which is riding a ship fitted with masts and sails; on the ship there appears a woman who throws herself into the sea; and, at the other side of the stage is a fine bedroom which can open and close, wherein there is a bed beautifully adorned with sheets." A later hand has added to the Mahelot specification in the manuscript the words, "some blood" — but this rather melodramatic accessory would not have taken up much room on the crowded platform of the Bourgogne. Everything else on Mahelot's list would suggest that he had in mind an outdoor stage for a mystery play on which could easily be placed a palace and a ship rocking on the waves. Laumann * felt that such a set was ridiculous for the stage at the Bourgogne and would literally use up all the available footage, thus leaving the actors no unoccupied spot in which to move. Such in all probability would have been the case if Mahelot's specified material had been placed in the space, twenty-three by seventeen feet, that Laumann assumed. However, the Mahelot drawing indicates that he had no such plan in mind, but that practically all of the area revealed by the stage opening would be at the disposition of the actors. The

* Some little time and space has been given to Laumann's statement on the Bourgogne stage because it has been frequently mentioned by critics of the French theatre — including Madame Deierkauf-Holsboer and T. E. Lawrenson — without analysis.

ship and the bed are only partially visible at the sides of the scene, and there is enough room left to set up doors, windows, balustrades, columns, and a very solid chair in the center of the scene at the rear. The only reason a décor of this kind could have been devised is the fact that the previously mentioned six feet were usable on each side of the stage for the concealed scaffolding or framework necessary to back up the set as it was seen by the audience. The performers, even if they had almost all of the visible boards at the Bourgogne to stride on, could not dash around in completely uncontrolled fashion. Nevertheless, it would have been unnecessary for the lady in Hardy's *La Folie de Clidamant* to leap off a ship and land in bed.[2]

The stage at the Hôtel de Bourgogne was in all likelihood no more than twenty-two or twenty-three feet wide, but it may well have been more than seventeen feet deep. The engraving of Abraham Bosse of the comedians on stage at the Bourgogne in the 1630's, it is true, would give the impression that the scene was rather shallow. Another of Bosse's works, depicting the interior of a theatre (very probably the Hôtel de Bourgogne) in the seventeenth century (see Figure 20), would create the impression that the five actors shown on the restricted stage had little room to move in any direction. There is other visual evidence, particularly in a picture * of the stage and parterre in the collection of Musée de la Comédie Française, which would lead to the conclusion that the scene at the Bourgogne had considerable depth in relation to its width. The illusion of a drawing, admittedly, can be deceiving and allow for no finality of judgment with regard to dimensions, but this one makes it look as though there was plenty of room for actors and properties upstage.

If the stage at the Hôtel de Bourgogne was only a trifle deeper than five meters, it was a good deal shallower than

* This engraving is frequently reproduced today in the programs of the Comédie Française.

similar installations in other theatrical halls of the same period. As has already been noted, the usable depth of stage at the reconstructed Théâtre du Marais was 9.75 meters, or nearly twice the similar distance proposed by Laumann for the Hôtel de Bourgogne. The newly built Marais, being a bit oversize, would have had all dimensions somewhat larger than those of the earlier jeu de paume on the rue Vieille du Temple. The older stage, then, might well have been only eight or nine meters in profundity. The depth of the scene in the Jeu de Paume de Mestayers, used by Molière in his first theatrical venture, has been estimated to have been 8.96 meters operationally deep, with a passage of a few meters in back of it. This building was almost the same size as the Hôtel de Bourgogne, though it was fitted out for dramatic productions much later. In a hall constructed at Fontenay-le-Comte in 1614 for presentation of plays, the stage was 6.50 meters deep, in a building some twenty-seven meters long and sixteen meters wide. But these dimensions are not in the standard three to one ratio of the Hôtel de Bourgogne or a jeu de paume and would not be typical: in other words, in a longer theatre the stage would be expected to be deeper and was so in several known cases. Lancaster's suggestion, therefore, that the stage at the Hôtel de Bourgogne had "somewhat the same dimensions" as the scene in the Fontenay-le-Comte theatre, which was sixteen meters wide by six and one-half deep, is untenable. The Laumann specifications of seven meters width by five meters depth for the Bourgogne stage are nearer to its original dimensions, though more than possibly it was seven meters wide by seven or eight meters deep.* The new Marais stage had the same inverted relation in the dimensions of the usable area of its first level: it was 7.80 meters wide and 9.75 meters deep. The old Bourgogne, then, which would have been imi-

---

* Lemoine, in the articles cited in Chapter VII, offered evidence that the Bourgogne stage in 1647 was more than ten meters deep; after remodeling during 1647 it was to be some three meters deeper.

tated by its burgeoning competitors, would scarcely have been too much out of line when compared to the newly constructed scenes.[3]

There is considerable reason to believe that the early stage of the Hôtel de Bourgogne had in back something of an upper level in the manner of the old mystery décors or of the reconstructed setting at the Théâtre du Marais. In a lease of 1616 of the Hôtel de Bourgogne by the King's own comedians is a clause specifying that the actors will not have any control over certain ground-level space which is "under the stairway of the *petit théatre* of the said main hall." The *petit théâtre* undoubtedly means here "little stage"; *théâtre* was a quite common term used at the time to designate the theatrical scene. A balcony stage was no complete novelty during this period since one existed in a theatre at Brussels; and it had a trap door from which either gods or demons could rise. Also, it should be emphasized that, with the renovated Théâtre du Marais's second-level scenic equipment, there was a series of circular steps rising up to it. Similar steps must have existed at the Hôtel de Bourgogne in order to reach the upper plateau there, however large or small it was. It probably was used for special effects in seventeenth-century plays, though it had been designed originally as an elevated "mansion" for the earlier religious plays. Many sketches in the Mahelot notebook would indicate that the higher platform was blotted out completely for some of the sets. If it were concealed by a backdrop, the space behind could have been used for the passage of actors or the movement of scenery or properties. All of which would lend support to the opinion that the over-all depth of the Bourgogne stage, even in its early years, was more than seventeen feet.[4]

As for the second-level Marais scene, which must have been an elaboration of previous constructions, it was rather a complicated affair. It rose thirteen feet above the floor of the first stage and was held up by some ten pillars of wood. Its total

width, like that of the lower scene, was thirty-nine feet —
most of which must have been usable, since, beginning some
six feet back from the front edge of main stage, it did not have
six feet cut off of each side by the loges. This upper stage was
indented in the middle and had a depth there of thirteen feet,
and a depth at the two sides of a little more than nineteen feet.
Its floor was cut off in back by a six-foot-wide hole extending about three fourths of the way across, and also by the well
of the circular staircase. This opening gave ready access to
the first level and was useful for hoisting properties to the
second scenic story. The upper plateau, too, was valuable for
the storage of scenery when the terrain was not needed to
show a god sitting on a cloud or for some other dramatic
illusion. There was plenty of room on the balcony stage for
all sorts of movement and effects. A two-foot railing went
around the inward curve of its front edge to prevent any
unwary spirit or divinity from toppling on his colleagues
below — which could also have been done through the hole
at the rear. Certainly the dual-level scene at the Hôtel de
Bourgogne was not so complex in its arrangement as the one
at the Théâtre du Marais. With such an installation, the
Marais turned quite easily in its later years to the production
of machine plays.[5]

The inner wall at the back of the Marais stage reduced its
depth to the previously noted 9.75 meters (or a little more
than thirty-two feet), but the acoustics of the building were
probably improved. This wall, which began at the bottom
level of the theatre, rose up only to the height of the floor of
the second stage, and thus offered no protection to a careless
actor who might back up too far and topple in the cavity
behind it. The whole balcony scene was, in fact, nothing but
a high table with indentions and gaping holes cut in it. It was
no place for a tipsy thespian or stagehand. Anyway, the inner
wall at the Théâtre du Marais formed, behind the stage, with
the end wall of the building a nice little nugget of space for

the use of actors. On the ground level were built against the end wall five loges that could be used for the comedians' dressing and general privacy; five more sat on top of these on the same floor as the main stage. Each one was fitted out with the rather minimal furnishings of a table and a bench. But the Hôtel de Bourgogne had no such luxurious and separate quarters for its performers. In one of the leases on the Bourgogne, signed by Bellerose and others of his companions, it was specified that the actors would have the "first room being above the main door of the said Hôtel in order to dress themselves in it and lock up their clothes there." From this statement it has been assumed in some interpretations that the men and women in the royal company at the advanced time of this lease — in January 1639 — dressed for their dramatic duties in the same room. This conclusion would seem to be unlikely: wherever the "main door" of the Hôtel de Bourgogne was,* the room above it was scarcely in direct connection with the stage — and thus there would have been a practical, if not moral, difficulty in having everybody take clothes off and on in this one spot. It must have been used for storage and more leisurely changing of attire. The Bourgogne unquestionably had back of its stage by 1639 facilities — crude, probably, and not as extensive as the ten loges of the Théâtre du Marais — for the players to do shiftings of costume.[6]

If it can be conceded that the first scene at the Hôtel de Bourgogne was something like twenty-three feet wide by twenty-five feet deep in open terrain for the actors, it was still not spacious enough for unmotivated wandering around or aimless promenading. In marking off the actors area, the stage at the Hôtel de Bourgogne during its early years, even as the trestle stages in the streets and squares, was hung with

* This "main door" quite probably was in the little building on the rue Française, visible on the Gomboust and Bullet maps. It was completely detached from the grande salle of the Hôtel de Bourgogne.

pieces of cloth or tapestries to make its décor. Charles Perrault, the famous teller of fairy tales, said in 1691 that he had
"heard from some older people" what the Paris theatre was
like in the first years of the seventeenth century. In a well-
known passage concerning settings, Perrault stated: ". . .
the stage was decorated with tapestries which gave at the
places where they were joined together entrances and exits
to the actors. These entrances and exits were very inconven-
ient and often put in disarray the coiffures of the comedians."
Perrault's opinion is twice removed from the realities of the
situation: his own memory may have deceived him and the
greybeards he consulted may have been fuzzy in their accuracy
of recall. Nevertheless, there is undoubted truth in what he
says. Lemazurier felt that a painted cloth was used as a backdrop, with three or four "frames" on each side. The tapestries,
as has been suggested by Bapst on the basis of Perrault's description, formed corridors on the outside of the stage set
where the comedians could pass or await their entries. Contemporary substantiation of this point comes from *Les Corrivaux*, a fairly scabrous play of Pierre Troterel which was published in 1612. In it, the prologuist who is seeking to be in-
gratiating to the audience is heckled by an actor "hidden behind the tapestry." The combination of the audience and the
heckler finally force the prologuist to give up his spiel and
leave the stage. Later in the play, Clorette, the warmly promis-
cuous daughter of one Mersant, is talking quite loudly in bed
with one of her suitors: their conversation wakes up the father,
who is asleep behind the back hanging, and he drives the
young man off. It would have been hard to put this play on
without a tapestry or two.[7]

Tapestry hangings to form a stage setting were not the
only technique in vogue at the Hôtel de Bourgogne in its
early years as a public theatre; box-like compartments that
could be moved around were also in use by the professional
companies of the first years of the seventeenth century. These

compartments or "mansions" were a legacy of the Confrérie de la Passion from their representations of mystery plays, which were mounted with a "simultaneous décor": that is, all places concerned with the action of the play were installed on stage — and visible to the spectators — at the same time. In the striking miniature of the Passion of Valenciennes of 1547, eleven or twelve mansions are stretched *across* the stage and they include, partially, paradise, a palace, a ship, the limbo, and hell. A tremendous width of planking would have been required for the setting of such a spectacle. Naturally, the mansions inside the Bourgogne were smaller and more compressed; also, the "little stage" in back would have allowed compartments on a second level. The actors that took over the Hôtel de Bourgogne with a different type of repertory necessarily employed the compartments in a different manner: they were set up on each side of the stage in two compact arrays and a tapestry or piece of painted canvas served as a backdrop. This was the only way that the mansions — which were well adapted to the wide outdoor medieval scene where there was little question of depth or perspective — could be utilized on the inside of the Hôtel de Bourgogne. Also, there was the question of saving a little money. The troupes renting the Bourgogne, in their struggles to make ends meet, were willing to try to adapt to their needs any properties that might be on hand when they took over the building.[8]

The Mahelot drawings of sets, along with the descriptive material accompanying them, give a good deal of information as to how the compartments were arranged. A maximum of five or six of them could be fitted into any given décor, or normally three on each side of the stage. The feeling once held that only compartments, and no tapestries or canvas, were employed at the Bourgogne by the first professional companies would be very much questioned today. There is no reason to object to the idea, already suggested, that medieval mansions and canvas backdrops or hangings were combined in the same setting. A very interesting description and drawing (see Figure 25) of the set for Du Ryer's *Lisandre et Caliste*, first produced around 1630, is to be found in the Mahelot memoir. To produce this play, there would be required on the scene: a building representing the Petit Châtelet (deep in the center); on stage right a cave, a hermitage, and a prison wall with a grilled window; and on stage left a butcher's shop with a window over it, and "a bedroom raised up two or three steps which one enters from behind." Here is fine evidence of the way the two six-foot passages at each side of the Bourgogne stage were utilized: they enabled an actor to make his entry into a compartment from the rear and then carry on his role in the portion of the mansion visible to the audience — or walk on out of it into the empty space in the central part of the stage. There is an indication, also, in the directions given by Mahelot for putting on *Lisandre et Caliste* that movable canvases could cover a compartment and thus change its identity. Lisandre was supposed to be able to talk, according to specifications, to Caliste through the grilled window of the prison. But, in the words of Mahelot: "It is necessary for that [the window] to be hidden during the first act, and it is to appear only in the second act and be closed in the same act; the closure (*fermeture*) will serve as a palace." In this instance the same mansion functioned in two, possibly three, capacities: it was both a window and a palace. The same piece of painted cloth that was to "serve as a palace" might also have hidden the window during the first act. At any rate, painted canvases of varying sizes were used in the early public theatre along with the medieval compartments: the cloth hangings could very quickly vary the dramatic illusion and denote a change of scene.[9]

Further confirmation comes from the first records of the budding professional troupes to show that they did not simply take over a collection of medieval stage sets in beginning their productions in Paris. A large amount of new scenery was

bought and paid for — or, at least, contracted for; the money
was not always at hand. On March 22, 1599, Nicolas Vattement, "master painter of Paris, living on the rue Saint Martin,"
agreed to furnish to Valleran le Conte "all the décors [*feintes*]
and painted materials that will be suitable and necessary for
plays." This arrangement was to last for one year and Vattement was to be paid one crown and twenty sous of Tours a
day by Valleran; it would be the master painter's duty to
provide "all the cloth and other things that will be needed."
Vattement promised on August 18, 1599, to supply Valleran
with "*feintes*, paintings, etc." from next "Saint Remy's day
[October 1] until Easter" for eighty crowns. Vattement was
also to paint "thirty ells of cloth" purchased by the actor.
On October 5, 1599, Valleran contracted with Bonniface
Butays, master painter, and with Sébastien Gouin, master rib-
bon weaver, both of Paris, for "all sorts of paintings of a city,
châteaux, rocks, *feintes*, woods, groves, grass-plots, artifices,
and in general anything else that might be required" for the
make-believe of the theatre. At this time, Valleran apparently
hoped to be successful in pastoral plays. The above assort-
ment of stage materials was to cost eighty crowns, twenty-
four of which had already been paid. Valleran guessed wrong,
it will be remembered, concerning Parisian tastes in drama at
the end of the sixteenth century; therefore, he fell into debt,
and in seeking to pay off the large sum he owed Estienne
Ruffin in 1606, part of the payment offered was "eleven pieces
of painted cloth for use in the theatre." Despite this financial
problem, Valleran hired on September 22, 1607, another Parisian painter, Jehan du Val, at the rate of twenty sous of Tours
a day to provide "nails for scenery and other things" until
the Lenten season of the following year. And in the contract
between Laporte and his troupe of February 21, 1608, all
profits were to be divided after the payment of expenses, including those for "painted scenery if any needs to be made."
It is more than obvious that the early professional companies,

in their too-great optimism concerning the theatre-going public in Paris, sank a considerable portion of their expected
revenue in new and freshly painted décors. Some of these
may have been left over when the Prince of Orange's troupe
under Charles le Noir rented the Bourgogne for a month on
August 27, 1624. Among other charges levied on the comedians were twenty-five sous of Tours a day for the "rights
of the concierge," and twenty sous for the "wood and orna-
mentation which are at present in the theatre." The "wood"
was the solid sets made of timber and scaffolding, possibly
some of them the old medieval compartments; the "ornamen-
tation" the lighter painted canvas that was more flexible and
easier to arrange.[10]

Whether he was working with wood or canvas, the decorator at the Hôtel de Bourgogne had his hands full when the
professionals first came to the Confrérie's antiquated hall.
He was a designer, an arranger of sets, and also a stagehand.
It was due to his skill that certain striking effects were produced, and it was in this capacity that he was called a *feinteur*,
or "creator of artifices." The name of the decorator Georges
Buffequin,* "Maître Georges," has come down from the
early years of the Hôtel de Bourgogne as a public theatre,
though no memoir of Buffequin is extant to match that of his
contemporary, Laurent Mahelot. The words *feintes* and *feinteur* were in regular usage in the older mystery plays, where
such things as effigies undergoing torture and angels flying
through the air were standard theatrical illusions. The *feinteur*
in the early seventeenth century did not have to be such a
prestidigitator as his predecessors, but he was still a busy man.
In a lease of the Bourgogne to the royal comedians from December 28, 1627 until the "week of the Passion" in 1628, the
company was held responsible for their *feinteur* "in case by
his negligence or otherwise he may set fire to some place in

---

* Buffequin assisted in bringing into France Italian ideas on central
perspective. His concepts are reflected in the Mahelot drawings.

the said Hôtel de Bourgogne." He was supposed, as another
duty, to remove from the back of the stage "flowered material
and serges" that had been used during the performance —
evidently another precaution against fire, which was an ever-
present hazard. Nor was the *feinteur*, in working out his
dramatic effects, allowed to "stop up and prevent the view"
from the first two loges * — that is, one on each side — at the
level of the stage. These two loges used up twelve feet of stage
frontage, and scenery projecting around them could have
interfered with their occupants' seeing the performance. The
feinteur had plenty to do in watching out for fires, unblock-
ing the first loges, and setting up and then striking the décor.
Gautier Garguille had all these problems in mind when he
advised Maître Georges to keep a sharp eye out for "pins" and
"nails" as he went about his varied duties.[11]

The lateral décor, with its compartments or boxes drawn up
in illogical and ill-assorted alignment down the two sides of
the stage, lasted for some plays until the 1630's. The farces,
the most popular early dramatic form, gave no great problem
to the decorator since their primary appeal was ribald dialogue
and uninhibited action. A door, a window, a listening post
for eavesdropping, a little open space in the center — and
the stage was set for the farce. However, for the pastoral or
tragicomedy that accompanied the farce, the lateral arrangement of mansions going off into the murky extremities of
each side of the stage was standard. Inevitably a number of
completely disassociated spots ended up next to one another
on the same scene — for example, a palace, a fountain, a wall,
a ship, two houses in reality leagues apart, and a cave. A
series of conventions, many of them deriving from the spectacles of the Middle Ages, made such an arrangement acceptable. An actor, by his presence in or departure from a given
mansion attached the ensuing episode to that geographical

* These loges were the probable ancestors of the present-day *avant-
scène* boxes at the Théâtre Français.

area. A different sequence of events could be initiated from another mansion. The central part of the stage was a sort of dramatic never-never land detached from time or space; the actors could move about in it freely after their immediate point of origin had been fixed. It was rather a confusing system and it fell before the renewed allegiance to the three unities of time, place, and action that began around 1630. With the many mansions all visible at the same moment, quite easily both the actors and spectators could get mixed up. One question raised during the century was how it was possible for the wall in Théophile de Viau's tragedy of around 1621, *Pyrame et Thisbé*, to be visible to Pyramus and to Thisbe, and invisible to the other performers in the play. Another point was made to the effect that more than one place shown on a stage at a given time was just as lacking in logic as a painting with two unrelated episodes on the same canvas. In further emphasis on verisimilitude it was claimed, against the protagonists of the all-inclusive décor, that according to reason even the Palais Royal and the Louvre could not be shown at the same time, one on each side of the scene and a square in the middle: such a set would be unacceptable because in reality there was no empty terrain between Richelieu's domain and the residence of the King.[12]

The *coup de grâce* was accorded the lateral stage set by the glowing triumph of Corneille's *Le Cid* at the Théâtre du Marais toward the end of 1636 or the beginning of 1637. It was not the artistic but the financial success of *Le Cid* that destroyed the compact nests of lateral compartments. So many people — and important people — wanted to see the play that they crowded into every unfilled niche at the sides of the stage in order to hear Corneille's young hero and heroine, Rodrigue and Chimène, struggle with their problems. In 1637, Montdory himself described the event in a famous letter to the writer and fine prose stylist, Louis Guez de Balzac: "The crowd was so great at our doors and our theatre turned out to be so small that the dim corners of the stage, which served in ordinary times as perches for the pages, became choice spots for wearers of the Cordon Bleu, and the scene was adorned regularly by the crosses of Chevaliers of the Order of the Holy Ghost." * Such was the beginning of the great vogue of seats on the stage in the French public halls of drama. Montdory's letter would indicate that under crowded conditions a slim and wriggling page had been permitted before *Le Cid* to slip into some small hole between compartments; but this was the first time that the stage of a public theatre had been invaded by such upper-bracket spectators, and it was destined to continue to be for many decades. The lateral décor, therefore, undermined by the dictates of fashion and increased revenue, was supplanted by seats and benches, which came to be spoken of as the banquettes on the stage. The compartment sets at the side would have probably disappeared anyway under the rising tide of respect for the unities and verisimilitude. In their turn the banquettes must have interfered with the reality of a play as much as did the compartments; in any event, they were a source of much greater noise and disturbance. Despite the hubbub that they led to, they were so popular throughout the seventeenth century that the Comédie Française in 1689 built something like a dozen rows of them on each side of the stage of its new theatre on the rue Neuve des Fossés-Saint-Germain.† With this installation hundreds of spectators were mixed up with the actors when a play was being performed. Art never really triumphed over economics in the matter of the seats on the scene: it was only because a wealthy nobleman reimbursed the actors for the loss of income from the banquettes that they were removed in 1759.[13]

---

* The Order of the Holy Ghost was founded in 1578 by Henry III to replace the Order of Saint Michael, which had ceased to be sufficiently exclusive.

† Now the rue de l'Ancienne Comédie.

The knottiest problem connected with the early public stage in France is the matter of the front curtain. It was certainly not used at the Hôtel de Bourgogne during the first years of the seventeenth century when the newly formed professional companies were still tied down by many medieval traditions. The older religious plays, whether presented indoors or outdoors, had not been staged with a front curtain — nor had the farcical skits put on by a wandering medicine man or street entertainer. It was easy for many of the accepted mechanics of the theatre to be carried over without too great a change into a later period. The audiences for the older plays of the Middle Ages had not been accustomed to the front curtain, and far on into the seventeenth century there was no application of it in the manner of the modern theatre. Many persons felt, in fact, that little real need existed for the contraption.

The Hôtel de Bourgogne in its original form not only omitted a front curtain because of theatrical tradition but also on account of the design of the building. Many complications would have arisen in trying to rig up any kind of a curtain at the front of a stage without a proscenium arch, and all the evidence is against the existence of this ancient Greek device in the Confrérie's original building. The proscenium ledge above the scene room of outdoor theatres like those of Athens or of Epidauros outside Athens was not continued in the Roman theatre or the Renaissance Italian, both of which had high and unimpeded stage openings. It would have been very difficult to fit a curtain into them. Palladio's beautiful Olympic theatre in the Italian town of Vicenza, for example, had no proscenium arch and a curtain to hide the stage would have been completely out of place. There was much to be said, admittedly, for the Greek scheme of a scene room, marked off at the top by a proscenium line that would frame the action. The Italians, recognizing this advantage, may have employed a front curtain on occasions before 1600. However, no in-

20. *Interior of a seventeenth-century public theatre*

'En fin lors que la nuit vient soulager les peines,
Les pourtraits animez des actions humaines,
Montent sur un Theatre artistement paré;

LE SOIR.

Il y voit de ses faits les viuantes histoires
Mais le feint et le vray de toutes ses victoires
Touchent egalement son esprit moderé.

21. *A play is offered to Louis XIII, in the* **Palais Cardinal**

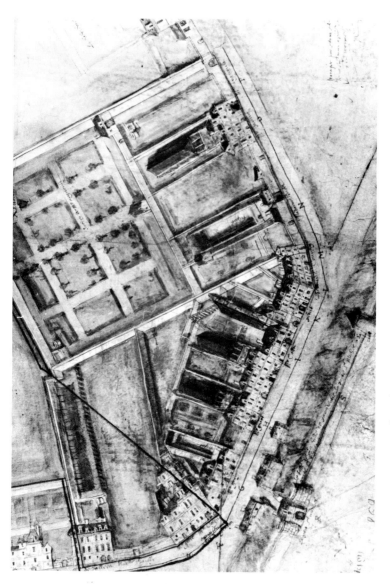

22. Jeux de paume *in the Luxembourg quarter, around 1615*

fluence from the Middle Ages in France nor from the adjacent Roman and Italian past, would have encouraged the Confrérie de la Passion to install in 1548 a proscenium arch in the Hôtel de Bourgogne.

Without a front curtain there was a greater spirit of informality and intimacy in a theatrical production. The players and spectators were more completely in harmony when no inanimate piece of cloth intruded from time to time to break the continuity of action. Much was to be said for an association of this type wherein the audience might share closely in the development of the spectacle, and at times almost encircle the stage. The older mystery plays — which, in theory, still contained elements of the ritual of the Church — fitted well into such a concept. It was effective, too, for the street entertainers who wanted their listeners to feel themselves to be so much a part of things that they would not resist too strongly the purchase of magic panaceas. On the other hand, the situation was entirely different inside the Hôtel de Bourgogne and the theatrical halls like it. No longer was the audience grouped in a semicircle around a platform of performers, but rather it was stretched out in a long line. The occupants of the distant loges or the far reaches of the parterre could not have thought themselves in any position to sympathize with the actors when they forgot their speeches. The very shape of the building demanded that everybody face in the same direction and focus their eyes on the same point of interest. The play became, because of the elongated rectangle of the Bourgogne, more detached and less personal for the spectators, and exacted greater concentration from them. Under such conditions, a proscenium arch and a front curtain made more sense. The machinery by which a theatrical illusion was being created could be better hidden in its workings. And, if the drama being enacted was regarded as an animated picture disconnected from daily problems like medicine and religion — as it was coming to be more and more — it was quite appropriate to frame it with a proscenium arch. Then, with the spectator's personal attachment to the scene broken, a curtain could, in theory, close at intervals without breaking the continuity of the play.

All of which is consistent with logic, but when did it happen? Certainly not during the golden era of the farces, while the farce-players still had their loyal followings. It is true that the compartments used at times by the *farceurs*, as can be seen from studying the engravings of several of them, might be constructed with individual curtains which could open or close. The same sort of closing of compartments had been employed in the earlier serious plays, where the mansions frequently had little sliding curtains to shut off their interiors whenever it was desired. Also, there was the standard device of a piece of cloth or painted canvas, which could be put over a compartment to denote a change of scene. But none of these processes involved the blotting out of the whole stage, as would be done by the use of a front curtain. If such a procedure did not happen with the farces, neither did it with the pastorals and tragicomedies of the early cenury, which continued the general processes of the curtainless, multiple-set stage of the Middle Ages. Since the compartment décor was not completely rejected until after *Le Cid*, it is safe to assume that the front curtain was not even in sporadic usage at the Hôtel de Bourgogne before the 1630's.

Many objected to the insertion of a curtain between the players and the audience, and it was argued back and forth even as was the question of the unities. There is a famous passage in the second act of Desmarets de Saint Sorlin's *Les Visionnaires*, published in 1637, which has to do with both matters. Sestiane, the girl who loves plays, is discussing with Amidor, the extravagant poet, a drama that violates the rules:

> The author deserves complaint, he has done me an outrage:
> I thought I was in Rome, he snatches me off to Carthage;
> It is useless to sing a song and draw the curtain,
> I am not deceived at all — I have not crossed over the water.

Such a statement would indicate that some use was being made of a front curtain at the time: in this case, to indicate the closing of an act and the shift of scene across the Mediterranean. A real-life theorist, the Abbé d'Aubignac, disapproves by implication of the front curtain when he says that the "stage should never be empty and the actors should never disappear" — unless, naturally, a given performer makes a motivated entrance or exit to or from the terrain of the drama. "One should always see the actors," says D'Aubignac, and he has no patience with those various apartments on stage "with curtains that can be closed and opened to make the actors appear and disappear." Such devices "render ridiculous those who invented them and those who approve of them." Obviously, at a fairly late moment in the dramatic history of seventeenth-century France, the most important practical critic of the period did not want any type of curtain on the stage.[14]

The acceptance of the unities made the front curtain in many ways not necessary. This was something of a paradox in dramatic development, since the more serious and sophisticated plays after 1630 had a greater detachment from the spectator's everyday life. They could most acceptably have been given a framed and pictural quality, with depth of perspective, that would have been enhanced by a proscenium arch. However, the front curtain was not needed to denote the end of an act and shift of scene, since all the action was supposed to be carried out in one place and within a period of twenty-four hours. The curtain, therefore, in some aspects was an opponent of the classical rules, since its closure might indicate a change of place and also an indeterminate passage of time. As such an instrument, it was considered dangerous and got little approval from supporters of the unities like Jean Chapelain and the Abbé d'Aubignac. Possibly because of the attitude of such disciples of regularity as these two, the front curtain was seldom pulled down throughout the seventeenth century to designate a change of time or place, in standard plays on the public stage. It had nothing to do with the separation of the play into acts, but helped in creating a unity of dramatic ensemble by being opened to reveal the setting at the beginning of a play and closed at the end. The effective use of a curtain for dramatic surprise was a device of the Italians and it may well have influenced the French. In any case, in the classical repertory of the Comédie Française today, the curtain is normally closed only one time during a five-act tragedy. This is done not to allow a change of scene, but to provide an interlude for the spectators to promenade in the foyer and do a little sipping at the bar.

The first theatre in Paris which incontestably had a proscenium arch curtain was in the Palais Cardinal of Richelieu. The Cardinal's handsome theatrical hall was dedicated in 1641 with the complex and ornate tragicomedy, *Mirame*; the frontispiece of the published play is an engraving which shows that the curtain was one solid piece of material and was raised or lowered by a roller behind the proscenium arch (see Figure 26).* The theatre of the Cardinal, it is true, was much too ornate to be compared with the public halls of drama, but it might well have been influenced by some of their technical installations. As for other nonprofessional diversions, a front curtain to mask the opening scene from the spectators was employed in the court ballets as early as 1610, a procedure borrowed from the Italians. The Italian theorician of theatrical design, Niccolò Sabbattini, in 1638 said that there were two manners of "lifting the curtain which hides the scene": it can be dropped to the stage floor (possible only once during a performance), or it can be raised up on a roller and hidden by the "sky" above. The French theatre operators early in the seventeenth century had few "skies," although Mahelot stated that for one of his décors a "night" would be required.

---

* Madame Deierkauf-Holsboer mistakenly assumes in her *Histoire de la mise en scène*, p. 140, that the *Mirame* curtain was made of two halves that slid to the sides of the stage. The center "break" was made by the engraving being folded in the middle in the *Mirame* volume; the "break" goes on down into the steps at the front of the stage.

In the realm of theory: the concept of the proscenium arch for scenic use was most likely furthered by the many triumphal arches that were built by the cities of France when a king and his court would make a royal entry into the urban areas. Such entries, very popular since the sixteenth century, involved considerable dramatic pageantry passing through the frame of the arch. In the realm of fact: there is textual evidence in the specifications for the repairs of the Hôtel de Bourgogne in 1647 that proves the old theatre had had a curtain before this date — heavier beams were to be installed for the support of "the curtain." It was to be raised and lowered, which would have demanded some sort of covering like a proscenium arch to hide it. Unfortunately, no curtain is mentioned in the list of renovations for the new Marais in 1644, even though a front curtain would have been needed for special effects in machine plays, soon to be the Marais' most popular offerings. As something of a last comment on the matter of the front curtain, it might be said that there is little doubt that one existed at the Hôtel de Bourgogne in the 1630's, but the proof of it is a long way from being absolute.[15]

When the stage was set for the productions of the early professional companies, it was scarcely lit up in dazzling splendor; this deficiency in illumination was another reason for a front curtain's not being necessary in standard plays to hide the mysteries that were arrayed on the scene. Though performances supposedly began in the early afternoon, very little light filtered through from the outside to the murky stage of the Bourgogne. And candles were deucedly expensive; therefore the Bourgogne and other public halls of the theatre remained in darkness until the last possible moment before the play began. Around 1600 the troupes, in their struggle to make ends meet, lit only the stage and assumed that a few weak beams would filter out over the spectators and corridors. Charles Perrault, who late in the seventeenth century talked about earlier theatrical events he could not have seen, made some provocative comments on stage lighting of an earlier period: "All the illumination consisted at first in a few candles on tin platters attached to the tapestries; but since the actors were lit up only from the rear and a little at the sides, which made them all look black, someone got the idea of making chandeliers out of two crossed laths, each one holding four candles, to be put over the front of the stage; these chandeliers, clumsily suspended by visible cords and pulleys, were raised and lowered awkwardly by hand when they were to be lit or extinguished." There were probably variations with different companies in regard to the placing the chandeliers — front, back, or at the sides of the stage in order to create a desired effect of shadows. Footlights (the *rampe*) were not in use during the early professional experimentation; they are not mentioned, in fact, by Italian theorists like Serlio and Sabbattini, both of whom were well-known in France. The origin of footlights, however, seems pretty certain: a row of candles was put along the front edge of the stage by a poor company that did not have time or money to hang chandeliers — and it worked fine both practically and artistically. It was much easier to light or snuff the candles in this location.[16]

Whether candles or oil lamps (both of which were discussed by Sabbattini) were the source of illumination for the scene, there was considerable trouble involved in keeping them going. They sputtered and went out, and also were smelly. Candles were less odoriferous than the oil burners, but the former very easily could ignite a costume. The wicks in both cases had to be trimmed from time to time in order to avoid smoking, and it was best if this could be done during some natural break in the dramatic proceedings. Candles were probably the lighting mechanism preferred by the actors since they were more manageable. This would be suggested in the

October 24, 1607, lease of the Hôtel de Bourgogne by the royal comedians wherein it is specified that the Confrérie de la Passion will furnish to the actors the "candles of wax which they have been accustomed to have." The candles were to be provided in this instance without extra payment of funds, a rather neat stipulation on the part of the troupe. It was a better, though less usual, situation than that revealed in the document of January 26, 1600, in which it is stated that Robert Guérin — or Gros Guillaume — will collect the "pocket change" at the doors of "the said Hôtel de Bourgogne" but out of it he will have to pay for the "torches, candles, and Fiacre Boucher,* master performer on instruments." [17]

Music and performing on instruments was a recognized item of expense for the early companies as they set the stage for a play. The Frères Parfaict made some informative comments on musical interludes between the acts of drama when they took up Garnier's tragicomedy, *Bradamante*, and the proper way it might be produced: for the choruses that have been omitted from *Bradamante* an instrumental divertissement could be inserted. Such has come to be the normal procedure, say the Frères Parfaict, since dramatists have abandoned the chorus to end an act; for the chanting voices, "players of instruments" have been substituted. As for the location of these performers, "they were first placed in the wings on stage, where they presented various melodies, before the beginning of the play and before each act. These *symphonistes* later changed position — they were put in the back of the third loges, then in the second loges, and finally at the Hôtel (de Bourgogne) where the comedians are producing at present, it was judged that the musicians would be better located between the stage and the parterre." According to the Frères Parfaict's statement, after the musicians left the stage

---

* The comedian, Fiacre Boucher, was called a "maître joueur d'instruments" when he was witness to a marriage contract on July 27, 1598.

they came all the way out of the third gallery (or paradis) into a pit in front; but this did not happen in the early years of the professional companies. The extensive directions for staging included in Antoine de la Pujade's *Jacob*, published in 1604, give some added information concerning the music needed for this tragedy as well as concerning operations "behind the canvas" (the backdrop). During Jacob's vision a "musician marrying his voice to the sound of a lute" will sing; then he will retire "behind the backdrop" and join all the "music" in making the voices of the angels. Despite the suggestions of the author of *Jacob*, the struggling troupes at the Bourgogne could hardly have afforded a very large celestial choir.[18]

Harmonious and dulcet sounds, certainly, helped the play along even if they did cost money. On January 4, 1599, Valleran le Conte in a contract with Benoist Petit agreed to furnish the "music and the playing of viols." In the document of February 21, 1608, forming Laporte's troupe, it was written that François Vautrel with his two brothers, Aubry and Claude, would "fill in the acts (*actes* here must mean intermissions) with their music, the instruments of viols." An orchestra of three pieces was about as large a musical combination as the troupes could afford, even though an actor, like Fiacre Boucher, might double in viols in the band. The prospective young players were frequently given training in music. Further connection between the musical and dramatic worlds of Paris in the seventeenth century was indicated in the obligation admitted by one Jehan Jacquet, "master instrument maker," on August 9, 1610, to pay Laporte six hundred livres of Tours before the following Easter — a rather unusual situation, indeed, for somebody to owe money to an actor. Some idea of the cost of the music to the companies can be gained from Valleran's contract with his troupe on March 31, 1612: one Jacques Vuaelte, "musician," was to be paid ten sous of Tours a day, and Pierre Pesant, "player of the violin," was to receive sixteen sous of Tours a day.

These artists were to get their promised daily stipends whether they performed or not. According to Perrault, the "symphony" of these early days in the public theatre was composed of a "flute and a drum, and two pitiful violins at the most." There was scarcely a lavish bank of strings in the Bourgogne and competing halls even later in the century. However, the situation seems to have been improved on occasions by outside assistance. Tallemant des Réaux tells a story about the dramatist, La Serre: "He composed several pieces in prose and when they were represented he furnished the violins to the Hôtel [de Bourgogne]; that is to say, there were in the end loges ten or twelve violins, which played before and after and in between the acts." [19]

The stage décors during the first years of the public theatre in France were not opulent, but neither were they makeshift scaffoldings or worn-out residues of a former age. The claim, made later in the seventeenth century, was not fully defensible that "in the recent past" plays were so defective as not to have even a "painted cloth to cover up the characters who were supposed to disappear;" in these earlier days those who were not needed for the action were just "considered to be absent." The reason for this somewhat imagined impoverished décor was, admittedly, a lack of public support; the comedians, who have been quite "incommoded in their business affairs," should not be expected to bear the whole expense of theatrical equipment. The Abbé de Marolles, a man with a great interest in the theatre, had a slightly different point of view. It was his opinion that "comedies," as opposed to ballets and machine plays, did not demand a wealth of decoration, since in them "the principal beauty consists in the things which are said, and in the actions of the personages, the rest being only an accessory which soon becomes boring." The Abbé de Marolles would, clearly, have agreed with many other critics before and since his time: in whatever way the stage is set, the play is still the thing.[20]

I X

THE AUDIENCE

INTO THAT "HOUSE COMMONLY CALLED THE HÔTEL DE BOURGOGNE," while the actors were giving a final check to their lines and coiffures, came a cross section of the people of Paris. They did not keep their movements very quiet, and this was in keeping with the raucous spirit that had permeated French dramatic audiences since the lusty farces of the Middle Ages. The noise-making propensities of the spectators in a French theatre have not lessened through the centuries; they have, indeed, remained more than obvious in many of the halls of entertainment in Paris. An overweight ballad singer has been hissed off the stage,* even though some of her hearers could still remember when her figure was trim and her voice less shrill; and actors have been booed because of a small mannerism or gesture. Since the beginning of time, French audiences — to put it mildly — have been among the most difficult in the world. Their beliefs in their unhindered rights to self-expression made it necessary, as the professional theatre developed in the seventeenth century, for an author to persuade his friends to go along to the opening of a new play in order to help it get a reasonably fair deal from the spectators. The *claque*, or paid applause, came into existence of necessity in the eighteenth century and has continued through the years in some Paris theatres where a few indi-

---

* Such a thing happened some few years ago to the Spanish singer, Raquel Meller, at the Casino de Paris. Also, a news commentator in a Paris movie house today will receive a round of jeers for being careless with an aspirate H.

viduals with heavy hands, strategically placed, have beat them together at every slight pause in the action on the stage. The public theatre in France, in its early gropings toward acceptance in society, definitely needed the financial and artistic support of the citizenry. But this paying clientele, whether it approved or disapproved of a dramatic offering, was certainly hard to handle.

One of the difficulties was inherent in the structure of the Hôtel de Bourgogne and in the theatrical mores of the time: both of these conditions created the parterre, the flat and seatless first floor of the Bourgogne where several hundred spectators formed a milling, jostling, and well-nigh uncontrolled mob. The Bourgogne and its customers had a bad reputation even before 1600 when the professionals had scarcely got their operations under way. The Frères Parfaict suggested, as has been noted, that the Confrérie de la Passion ceased producing — in 1588, according to the Parfaict brothers — because the "best people stopped going to their performances." It was in 1588, indeed, that was printed one of the most bitter attacks on the Hôtel de Bourgogne and those who were its patrons — the *Remonstrances très-humbles au Roy de France*, a complaint destined to be presented at the sessions of the States General in Blois. In this anonymous pamphlet, objection was raised to plays and spectacles on Sundays and festival days; and the Hôtel de Bourgogne was labeled a "sewer and house of Satan" which had been rented out to players by a group "abusively" calling themselves the Confrérie de la Passion. In the Bourgogne, "a thousand scandalous assignations are made, to the prejudice of the honor and modesty of women, and to the ruin of the families of the poor artisans with whom the low hall [the parterre] is quite full, and who more than two hours before the play spend their time in immodest carryings-on, in dice games, in gluttony and drunkenness — all right out in public, and therefrom several quarrels and fights arise." The badly lit parterre of the Bourgogne and dark areas around the side walls undoubtedly lent themselves most easily to all sorts of excesses before the show began. The sharp attack leveled at the Confrérie's theatre in the *Remonstrances* may have had some effect, since there is no evidence that the Hôtel de Bourgogne was being leased to dramatic companies between 1588 and 1598. During this difficult decade in the city of Paris, audiences in the provinces got a look at the first professional troupes.[1]

The nature and quality of the audience that went to the Hôtel de Bourgogne during the first thirty years of the seventeenth century is a provocative question. Beauchamps felt, as he looked at the earlier era, that the building improvements in Paris begun around 1600 by Henry IV, including the reopening of the Hôtel de Bourgogne, encouraged all classes to get out of their houses and go to the theatre. Before that time the solemn city dwellers like "merchants, ecclesiastics, and magistrates" had been "too scrupulous to be seen publicly at the silly performances of a buffoon." The "people of quality," before the first of the Bourbons took over Paris, had "spent their lives either at war or in their châteaux." Beauchamps' estimate is probably an oversimplification of the situation, but there is evidence that all types of Parisians toward the end of the sixteenth century began to take an interest in what was going on in the Hôtel de Bourgogne. Traffic around the place was beginning to be heavy, since on October 6, 1599, the city authorities gave the actors permission to put up barriers "in front of the door and entry of the said Hôtel to withstand the pressure of the people whenever it is desired to put on a play inside." And, in Thomas Platter's enthusiastic description of his visit to the Hôtel de Bourgogne in 1599, there were "so many people" and the comedies lasted so long that they were not finished until after dark. A person could stand up for half price on the floor, but it was full price for a seat in the galleries — and "it is there that the ladies are accustomed to go."[2]

Just how ladylike were these "ladies" who went to the early public plays might be a matter for discussion. Tallemant des Réaux made the much-quoted statement that before the reforms of Cardinal de Richelieu in the theatre, "virtuous women did not go to it." A slightly less positive opinion was expressed in 1666 when it was said that "fifty years ago a woman of gentility did not dare to go to the theatre, or if by chance she did she had to be masked and completely invisible." The pleasure of playgoing, so the opinion ran, at this time was reserved chiefly for *débauchées* who allowed themselves to be seen at spectacles "with their faces uncovered." The solid bourgeois of Paris most logically left their wives at home when they went to see the bawdy farces of the first professional years at the Hôtel de Bourgogne; nor was it likely that the fastidious ladies — or gentlemen, for that matter — of the Court made a habit of listening to the heavy humor of Gros Guillaume or Gautier Garguille. Nevertheless, it seems invalid to assume, as did such a critic as Eugène Rigal, that ladies in the first years of the seventeenth century avoided the theatre completely. Certainly, in the retinue of the uninhibited Henry IV, they went with the King to the Hôtel de Bourgogne even as they were a part of his cheering section when he was smashing racquets in some unrefined jeu de paume. It will be recalled that on January 26, 1607, Henry IV attended the Hôtel de Bourgogne to see a "pleasant farce"; and with him were "the Queen, and the greater part of the princes, noblemen, and ladies of the Court." This might well have been a private performance for royalty, but it was done in the public hall of Paris by the same farce-players who amused the rabble whenever the Bourgogne was open for business. At the end of the clammy month of January, the *salle* would have needed to be well filled with relatively warm bodies to keep the royal audience from being chilled to death.[3]

There is considerable visual evidence to show that ladies lent their presence to a variety of theatrical spectacles in Paris during the early years of the seventeenth century. Three different engravings of the period (see Figures 10, 12, and 20) portray three popular areas of entertainment in the capital city: the Place Dauphine with Tabarin, the *opérateurs* (their sign is visible over the stage) and their medicine show at the Foire Saint Germain, and the parterre of one of the public theatres. No more down to earth spots for relaxation could be located in Paris, but the artist in all three of these pictures has drawn in the groups of spectators several very elegantly costumed ladies, who appear in no sense of the word to be ill at ease. One, in the engraving of the scene at the Saint Germain fair, is walking a little nearer the stage as though she did not want to miss any of the wise and pithy sayings of the performers. The audience, it is true, in these three cases is an imagined one; but it is not likely that the artist would have clothed all the scullery maids present in the elegance of ladies at the Court.

Ladies, beyond little doubt, went on occasions to the rough farces at the Hôtel de Bourgogne. They may have done it for the novelty of the thing, or in a gesture of emancipation — or, as has been suggested, they joined their gentlemen escorts in a "taste for dirt." The larger portion of the feminine patrons of the farce, admittedly, was made up of the lower stratum of society, intent on finding a man; but the women in the audience even during these early years were of a mixed category.* One of the comedies lowest in moral tone of the earlier time was Pierre Troterel's *Les Corrivaux*, which came out in 1612; the author in his announcement to the reader feels that he has to make it clear that there is no purpose in the play to "instruct in vice," a purity of concept that might well be missed in the play itself. In any case, the prologue to the comedy is addressed to a mixed audience, to men as well as to all branches of femininity:

---

* As they have been in later years at the Folies Bergère or at the vaudevillian skits of the Olympia on the Boulevard des Capucines.

Gentlemen, my God give joy to you; and to you also, my ladies,
And likewise to you, beautiful *filles* and *femmes*.

The prologuist goes on to say, in a burst of optimism, that
the actors are not a collection of "old antiques," and that the
spectators will be edified by the drama if they will only
"bring us a little silence." The request for silence was a
standard one in a theatrical age of constant noise and uproar.
Other evidence of feminine patronage of the theatre in these
early years is in one of the speeches of the most famous of the
prologuists, Bruscambille. In *Des étranges effets de l'amour*,
Bruscambille addresses himself specifically to "my ladies,"
and hopes that they will find the play "agreeable," that they
will "listen to the actors," and that their "patience will not
be deceived." [4]

One of the most turbulent incidents involving ladies attending the theatre early in the seventeenth century happened in Bordeaux, where a troupe of comedians were presenting their repertory in the Jeu de Paume de Barbarin. A
very "tough young man" named Tarneau was angry at a
certain young gentleman called Rochemaine and was search-
ing for Rochemaine in the hall where the play was in progress. There Tarneau insulted a friend of Rochemaine and was
stabbed by the friend as well as by a lackey who was in the
service of the archbishop. Tarneau died "in the arms of some
young ladies who were watching the comedy, which
stopped." The *lieutenant criminel* of Bordeaux, who "was
also present watching the representations of the comedians,"
arrested the friend of Rochemaine for the stabbing of Tarneau. The young gentleman later escaped. It would appear
that on this occasion everybody in Bordeaux was at the
Jeu de Paume de Barbarin, including several nonsqueamish
demoiselles.[5]

The farces between 1600 and 1630, it is true, were not
aimed primarily at a feminine ear, and if they had remained
throughout the century the principal dramatic offerings of the

professional comedians the theatre would never have been accepted in the best circles of Parisian society. The few ladies who put on their masks around 1615 or 1620 and went to the Hôtel de Bourgogne — along with some gentlemen from the Court and a few intellectuals — assisted in raising standards of taste. Yet it is doubtful that, in an age when a spade was pretty definitely called a spade, they were too greatly shocked by the grossness of language and pantomime in the farces. Some of the plays as late as the 1630's were quite scabrous, none more so than Jean de Mairet's *Les Galanteries du duc d'Ossone*, performed in 1632. Rather surprisingly, in the dedicatory epistle of this series of bedroom escapades, Mairet welcomes his female auditors by saying "the most virtuous women are now frequenting the Hôtel de Bourgogne with as little scruple or scandal as would be attached to their going to the (Palace of) the Luxembourg"; all of this is possible, says Mairet with tongue-in-cheek seriousness, because the moral tone of the theatre has been so much elevated by him and his contemporaries. In Scudéry's *La Comédie des Comédiens*, also presented in 1632, one of the wives in the play defends her slow-talking spouse by saying: " . . . if my husband does not have his tongue too well hung, he has other parts about him worthy of recommendation." And in Véroneau's play, *Impuissance*, published in 1634, there is line after line of lamentation over the impotence of a husband, who is unable to give his wife any amatory attention in a normal way. All had not been completely refined by the 1630's, though the audience was certainly becoming progressively more mundane. Women were going out more and more, if L. C. Discret's comedy of 1637, *Alizon*, can be believed. In it an old soldier has given up warfare because of his infatuation with a certain lady, but he can never find her at home: "Now a president of the assembly is taking her for a promenade, now a counselor is having dinner with her, often she is in a lecture hall or attending the theatre."

Woman's place, in seventeenth-century Paris as well as in later epochs, was not limited exclusively to the home. A combination of the theatrical and domestic was made a little later in the century by the noted lady about town, Ninon de l'Enclos: one Des Mousseaux "made her acquaintance *à la comédie* and went to call on her: she was in bed." [6]

The chief problem of audience control at the Hôtel de Bourgogne was the unseated and boisterous parterre, which made up over half of the spectators. Estimates have been made that close to one thousand persons could be packed onto the unslanted floor of the Bourgogne, and this would seem to be a reasonable figure. The salle for the standees was about seventy by thirty-five feet, if some thirty-five feet were taken off the building's more than one hundred feet of length for the stage and possible foyer — a liberal allowance. More than two thousand square feet were therefore available to the downstairs customers, counting footage extending up to the side walls. A noncorpulent spectator, if the play were exciting enough, could fit into two square feet — certainly not a preferred position from which to watch a drama, but it would be possible. And, too, only on the rare occasions of a hit show would such stuffing of human anatomies into this restricted space be necessary. Lemazurier quotes from a "contemporary author" (unnamed)* in the earlier seventeenth century a passage suggesting that the parterre would contain more than a thousand persons and that most of them were bad: "The parterre is very difficult because of the pressed-in crowd: in the space are a thousand roughnecks mixed in with honest citizens at whom from time to time the low types hurl insults. A quarrel arises out of nothing, swords are put to hand, and the whole comedy is interrupted. In their

---

* The passage used by Lemazurier is in Les Frères Parfaict, *Histoire du théâtre*, VI, 128, where Lemazurier probably found it. The Frères Parfaict took it from the seventeenth-century author, Charles Sorel.

most perfect repose these rascals never stop talking, yelling, and whistling; and because they have paid nothing as an entree (which shows that this statement comes from an earlier century), and because they come there for lack of any other occupation, they scarcely bother to listen to what the comedians are saying." With the loges, galleries, amphithéâtre, and possibly a few seats on the stage, the Hôtel de Bourgogne would hold fairly comfortably around sixteen hundred customers. The Abbé d'Aubignac used round numbers when he advised an actor to become so wrapped up in his role that he would forget he was "in the Hôtel de Bourgogne in Paris" and that everything was being said and done "in the presence of two thousand persons." Whatever was the exact count, many hundreds of them were turning and twisting and not watching the play.[7]

Bruscambille in his *Prologue de l'impatience* has aimed an excellent bit of badinage at the uncouth and noisy customers who push their way into the parterre shouting impatiently "start the show" — while "we have indeed had the patience to wait for you calmly and receive your money at the door." Some of the audience are "more impatient than impatience itself," and insist that the comedians hurry up and get things under way. But it is not a good time to begin while "one is coughing, another is spitting, another is breaking wind, another is laughing, and another is scratching his rear." Also, the pages and lackeys are throwing stones — the actors on stage were exposed to bodily damage as well as verbal abuse — for which their masters should apply a little something to their "posterior parts" later in the day. The audience ought to remember that "the bed is for sleeping, the table for drinking, the Hôtel de Bourgogne for seeing and hearing whether seated or standing, and without budging any more than would a new bride." If an "excellent pastoral" is being presented some find it too short, others too long. There is too much stamping of the feet and at times is heard the "grunting of a badly stuck pig." The rabble out front might well have the patience of Socrates, and Bruscambille quotes some Latin and "two words of Greek" to prove it. On other occasions, Bruscambille would vary his technique and try to calm the restive spectators with a bit of rapid patter: "Ladies and gentlemen, I should desire, expect, wish, demand, and require desirously, wishfully, expectantly, demandingly, and insistently . . . that you might be illuminated, irradiated, and so clarified that you could penetratively, secretively, and with divination look through a little hole which is in the window of the buffet of my conceptions . . . to see the method that I wish to employ today to thank you for your delightful presence and audience." Any system that would gain for the actors a little preliminary peace and quiet was worth trying on the unpredictable parterre.[8]

The pages and lackeys were a large portion of the noise-producing element at the Hôtel de Bourgogne, but they were not all of it. A great deal of the disturbance occurred on the outside of the theatre, as the crowd was milling around and pushing its way in. An idea of the mixed nature of the multitude may be gained from the sentence of the Châtelet court on February 4, 1611, forbidding "all pages, lackeys, and any other persons of whatever quality or condition to employ force or indulge in any insolences at the doors of the said Hôtel de Bourgogne." The injunction against "insolences" in front of the entrances to the Hôtel de Bourgogne was repeated much later, probably with very little effect, on September 3, 1624. Once they were on the inside, the pages and lackeys apparently had their throwing arms in good condition, and an adequate supply of missiles. This would be suggested in the *Testament* of Gautier Garguille, where a certain Tibaut Garrau is threatened with solid punishment if he continues to copy the mannerisms of the great farce-player: Garrau will be "hissed by the pages and lackeys" and "battered with volleys of cooked apples" — which should have been less damaging, incidentally, than chunks of plaster or fragments of paving stone.[9]

More serious injuries could be caused by the royal guardsmen, gentlemen at Court, or plain Parisians, who came into the theatre wearing swords or shorter daggers. As late as 1641, in a mob of bigwigs from Brittany who were pushing their way into the Théâtre du Marais, the actor Laroque was wounded by a sword-thrust in the shoulder. Much earlier at the Bourgogne on March 19, 1608, when an Italian company was there, a French gentleman forced his way in without paying and gave the Italian actor, Battistino (who was collecting the money at the door), a slap as he went by. Battistino followed the gentleman to the loges, still requesting the price of the entree; when it was refused with a scathing remark, Battistino punched the gentleman solidly in the nose. The blood flowed freely and several swords were drawn, but Battistino managed to escape with the assistance of some fellow Italians. Obviously, not all of the tumult and disturbance at the Hôtel de Bourgogne could be blamed on the parterre; swords and other weapons were dangerous in any part of the theatre. It was pointed out during the period that "several bad characters" wore their swords into places destined for "public diversion" and while there insolently attacked "persons of respectability." It was dangerous, therefore, for women and children to go to the theatre, as they had done in ancient times. Part of the trouble in France came from the bad arrangements for seeing a play — especially in the parterre, where there were "no seats and no elevation." Under these unfavorable conditions, performances have been constantly disturbed by "debauched young men, who go to the theatre only to show their insolence, who scare everybody around them, and who often commit murders while they are there." [10]

Even later in the century audience conditions were far from ideal in the theatres of Paris. The uproar from the par-

terre and the noise from the loges and galleries were supple-
mented by the distractions created by the spectators sitting
on the stage. These seats on the scene itself — which, it will
be remembered, became fashionable with the popular success of Corneille's *Le Cid* — were always a liability to a
dramatic production. Tallemant des Réaux summed up the
situation rather well: "There is at this moment a terrible
inconvenience in the theatre: it is the fact that the two sides
of the stage are completely filled with young men sitting on
chairs of straw [cane bottoms?]; they sit there because they
do not wish to go into the parterre, although there are often
soldiers at the (entrance) door, and although neither the
pages nor the lackeys carry swords any longer. The loges
are quite expensive, and it is necessary to plan (for seats)
well in advance. For a crown, or for half a louis, one can
be on the stage; but that spoils everything, and only one in-
solent fellow is needed sometimes to ruin the whole show." [11]

Not only was there noise and confusion inside the theatre
and at the entrance doors, in connection with the presentation of the early professional plays in France, but an equal
amount of disturbance was in the general environs. This condition was revealed in the sessions of Montdory and Charles le
Noir at the Jeu de Paume de la Fontaine during 1632 and
1633. Their performances seem to have attracted large
crowds, but the neighbors surrounding the theatre objected
to the increased traffic on the streets. As a result of these complaints, the Parlement of Paris issued a decree on March 22,
1633, stopping the production of plays at the la Fontaine hall.
The inhabitants of the rue Michel-le-Comte, where the theatre
was located, claimed that the street was quite narrow, had a
number of portes-cocheres on its houses, and was populated
by "several persons of quality." On the days that plays were
being given, these estimable people could not get home until
nightfall because of the "confusion of carriages and horses
meeting one another in the said street." Also, the occupants

of the fine dwellings in the area, in seeking their way home after dark, suffered "great danger to their persons from the insolence of lackeys and pickpockets accustomed to look for such pretexts and occasions to practice with impunity their thieveries." Many persons had been "beaten and maltreated, with the loss of their coats and hats." By implication, in the complaint of the good bourgeois of the rue Michel-le-Comte, the lackeys and the pickpockets earlier in the day had been patrons of the dramatic company at the Jeu de Paume de La Fontaine — which might very well have been the case. But these impecunious lovers of drama hardly would have clogged the streets with their horses and carriages; indubitably, the public theatre was drawing its clientele from all classes.[12]

The doors of the Hôtel de Bourgogne, when the seventeenth century was new, opened at one o'clock in the afternoon. This was in keeping with the police order of November 12, 1609, which specified one o'clock as the hour for unlocking the doors of theatres on regular days, two o'clock as the latest moment for the play to begin, and four-thirty as the time for everything to be finished up and for the audience to be on its way home. During the wintry period of the year, when the sun was far away, the above schedule was supposed to be in effect — "from Saint Martin's day [November 11] until the fifteenth of February." Undoubtedly, there was much abuse of the edict and variation in its application. The official policy was to have public amusements like the theatre completed before nightfall, when the streets of Paris became the domain of thieves and robbers. On the other hand, the dramatic companies would delay a performance until all possible clients had come into the hall. The interlude before the play could be passed, as may well be imagined, in gaming, fencing, or wenching. Early comers who lacked initiative and insisted on stage entertainment immediately had to be diverted by the prologuist or the *orateur* of the troupe. Preliminary noise at the Hôtel de Bourgogne must have prompted the inhabitants of the "rue de l'Hôtel de Bourgogne" to request that the Confrérie de la Passion be compelled "to have plays start at exactly three o'clock." This happened on January 27, 1609, many months before the edict specifying two o'clock as the beginning hour. Some few years later, on January 7, 1625, the comedians at the Bourgogne were permitted by the authorities to swing wide the doors on "legitimate days" at any hour, except on Sundays and feast days: then the place could be opened only at three o'clock. The companies, for their part, had long objected to the Hôtel de Bourgogne's being locked up until three o'clock on Sundays and festival days. As far back as 1572, a decree of the Châtelet said the hall would be closed on Sundays until "after the saying of Vespers." The Confrérie maintained they could not get ready for a performance unless they were let in earlier, but they promised not to start the show before "three o'clock has rung." The Parlement of Paris acceded to their request, though the Confrérie was held responsible for any "scandal that took place at their plays." In a company's lease it might be written that the actors were to perform "at the licit and accustomed hours" — which clause was in the royal comedians' document renting the Hôtel de Bourgogne from December 28, 1627, until Easter 1628. No general agreement existed, however, as to what the "licit hours" were.[13]

In view of the official edicts permitting the public theatres to be open only in daylight, there is grave doubt that the first visits of the future Louis XIII to the Hôtel de Bourgogne were for regular performances. The much quoted diary of Jean Héroard, in its staccato reporting of every detail of young Louis's life — Tallemant said the good doctor Héroard wrote down every time the Dauphin belched or went to the bathroom — lists several visits to the Hôtel de Bourgogne before Louis had passed the age of ten; but they are all quite late in the day. The first time, according to Héroard, that young Louis went to the Bourgogne was on February 6, 1609: it was at five o'clock and he returned to the Louvre at six-thirty. Eight days later, on February 14, 1609 (it was a Saturday) the Dauphin went back to the Hôtel de Bourgogne at four o'clock in the afternoon and stayed until eight o'clock, by which time he was practically frozen. Other early visits to the Bourgogne by young Louis were on September 11, 1611, on which occasion he was back home for supper at six-thirty; and on September 25, 1611, when he arrived at the theatre at four-thirty. Both of these dates were on Sunday, and it is most unlikely that the old Bourgogne had been opened to the general public at any time on either day. The parterre could, therefore, have been set up well in advance with proper seating accommodations for the royal household and other ladies and gentlemen of the Court. Command performances for royalty, to be sure, did nothing to interfere with the drawing power of the comedians as public entertainers. The city authorities, on the other hand, would have objected strenuously to the people of Paris staying in the Hôtel de Bourgogne after dark as did Henry IV or Louis XIII. The normal starting time for a play was illustrated by a performance in Lyon, much delayed because the customers were very slow in arriving; the actors finally began the first act at five o'clock, although, they said, "we have been accustomed elsewhere to finish at this hour." [14]

The problem of publicizing the play and of getting a fair percentage of the spectators into the theatre on time, or even an hour late, was a serious one. Advertising, as the professional companies were getting under way, was rather elemental in nature and smacked of the procedures of a carnival or small circus. During the Middle Ages, the mystery plays had been announced by a parade through the streets of the actors in their costumes, with much shouting and proclaiming. Some of the same processes carried over to the professional troupes, though the actors were not willing, for many reasons, to walk the dusty streets in stage regalia. The Italians would send around a Harlequin and a couple of acrobats to inform the loiterers in public squares that a dramatic master-piece was about to be shown. The French companies used similar techniques in letting the public know about their proposed exhibitions. They, too, sent out a Harlequin and also a man with a drum to inform the populace of an immi-nent performance. In Scudéry's *La Comédie des Comédiens* of 1632, both a Tambour and Harlequin (see Figure 16) were used to drum up a crowd, though the procedure is described in the play as being that of "little troupes in little cities." Neither the Tambour nor the Harlequin, in any case, was effective in creating an audience — "the noise that they made through the streets being no more persuasive than the exag-gerations of the poster." The Harlequin reported that he has been through all the streets where people might be — "what the posters have shown their eyes I have made resound in their ears" — but that he could get no crowd. He concluded that everybody must have gone to Egypt.[15]

Posters (*affiches*) had limited use during the beginning years of the public theatre. The earliest one that has been preserved announced the performance of another of Scu-déry's plays, *Lygdamon et Lydias*, published in 1631. It was presented by "la Troupe choisie," whatever that organization was. Posters had been tried, certainly, many years before the one announcing the staging of Scudéry's work; but they were expensive and many companies doubted their effective-ness in an age when the power of display advertising for selling goods had not been fully tested. They were in exist-ence, nevertheless, as early as January 4, 1599: * in the agree-ment between Benoist Petit and Valleran le Conte of that date, the former wanted to be sure that Valleran would per-form in farces; otherwise, "the said Petit will not be able in

* They were in use even earlier to advertise school plays.

any way to name the said Valleran in the posters that will be put up." Benoist probably did not stick up enough of them to do much good; and, too, they had at this early date no more protection from the elements or a lackey's defacement than a handbill on a present-day telegraph pole. Therefore, more noisy and visible methods were preferred during the first part of the seventeenth century for the publicizing of operations at the Hôtel de Bourgogne. On the other hand, the Abbé de Marolles mentions at least twice in the 1656–7 edition of his *Mémoires* how he had seen in his earlier years in Paris "the posters of the comedians." By the time of Chappuzeau's *Le Théâtre français* in 1673 posters must have been quite common, since Chappuzeau, in listing the functions of the various members of a theatrical troupe, includes those of the *afficheur*, or "poster man." He should be certain that the *affiches* are put up punctually at "all the crossroads and necessary places." According to Chappuzeau, a system of color had been evolved: the posters were "red for the Hôtel de Bourgogne, green for the Hôtel de la rue Mazarine [the Théâtre Guénégaud], and yellow for the Opéra." By this date posters had become a standard accessory to the presentation of a show, and an author might expect to have his name exhibited along with the title of the play, which was not the case earlier in the century with an *auteur de troupe* like Alexandre Hardy.[16]

Once the prospective customer was convinced by fair means or foul that he should attend a performance at the Hôtel de Bourgogne on a given afternoon, his money was collected at the door by the *portier*. This porter had to be a rather capable and astute fellow in order to keep the soldiers and lackeys, or ribald young gentlemen, from running right over him without contributing an entrance fee. It was something of a sporting proposition to push by the *portier* without paying, even though the matter of saving a few sous was unimportant. In view of his many financial and physical problems, the porter normally carried a sword; but it was insufficient to maintain order or protect his own health when the approaches to the Bourgogne were under major assault. All through the century porters at the entrances to theatres suffered injuries and several were killed. The King's own guardsmen traditionally went into the theatre free; it was a difficult maneuver to see that this privilege was not assumed by all the military. In the early years of the century the actors themselves doubled as *portiers*. On January 26, 1600, Gros Guillaume along with two other comedians agreed that "one week from Sunday" they would collect the money "at the doors of the said Hôtel de Bourgogne." Valleran le Conte and other leaders of the first struggling troupes acted as porters from time to time when no one else was available.[17]

The *portier* in Scudéry's *Comédie des Comédiens* is an important personage in the play and he gives some ideas as to the nature of the job. The very first scene of the piece shows him philosophizing on his duties: ". . . although the role I play at this door is not the most honorable it is nevertheless the most useful; and if I give a share (of the money) to my companions, my memory is not so poor that I forget to put aside a goodly portion for myself." The famous engraving accompanying Scudéry's piece apparently depicts the end of this speech of the porter's, and the arrival of the Tambour and Harlequin after their fruitless search for customers; it is to be noted that the porter's sword is an enormous weapon and the Harlequin's sword is also, for him, oversized. The exaggerated dimensions of the side arms were expected to help keep down trouble at the entrance doors of the theatre. At any rate, the general conclusion in this drama on the lives of comedians is that the terms "porter" and "thief" are almost synonymous. The suggestion is made, then, that the troupe might make better progress if the successor to the present porter decides to show that a "portier de comédie" can be an honest man. All of which ignores the indignities and physical danger a porter had to endure out in front of the Hôtel de Bourgogne. In Gabriel Guéret's delightful bit of banter between authors of all ages, *Le Parnasse réformé*, the rather feeble French dramatist, La Serre, boasts to Seneca and Tacitus that he had one play so tumultuously successful that four *portiers* were killed, and that he would yield to Corneille only when the author of the *Cid* had killed five. A porter's job was not one for a weakling.[18]

The admission prices into the Hôtel de Bourgogne, whether or not they could be collected, increased as the century grew older. Both Bruscambille and Gautier Garguille speak of the customers who "bring a *teston* to the Hôtel de Bourgogne"; this coin, obsolescent by the time of Louis XIII, must have been a symbol of an entrance fee in the early seventeenth century and not a specific piece of money. The *teston*, which before 1600 had had a value of ten sous, would have easily bought one admission to the loges. In normal practice, entree to the loges cost twice as much as standing room in the parterre. On gala or special occasions, the prices could be doubled all around — a neat system that has lasted down to the present-day *soirées de gala* in French theatres. In the sixteenth century, a client could get into the parterre for two sous — or, according to Lemazurier's previously quoted anonymous informant, for nothing at all. Free performances, it is true, were offered on certain dates, even as nowadays the Opéra presents a no-charge spectacle on July 14. For example, in a lease of the Bourgogne to the royal comedians on August 6, 1607, it was stipulated that a free show would be given to the parterre on Mardi gras, "in the accustomed manner." The ordonnance of 1609, which regulated the opening and closing hours of the Bourgogne, also fixed the price of admission to the parterre at five sous, and at ten sous for the loges; by the 1630's the parterre cost ten sous to get into, and the loges twenty; prices continued to go up later in the century, with progressive monetary devaluation, until an entree into the parterre for a gala performance with double tariff could cost thirty sous or more. The authorities assumed that at any given level of prices the professional theatre was making some money, since the Parlement of Paris on January 18, 1610, decreed that the "surplus of pennies" from the Hôtel de Bourgogne, along with that of a few other institutions, should be used for the nourishment of the poor. The "right of the poor" levy on theatrical performances began to be made in the sixteenth century because the public, supposedly in its distraction by mystery plays on Sundays, failed to give its usual alms to the needy.[19]

The professional troupes welcomed all the paying customers they could get into the Hôtel de Bourgogne, since the Confrérie de la Passion did not like to wait for its rental money. The Brotherhood usually demanded around two hundred livres a month for its hall, as is indicated in a joint lease of the Bourgogne by Valleran le Conte and an Italian company on March 9, 1612; half of the money was to be paid at the signing of the lease and the other half a week later, whether the comedians performed or not. The Confrérie, as has been seen, kept a good deal of free space inside the theatre for its own use. It retained, in addition, some little shops on the outside "underneath the stage" to be rented separately. These must have set the mold for later shops and stalls attached to theatres.* The little stores at the Bourgogne encouraged the customers to browse around a bit before and after the show, and spend a few extra sous. At any rate, the monthly or annual rental of the Hôtel de Bourgogne remained rather stable throughout the first decades of the seventeenth century. The annual figure varied from two thousand to twenty-four hundred livres. In 1629, it was twenty-four hundred livres a year but by 1639 it was two thousand, which would imply a recognition of the dilapidated condition of the

---

* Like those which have for so many years rimmed the exterior arcades of the Odéon.

hall as well as a realization that other troupes were competing for the customer with some coins in his pocket. With an almost static rate of rental from 1600 to 1640, and a doubling or more of the tariff for the parterre and loges, the royal comedians ought to have been making quantities of money. On the other hand, their old box of a theatre must have been at times very sparsely filled, since the aggressive Théâtre du Marais during many of these years was making a strong bid for interested and solvent spectators.[20]

A troupe of professionals, as they were striving to make a groove for themselves in Paris during the first years of the seventeenth century, opened their doors to customers two or three times a week. One is inclined to wonder how the good bourgeois of Paris could get away even this often to go to a place of amusement at one or two o'clock in the afternoon. Idleness, however, has always been a problem in areas of urban concentration; in the Paris of the sixteenth and seventeenth centuries, it affected, in particular, soldiers, pages, lackeys, students, prostitutes, gamblers, and the upper classes — out of which groups for the most part the audiences for the first professional plays came. Without insisting too strongly on the similarity, it might be claimed that the same type of clientele, with possibly a few additional housewives, would today be in a Broadway or Paris movie house on a Tuesday afternoon, and at Belmont Park or Longchamp making a hopeful wager on a prancing thoroughbred. The nine to five storekeeper, brick mason, or librarian in any age would most probably be unable to get off from work on many Tuesday afternoons. Nevertheless, one of the arguments advanced for the theatre in the seventeenth century was the fact that it filled in most splendidly the idle moments of the people: at a dramatic spectacle "their unoccupied hours flow by without any feeling of regret." However that might be, the halls of the comedians were most likely open only twice a week during the first years of the seventeenth century. A slight argument on the other side is the paper signed by the royal comedians on December 2, 1611, wherein it was agreed that they would perform "each week at least three times." This was undoubtedly a gesture of optimism; even in the second half of the century a given company would produce only three times a week — Molière and the Italians, for example, alternated days. The best three days for audience appeal, according to Chappuzeau, were Fridays, Sundays, and Tuesdays. In 1692, Abraham du Pradel, the man who knew all the best addresses in Paris, said the "French Comedians who have their Hôtel on the rue des Fossés Saint-Germain-des-Prés (now the rue de l'Ancienne Comédie) are performing every day, with tragedies one day and comedies the next." But, it must be remembered, this was after three companies had been combined by royal order in 1680 to form the Comédie Française.[21]

Wherever the Frenchman of any age has taken his leisure, he has always liked it better with a little food and drink. The early public theatres in Paris were cognizant of this fact and sought to take proper measures to assuage the ravages of hunger and thirst before an audience was beaten down. The widow Dellin, in the 1621 contract previously mentioned, sold in the parterre of the Hôtel de Bourgogne her macaroons, bread, wine, and "other things." The list must have been fairly inclusive, but constant effort toward addition to it continued to be made, and the *distributrice*, or salesgirl with her buffet, came to be a standard item of theatrical equipment. Chappuzeau sang her praises later in the century — in fact, he said that there were two *distributrices*, "one near the loges, and the other in the parterre." On the buffets was found in summer "all sorts of refreshing drinkables, lemonades, lemon sherbet, strawberry, currant, and cherry waters, dried confitures, lemons, Chinese oranges; and in winter drinks which warm the stomach, such as rose liqueurs, wines from Spain, etc." There was a time when a spectator could get "only beer and weak infusions," but all that has been improved. The *distributrice* was necessary to a theatre because, however much a person might love the halls of drama, he could not "stay therein three hours without soothing his palate with some pleasant liquid." [22] Chappuzeau, noticeably, has placed his emphasis upon liquid rather than solid nourishment.*

The heterogeneous mixture of society that made up the audience for the first public theatrical companies in France was important, crtically as well as financially, to the development of French drama. If the spectators' tastes had not changed and improved, there would have been no platform for the more finished products of Corneille, Molière, and Racine. The paradox in the evolution toward that most polished of all French dramatic forms, the tragedies of Racine, was the parterre: so motley and rowdy that an iron grill had to be erected between it and the stage, and yet not unlacking in critical judgment of what a play should be. Its combined efforts could certainly make or break any dramatic creation that was served up to it. At times an actor would have to come out of character to beg it to make a little less noise, while Bellerose in Gougenot's *Comédie des Comédiens* makes a special point of praising the "silence" and well-behaved quality of the audience. Beauchamps discussed the parterre at length and had considerable respect for its opinions; he felt that an author could not be "too careful about going against its ideas." On the other hand, Desmarets de Saint-Sorlin makes it clear in his play, *Les Visionnaires*, that he is not interested in the decisions of the rabble — in which

---

* The theatres of Paris from the seventeenth century down to the present time have continued to provide arrangements for quenching the thirst of their customers. In this they preceded the Dutch, who before 1638 did not even allow beer in the National Theatre of Amsterdam. Incidentally, to Chappuzeau's list has been added in recent years, for better or for worse, another libation for patrons of the theatre — Coca-Cola.

IODELET ESCHAPE DES FLAMES.

Ie me Saue du feu plus guère qu'un rat d'eglise.
Si vous ne m'assistez ie me vois en chemise
Tous mes biens sont brusles auec nostre tripot.
Rendes moy par vos dons mon humeur ordinaire
L'oublieux perd et chante et moy tout au contraire
Si ie ne gaigne au jeu ie ne puis dire mot.

23. Jodelet escapes from the burning **Théâtre du Marais**

24. Mahelot's set for Hardy's Folie de Clidamant

25. Mahelot's set for Du Ryer's Lisandre et Caliste

category the greater portion of the parterre would fit; Desmarets says he is primarily concerned with offering a banquet to the nobles and any crumbs that fall off the table will be good enough for the valets. And Guéret in his *Le Parnasse réformé* has Tristan l'Hermite, the well-known author of *Mariamne*, speak scathingly of the tastes of patrons of the Hôtel de Bourgogne like "the merchants of the rue Saint-Denis." But Saint Sorlin and Guéret both came from a slightly later and more refined era, when everything theatrical was on a somewhat higher plane. During the first part of the century, when the audience at the Hôtel de Bourgogne was more of a milling mass of uncatalogued humanity, it was a very necessary thing for an author and the actors to have the parterre on their side.[23]

COURT AND PRIVATE ENTERTAINMENTS

AS THE PUBLIC THEATRE MADE PROGRESS IN FRANCE, with its rather easy availability to all classes, the problem of leisure and boredom in the land was somewhat alleviated. But before the professional comedians had created a niche for themselves in the social framework, at the royal court and in the châteaux of the great nobles, efforts were made to relieve the tedium of existence by putting on plays and other types of entertainment. In earlier times a *jongleur* might present his repertory to a nobleman and his friends in a Normandy château, or a troubadour might chant his complicated rimes to a courtly audience in sunny Provence. By the sixteenth century provincial cities like Rouen or Lyon looked forward to the dramatic pageantry that accompanied the entrance of royalty into the urban area — the floats, the triumphal arches, and the episodes acted out from classical mythology. These scenes, in general, were open to the populace as a whole, even as had been the medieval farces or mystery plays enacted in a public square. Inside the great palaces and châteaux of the Valois monarchs, along with jousting matches and other types of simulated warfare, plays and ballets were staged during the sixteenth century by young ladies and gentlemen in the service of royalty. Even after Catherine de Médici turned her back on the production of tragedies at Court, she still favored enormously complicated and expensive ballets. Many of these spectacles, as well as concerts of music and dancing, were aimed at diverting the young nobles and keeping them from fighting senseless duels, a purpose that had only limited success. Plays and ballets in the seventeenth century continued to be performed in the royal palaces and in the houses of the wealthy chatelains. Neither these representations nor the attractions of the public theatre nor official edicts threatening punishment kept a fiery young gentleman from issuing a challenge over some triviality and fighting a duel unto death.

Gambling, under the leadership of Henry IV and his favorites, came to be in the seventeenth century very much of an upper-bracket diversion. All classes, it is true, were fond of risking a few sous on the roll of the dice at the fair, but the King and his courtiers really set the fashion. On the general question of gambling in the early 1600's, a critic like Emile Magne thought it was an all-inclusive malady: "The whole of society from princes to priests, from priests to bourgeois, was smitten by this shattering vice. There were in the different milieux [of Paris] professional handlers of dice. A man might put up everything he had, including his shirt — which is what happened to [the writer] Dassoucy." It will be remembered that Henry IV wagered regularly on his skill at smashing a tennis ball, and that the tripots, like the Foire Saint Germain, were open to the public for wine-sipping and games of chance. But the most impressive homage to the goddess of fortune was paid by the King's gentlemen, in the semiprivacy of the royal court, and with the approval and participation of His Majesty. These companions of the King, along with the King himself, gambled in a big way; and Henry IV had no scruples about subjecting his courtiers to large losses. In March of 1597, according to a contemporary report, "the King won last night from monsieur Lesdiguières five thousand crowns, playing at three dice, and from monsieur Sanssi a string of pearls estimated at being worth eight thousand crowns." These sums could scarcely be called pin money.[1]

A worthy competitor of Henry IV either in the bedroom or at the gaming table was the lusty friend of the King, the Maréchal de Bassompierre. In the journal of his own life, Bassompierre kept a rather good record of both his amorous and financial accomplishments. In 1608, says Bassompierre, "we spent several days at Fontainebleau, indulging in the most furious gambling that anyone ever heard tell of . . . I won that year more than five hundred thousand francs, although I was distracted by a thousand follies of youth and of love." When the King was ill with the gout early in 1609, Bassompierre and other gentlemen at the court sat up and read to him, of all things, Honoré d'Urfé's insipid pastoral novel, the *Astrée*, "which was then in vogue." Such emasculated amusement evidently was not adequate for Henry IV even when he was indisposed, since in February 1609, "the King played at three dice according to his custom, having had a table put in the space next to his bed." By March 1609, Henry IV must have recovered from his attack of gout, because at that time "debauchery and gambling" were going on at Court "as customarily." During this period Bassompierre did some wagering with the King's money and lost, which irked Henry IV and caused him to doubt Bassompierre's capabilities in either a game of chance or one of love. The Maréchal, who had been infatuated with a certain lady at Court and contemplated marriage with her, was told by the King that through his [the King's] own personal efforts Bassompierre after the ceremony would become "the greatest cuckold in France." Bassompierre modestly suggested that he thought he would be able to defend his bedchamber for a time, even against royal invasions. And such was a bit of conversation in the King's palace while another roll of the dice was awaited. Bassompierre's luck continued with him as late as New Year's Day of 1617: during the previous twelve months he estimated that he had won "in the game of tricktrack one hundred thousand crowns," from a variety of persons. His reputation as a "man of the world," with its many implications, was mentioned on into the second half of the seventeenth century. Among other personalities of the period the poet of the salons, Vincent Voiture, was credited by Tallemant des Réaux with being successful both in love-making and gambling — but Voiture preferred the halls of chance. Louis XIII, for his part, was not the vigorous patron of gambling that his father was, and it was a good thing. Though royally sponsored ballets and dramatic performances existed in the reign of Henry IV, they got a better chance in the slightly more refined era that followed.[2]

The court ballet, in high esteem in the late 1500's with the last of the Valois kings, continued to find favor throughout the seventeenth century with the Bourbons. It was the one form of representational entertainment that had not lost "magnificence" when compared with the stylized dances of the ancients — so ran one opinion of the period — although the tragedy and comedy of the present lacked the perfection of the equivalent dramatic genres among the Greeks and the Romans. Many of the court ballets were extremely lavish and the salle du Petit-Bourbon, adjacent to the royal quarters of the Louvre, was large enough to contain any of them. Sauval gave a description of the Petit-Bourbon hall: "It is eighteen normal paces wide by thirty-five toises long and the roof is lifted so high that the summit seems to be as elevated as those of the churches of Saint Germain and of Saint Eustache; which was the reason that under Louis XIII a place so vast and so near the Louvre was chosen by him for the staging of balls, ballets, and other magnificences in connection with his marriage." The salle du Petit-Bourbon was, then, around forty-five feet wide by two hundred twenty-one feet long; * it had on each long side two superimposed galleries divided into loges, and it made a splendid setting for balls,

---

* These measurements are based on the assumption that a *pas commun* was thirty inches and a *toise* six feet four inches.

pageants, ballets, or any official function. It was, however, much too long and too high for effective use as a theatre, although Molière and his troupe occupied it upon their return to Paris in 1658 until the building was torn down for the enlargement of the Louvre. In any event, at the Petit-Bourbon, at the Louvre, in the hall of ballets and comedies at the Arsenal, at the great château of Saint Germain en Laye on a hill outside Paris or in any other château that the King and his court might be visiting, royal and genteel audiences found relaxation in ballets, masquerades, and similar diversions.[3]

Although Henry IV was not a primary patron of so prettified a form of entertainment as a ballet, he was willing to look at them if no more exciting amusement were at hand. In a collection of *mascarades* for the carnival season of 1607, there was an opening statement to the effect that courtiers in their finest clothes would seek to divert His Majesty in a moment of peace just as they would give him "valorous support in time of war." One of the divertissements was called *La Foire Saint Germain*, in undoubted recognition of Henry IV's fondness for the Saint Germain fair. It was introduced by a small boy as the "oracle of Saint Germain." In 1608, there were numerous ballets at Fontainebleau and in Paris, all well seasoned with "blondes." One of the last ballets done for Henry IV occurred early in 1610: it would have been a dull affair if only the "petits enfants" had participated in it, but it was considerably pepped up by the "gallants of the Court."[4]

Other ballets in and around the royal palaces before the sad day of Henry IV's assassination in May 1614, were unquestionably more to the King's liking. They had more zest or pleasant aftermaths. On January 15, 1602, "monsieur le comte d'Auvergne, monsieur de Nevers, the comte de Sommerive, the comte de Cramail,* and several other princes and

---

* The comte de Cramail was, along with the duc de Montmorency, a

seigneurs created a ballet of *Seven Fools and Seven Wise Men.*" It was presented at the Louvre and a number of other places, including a performance before the "Lieutenant civil Miron" and an audience of "gallant ladies and demoiselles." On this occasion, "messieurs de Victri, Créqui, and other gentlemen" broke into the hall with swords in hand, after having "set fire to the door." The prince de Condé who was there was much upset by the intrusion, so Henry IV compelled the "gentlemen" to tender their apologies. A little later on January 3, 1604, a ballet was in progress at the house of the first president of the *Cour des Aides* in Paris. Some of the gentlemen there got into a quarrel, with "swords drawn," and several persons were wounded. Also, an "honorable demoiselle" in the assembly was so upset that she gave birth to a baby that was four and one half months premature. It is almost a paradox that a refined art form like the ballet could be the setting for such violence and upheaval. One of the reasons for the precipitating of noise and disturbance at a ballet might be seen in the one staged by the Queen on January 31, 1609. This was a large affair which had been a long time in planning and preparing. It was given at the Arsenal and was preceded by a bounteous collation "at the home of la Reine Marguerite." * The whole occasion was ornate and complicated, and lasted until six o'clock in the morning. The star of the festivities was a demoiselle called "la petite Paulette," who caused considerable excitement: "La petite Paulette carried off the honors of the ballet, as much by her graceful charm as by her harmonious and delicate voice, combined with the fact that her white, smooth, and delicate skin covered with a single thin and loose garment, through which appeared the markings of a secret part even less restricted, aroused the feelings and appetites of several

---

patron of Jean de Mairet, whose *Sophonisbe* was the first regular tragedy on the public stage.
* The first wife of Henry IV.

persons." This 1609 ballet was remembered later by Tallemant des Réaux, who said "madame Paulet" was very good
in it. Afterward she spent some agreeable nights with Henry
IV, but never with the Dauphin who was a "poor bedroom
campaigner." [5]

That the ballets and similar divertissements of the first
decades of the seventeenth century were not always on the
highest and most ethereal artistic level was intimated by the
Abbé de Marolles in the ninth of his *Discours*. In it he seeks
to distinguish between the lofty art of the ballet and the
"crude masquerades that fill the streets of Paris" at carnival
time. He would also rule out of the category of ballets those
"shameless dances" which were held in some of the private
houses of the capital city. One of the more earthy ballets was
the *Ballet des Quolibets*, the verses of which were attributed
to the satiric sieur de Sigogne, and which was presented and
"danced" by the King's brother, Gaston d'Orléans, at the
Louvre, the Maison de Ville, and the Arsenal in 1627. In it
one Maître Mouche boasted that he had more tricks to teach
the ladies than could have been learned from the Italian master, Aretino; also, Mouche felt that he was more clever than
Francis I's entertainer, Maître Gonnin, or the descendant of
Gonnin, who was supposed to be hanged but by his magic
art tricked the hangman into suspending the "mule of the
first president" in his stead. The *Ballet des Quolibets* was full
of smut; any diversion staged under the auspices of Gaston
d'Orléans could scarcely be expected to have its emphasis
on purity.[6]

Louis XIII was much more interested in ballets than was
his father, and in the more legitimate form of the art rather
than in the demoiselles who performed in filmy and loose
costumes. The second of the Bourbons lacked the grace of
movement and muscular coordination that his father pos-
sessed; nevertheless, he was very fond of dancing and was
still taking ballet lessons at the age of twenty-two. The ballet

in all its intricacies was, then, a favorite indoor diversion of Louis XIII as it was to be later with Louis XIV. Of Louis XIII it was said during the century that he "danced fairly well in ballets but he never played in them anything but ridiculous personages." Though this estimate was a trifle harsh, it is true that young Louis was dancing a *commedia dell 'arte* Pantalone — a leering and suspicious old man — in the quarters of the Queen Mother, Marie de Médicis, before the Dauphin had reached the age of ten. A few months later in the same year, on August 2, 1611, a very spectacular version of Garnier's *Bradamante* was presented in a specifically constructed theatre at Saint Germain en Laye; it included such a large number of ladies and gentlemen of the Court that the story had most probably been turned into a ballet. Mademoiselle de Vendôme played the part of Bradamante, the vigorous young lady who would not marry any man until he had conquered her in the lists. Young Louis was there and may have essayed the role of Charlemagne, which he had tried a little more than two years earlier at Fontainebleau without great success. The casting would seem to have been a trifle faulty on these occasions, when a nine-year-old was asked to play Pantalone and a seven-year-old the great emperor Charles. But it must be remembered that royal childrens' performing privately in grown-up roles was a part of the badinage of the court.[7]

An indication of the popularity of ballet during the time of Louis XIII might be noted in a story of the pillaging of the conniving Maréchal d'Ancre's house, in the faubourg Saint Germain. The Maréchal d'Ancre, it will be remembered, was hostile and disdainful of his King; Louis XIII destroyed him in 1617, in an early gesture of royal prerogative. At the ransacking of the Maréchal's quarters, one eyewitness said: "I saw thrown out, from an upper window that looked down on the street, more than eight hundred masks for ballet or comedy." If such a collection was to be found in a private dwelling, it would be hard to estimate what stores of dancing costumes and dramatic accessories were available in royal warehouses — or, a bit later, in Cardinal de Richelieu's extensive domain. There are still extant many drawings, water colors, and engravings that show how elaborate many of Louis XIII's ballets were. Three successive ballets, for example, in 1628, 1629, and 1630 were devoted to national subjects and called the *History of France*. In the second of these was one unit described as "the ballet of the four parts of the world, danced by King Louis XIII at Saint Germain en Laye on January 17, 1629, and the days following." In one of the scenes of the spectacle was an "actor in a short costume of a woman, wearing a headdress of feathers," an obvious effort at depicting an American Indian. The performer was to give a "recital about America," to the accompaniment of "music from America." It is to be wondered what concept of melodies from the New World was current in 1629 at the royal court of France. At any rate, music was a prominent feature in the ballets and could be symbolized visually. For the *Fairies of the Forests of Saint Germain* — this title was inspired by the great wooded area surrounding the château of Saint Germain en Laye — there was a large number of entrees and one of them had in it a tall woman with a "machine representing the sum total of all music." This complex affair was danced at the Louvre on February 11, 1625, while "the King was still young." It was under the general direction of the duc de Nemours and many prominent persons were in attendance. The King's youthful vigor, according to contemporary report, continued on as late as December of 1633, since he was hunting at this time in the broad expanse of terrain at Saint Germain en Laye, in spite of the bad weather. And on December 30, 1633, from Saint Germain, the news was: "The King is feeling so well that they do not talk about anything else here except the arrangements for a royal ballet, in which all the Court is participating." As for the Maréchal de Bassom-

pierre, who went on to enjoy the diversions around Louis
XIII after the death of Henry IV, he described one carnival
season as a period "accompanied by splendid comedies and
magnificent ballets." At such a moment, "the Court was very
beautiful, and so were the ladies." A slightly more critical
attitude was that held by the Abbé de Marolles apropos of a
ballet staged by the King during the carnival of 1626: "Dancing is nothing but pure fiction for entertainment; the same is
not true for comedy, which comes nearer to being like nature." Comedy, in Marolles's opinion, could therefore have
in it at times real animals, while ballet must use always men
and women thinly disguised as birds and beasts. Such a
criticism found little acceptance among the courtly spectators
that looked on at a ballet; they preferred the stylized movements of handsomely costumed gentlemen and ladies.[8]

Not all the ballets were performed at the Louvre or in a
royal château like Saint Germain en Laye; many would be
represented in the houses of the great noblemen of the realm,
with members of the King's household among the onlookers.
The Arsenal was frequented by Henry IV and his entourage
both for the purpose of consulting with the finance minister,
Sully,* and to see ornate ballets. There was one hall, in fact,
in the intricate structure of the Arsenal given over regularly
during the early 1600's to the presentation of ballets and
comedies. One of the numerous historians of the city of Paris
still remembered in 1685 this hall, which he said was "formerly
the *salle des comédies* in the time of Henry IV." Of the
private establishments in favor during the period for the staging of ballets, one was the town house of the duchesse de
Retz, who was described by the gossiping Tallemant des
Réaux as being a creature of warm blood; the old archbishop
Bertrand de Chaux liked to sit next to her at sophisticated
gatherings and gently rub her thighs. An excerpt from the
calendar of 1634 will show how the royal family moved

* The rigorous Sully also liked ballet.

around the city of Paris sharing the diversions of the nobility: "On the same day [January 23, 1634] the Queen was present at a ball and a comedy at the hôtel d'Angoulême; and on January 26 she went to see a ballet at the hôtel de Chevreuse." The ballet, to some degree, helped keep the upper classes from getting bored.[9]

Even more than ballets, plays of various sorts were produced in palaces, châteaux, and in the nobles' *hôtels* in Paris during the first decades of the seventeenth century. All over Europe, indeed, in the households and at the courts of the great families there existed at the time a sort of *théâtre de société* — which was, like the Jesuit instruction, a valuable training in memory for the youngsters and a "delightful remedy for idleness and boredom." One little Dutch princess, to show her knowledge of French and to impress her older sisters, learned all of Corneille's tragedy, *Médee*, by heart when only eleven. She was more adept than was the little Dauphin Louis in 1608 when he was playing the role of Charlemagne, in Garnier's *Bradamante*, before Their Majesties at Fontainebleau: he had seven verses to say and could think of none of them, whereupon he remarked tearfully, "I have forgotten all my part." The future Louis XIII from the age of three had watched at Fontainebleau and the Louvre English, French, and Italian comedians of professional stature; it is understandable, then, that he might have been histrionically precocious and, after having seen a performance in the "great new hall" at Fontainebleau in 1604, put on a masque and a wrapping of white cloth to "imitate the comedians." When he was a little older and had returned from the Tuileries to the Louvre on December 6, 1609, "he had a comedy performed by his little gentlemen." Some time later, on February 3, 1610, Louis "studied, did some writing, practiced with weapons, and danced"; then "he amused himself by playing some comedies." On February 26, 1613, he had presented in his room by his "little friends" a tragedy based on Ariosto, with the Queen in the audience; and on May 28, 1613, there was another play "by his *enfants d'honneur*" staged in the Queen's quarters at the Louvre. Young Louis was probably little more of a participant in acting or in mounting plays than many other royal or noble youngsters; he simply had a better chronicler of his activities in the good doctor Héroard. There was, for example, in 1608 a great assemblage of guests at the home of the marquis de Coeuvres, "where a comedy was played with no other performers but the women in the family of the said marquis." [10]

The professional actors were invited on occasions to the palaces and the châteaux for the private entertainment of chosen audiences. This was good advertising for the rising professionals, and might lead to the sponsoring of a troupe by some person in high position — like the support given by the prince d'Orange to French actors in Holland and that of the prince de Conti, some years later, to Molière's first theatrical venture. And, too, a financially solid nobleman might prefer to pay for entertainment of professional caliber in his own home rather than risk the mud outside and the hurlyburly inside the Hôtel de Bourgogne. In 1626, Gaston d'Orléans had Gros Guillaume and other "companions" for thirteen days' performance at the fine and spacious château of Chantilly, some twenty-five miles north of Paris. These amusements for Gaston d'Orléans were not done free of charge, since his accounts of 1627 carried the item of one hundred fifty livres owed Gros Guillaume for "performances." Gautier Garguille entertained the King and his retinue at the Louvre, where the lanky *farceur* would lean and "scratch his backbone against the pillars." The great farce-player remembered these visits to royalty when he said in the dedication of his published songs that he would be glad to see any of his readers "at the Louvre or in our usual theatre." There were certainly plays in the Louvre for both the young and the old.

On January 13, 1613, the Queen had a favored courtier, monsieur d'Eperson, sit down by her (she had a chair brought in for him, in fact) and "invited him to the comedy," which was also attended by the princesse de Conti escorted by the Maréchal de Bassompierre. A trifle later in January the Queen had a small supper party in her own private rooms at the Louvre, and then everybody went "to the comedy" — where, said Bassompierre with his usual modesty, "a Greek beauty appeared because of me." The halls of the Louvre must have been cold and damp during the month of January, however sprightly the comedy might have been. It could have been given by either French or Italian professionals; in 1614, it will be remembered, Louis XIII was paying the celebrated Tristano Martinelli six hundred livres a month to divert the Court. Another mixture of food and dramatic entertainment was made some years later in 1634 in the hôtel de Silleri for the nuptials of the marquis de Coislin and "the elder daughter of the Garde des Sceaux": at this celebration "the comedy was given before supper and the ballet came afterward." [11]

One of the biggest parties of the first decades of the century was the celebration at the Arsenal for the triple wedding of the duc de la Valette, the sieur de Puylaurens, and the comte de Guiche. The splendid affair took place on November 28, 1634, and was attended by the Queen * with a large retinue. Booming salutes of artillery pieces welcomed the arrival of the Queen at the Arsenal; then all the ladies attending Her Majesty were escorted by handsomely dressed gentlemen into the "grand ballroom where the comedy was to be presented." This hall was eighteen toises long by eight toises wide, with a double gallery, and seats arranged in an amphitheatre — and "it was completely filled with princes, princesses, and other ladies and gentlemen of the Court." When the Queen arrived in the hall, fifteen hundred candles

* The Queen was now Anne of Austria.

(*lumières*) were gleaming. Also, there was a big illuminated wheel which turned to welcome the Queen. The full description of what followed, as it was told by Théophraste Renaudot, is worth repeating: "The Queen was no sooner seated on the elevated dais which was prepared for her at ten paces from the stage (the artificial light of which lit and made clearly visible the whole scene, without the source of the light being seen), when Montdory's troupe of comedians, which had been chosen on this occasion to give pleasure to Her Majesty, began the show with three entrees, that they preferred to call nothing but buffooneries, although they well deserved the name of ballets." It is of interest to note that Montdory's troupe was invited to entertain such a high-level audience — and, too, that members of the company could dance in skits that might be described as ballets. The full program presented by the troupe was a long one: the three entrees, a comedy in prose, a comedy in verse, and a farce, all with incidental music to fill up any dull gaps.[12]

The three entrees were far from being subtle: "The first one was of four well dressed servants who came to sweep out the place, while dancing gracefully, and prepare it for the first comedy which was in prose. The second entree, between the first and second acts of this comedy, was made up of six ridiculous characters, two of whom represented a householder and his pregnant wife who was not prevented by her belly from dancing to perfection, although she was so far along in her term that she gave birth to a child behind the stage. The third entree, between the end of the comedy in prose and the one in verse, had in it ten persons; among them was a nurse carrying the newly born child and she gave it a bottle while dancing; then all of a sudden the child came out of its swaddling clothes apparently naked, so delicate and well applied was the flesh-covering with which it was dressed. The infant did marvels of all sorts of dancing, to the astonishment of everybody." The Queen, who was no more than twenty-five feet away, should have missed none of the details of this remarkable performance.[12]

In the prose comedy, Montdory took up the question of plays and players, and the position of those in the acting profession. The great actor evidently put in a few licks of propaganda to a group of listeners that could have had some influence in improving the status of the comedian. The comedy in prose, then, looked at what a drama should be, rejected prologues, and examined "the conditions of good actors." The comedy in verse was "the *Mélite* of Scudéry * where twenty violins played in the intermèdes." Between the verse comedy and the farce was a "miraculous concert" of sixteen lutes. As for the farce itself, which was excellent: "It began with a genteel sarabande, in the Spanish fashion, and ended with a second volley of muskets, and a new salvo of mortars and cannons which gave the warning — hunger did not do it — that it was time to go to supper." And such were some of the festivities when three of France's great noblemen decided to get married, even though the chronicler did not bother to give the names of the brides.[12]

One of the most turbulent and exciting private theatricals took place some time later at the Hôtel de Bourgogne when a widower and "overseer of finances" by the name of Foulé reserved the old theatre one evening to "give the comedy . . . to a widow whom he was courting," and also to entertain one mademoiselle Garnier. The place was so crowded with a large number of uninvited gate-crashers that the two guests of honor could find no seats. Many of the other legitimate customers were unable to locate a place to sit, even though for special performances "chairs were put in the parterre." Much irritated, mademoiselle Garnier, who was a "kind of colossus," grabbed a candle from underneath a loge

---

* Renaudot corrected himself later and said "the comedy in prose was Scudéry's [probably *La Comédie des Comédiens*] and the *Mélite* in verse was Corneille's." The printer was blamed for the error.

and angrily strode out of the hall, with the remark that she and her friends felt out of place in the midst of so many "handsomely adorned women." The intimation was that the latter had come to the party without being asked. Soon after the departure of mademoiselle Garnier and her entourage, the play began; but the theatre was almost immediately filled with smoke. A fire had been started at the entrance door of the Bourgogne by the lackeys of mademoiselle Garnier, most likely at her urging, and "bunches of wet straw" had been piled on the blaze. The actors managed to get through the first act, but the smoke started pouring in again during the second, throwing the audience into something of a panic — and "everybody pushed and crowded to get through the little door which is at the side of the stage." Tallemant des Réaux, who was there with some ladies, said it could have been a tragic affair: ". . . if the fire had started through such an old building, it would have spread very fast, and in the uproar people would have been smothered." At the risk of burning the Bourgogne to the ground, mademoiselle Garnier enjoyed a bit of revenge for having been kept standing when she was due a seat of honor. The whole episode gives a little added information on the structure of the old Hôtel de Bourgogne, and shows, also, that theatres as well as theatrical troupes could be rented for private celebrations.[13]

In the more spacious homes of well-established Parisians, aspiring amateurs performed in plays and sought to imitate the techniques of the better known professionals. Marolles said he went two or three times a week during the winter, with a chosen audience, to see comedies staged in the residences of "several ladies of high position." At the house of one monsieur Guiet in the Saint André quarter, it will be recalled, some young gentlemen did rather well in copying Gros Guillaume and Gautier Garguille. It was at this party, incidentally, that both a pastoral and a farce were presented, and the whole program lasted until after four o'clock in the morning. An Italian who was present enjoyed the affair so much that he forgot that he had had no supper. One of the more unusual nonpublic entertainments was that presented at the home of a *maître de requêtes* in homage to a lady of whom he was enamored. He "gave her the comedy" — undoubtedly by hired entertainers — although his wife was at the time ill with a confinement. The incident, quite understandably, "made the delicately conditioned lady almost go mad." Fortunately, not all the dramatics done privately, whether by professionals or amateurs, were scheduled so badly.[14]

Outside Paris comedians of all types entertained in whatever château might be in momentary prominence because of the presence in it of a genteel audience. The château of Nogent-le-Roi near Chartres might have a visit from the Italians if the Court were there; or Blois could be the scene of operations if Marie de Médicis were in residence and wanted a little relaxation. A Frenchman of high station might pass through the Italian city of Florence and see some "comedies and the festivities of a wedding" along with the spectacular horse race known as the *palio*. The governor of Lyon might make certain that an important visitor was regaled with "the comedy," and the Jesuits in Avignon or Rouen might perform a tragedy for noble and royal spectators. On a slightly lower social level, a "rich bourgeois" of Le Mans could invite the wandering band of comedians in Scarron's *Roman comique* to put on a play "after dinner" at his house, and set aside two rooms for their specific use. An earlier troupe in Scarron's story was received at the château of one baron de Sigognac in Périgord, where they were well treated and where they acted for "a great number of the nobility of Périgord." These comedians stayed on the baron's estates for a month, and he ended up by wanting to marry one of the actresses.[15]

One of the most spectacular of the private theatricals was

the staging of Nicolas de Montreux's pastoral, *Arimène*, at the château in Nantes of Philippe Emmanuel de Lorraine, duc de Mercueur. It was put on in 1596 by members of the noble families of Brittany living in the environs of the duke's castle. Whatever might be the merits (and they are doubtful) of *Arimène* as drama, it was given an incredibly lavish presentation: there was a large stage, magnificent costumes, music, intermèdes, brilliant lighting, and plenty of seats for the carefully selected audience. The most amazing feature of the décor, which was explained in the printed edition of *Arimène* of 1597, was a series of four five-sided standards that could be turned simultaneously by an apparatus underneath the stage and thus give five different settings. The complicated device required an excellent mechanician to make it work, and might well have been inspired by the *periaktoi*, the adjustable prisms of the ancient Greek scene. It was something that a wealthy noble could use to dazzle his friends, but it was hardly a setting for expense-minded managers at the Théâtre du Marais or the Hôtel de Bourgogne.[16]

The private amusements of the Court and the surrounding nobility could be of the most lavish or they could be nothing more than a stroll through the Tuileries gardens. A tremendous peak of splendor was reached in 1612 with the betrothal of Louis XIII . . . to Anne of Austria. The pageantry during this period of celebrations was most ornate, as was illustrated by the carrousel in the Place Royale, called in the contemporary painting at the Musée Carnavalet *Le Roman des Chevaliers de la Gloire* (see Figure 27). It was the essence of pomp and circumstance, embellished at night by displays of fireworks in the sky. On the other hand, Henry IV encountered the elements of drama while wandering over the streets of his beloved Paris. One day in 1609, he was on the way back to the Louvre with his accompanying retinue; they met a woman leading a cow which the King admired and offered to buy. The woman was unwilling to sell because the suggested purchase price was too low — and she intimated that the King, not being a "cow merchant," knew little about such animals. Henry roared with delight and wondered why he was not an expert in matters bovine, since he had a troop of "calves" (his courtiers) following him. Then there was the Abbé d'Armentières who was infatuated with the actress, La Valliot, and found satisfaction upon her death in decorating his room with her skull.[17]

TYPES OF PLAYS

MOST OF THE PLAYS THAT CAME OUT OF THE SIX-
TEENTH CENTURY had little practical value for the early professional actors as they were opening the theatre to the
general public in France. The moralities and mysteries of
the Middle Ages were outmoded and too complicated in their
requirements for staging. The first tragedies and comedies of
the Renaissance, written for the most part by schoolboys under the direction of their professors, were stilted and limited
in audience appeal. These compositions were important in re-
viving an interest in the drama of Greece and Rome, and were
at times well presented before an admiring group of relatives
and friends. But they were scarcely adaptable to the public
stage and were no longer produced even in the colleges by
the beginning of the seventeenth century; productions of
Renaissance tragedies at Court had ceased several decades
earlier. The Jesuits, it is true, continued their rather elaborate mounting of plays on into the seventeenth century; their
scripts, however, were of a specialized nature and were never
available to the professional companies. The only form of
drama from previous centuries that found solid favor with
the actors in the public theatre was the farce. The lusty spirit
of the medieval farces never died, though few examples of
them have come down from the sixteenth and seventeenth
centuries; they were acted but seldom printed. On the other
hand, the learned tragedies on beyond 1600, with their long
and erudite speeches, were printed but rarely acted, even
after a public stage had been established. The Frères Parfaict

said that the reason for these tragedies not being dramatically acceptable was that they were tinged with the "barbarism" of Ronsard and the "inflation" of Seneca, an accusation that would fit the rhetorical plays of the Latin writer better than the verses of the great Renaissance lyricist.[1]

A casual group of performers in a provincial town, or possibly in Paris, did not designate before 1600 the plays in their repertory very exactly. The pieces might all be lumped together as "plays" (*jeux*), or "pastimes" (*passe-temps*) or "histories," or just as "comedies." There was never any sharp distinction between the moralities, fools' plays (*sotties*), and the farces as they began in the Middle Ages; all the medieval comic versions were eventually blended into the farce. In the 1515 edict of the Parlement of Paris against the students' producing anything derogatory to the king, the forbidden offerings were called "farces, *sotties*, or any other *jeux*." A little later in the century the repertory of Lepardonneur's company in Rouen was described as "farces and moralities." A Biblical play presented in Clermont in 1579 on the life of Herod — possibly a suggestion for Alexandre Hardy's tragedy, *Mariamne*, and Tristan l'Hermite's later one of the same title — was simply called a "drama." A few years earlier in Amiens a series of plays were catalogued as "tragedies, moralities, and farces," while a schoolboy repertory in Poitiers in 1581 consisted of "tragedies, comedies, and farces." In 1585, a small troupe was permitted by the consuls of Agen to "play a bit of their comedy," but some time afterward "farces and pastimes" were not allowed in the town. On Valleran le Conte's visit to Bordeaux in the 1590's, when he acted with the beautiful and chaste actress, he produced "tragedies and farces" — which terms were probably quite accurate. Nevertheless, throughout the sixteenth century, wherever there was an occasional performance of a play in the land of France, the designation of the type of drama being staged was seldom very specific. The clearest descriptive term was "farce"; any play with this title could be counted on to have in it plenty of rough action and language.[2] The question of terminology was not completely resolved by the first decades of the seventeenth century. In 1599, Valleran le Conte hoped to present on successive Sundays in Paris a "romance," which must have been something like Hardy's later *Théagène et Chariclée*, a lengthy spectacle of eight "days" of five acts each. A few weeks later in 1599, Valleran indicated in an agreement that he would prefer to put on a "tragedy" instead of the "romance"; unfortunately, neither tragedies nor extended romances had much appeal for Paris theatre audiences at this time. Before the end of 1599, Valleran listed a more varied repertory consisting of "romances, comi-tragedies (a strange hybrid), pastorals, and comedies." Comedies in this case must have also included farces; a few years before, Valleran had been permitted to present some "Biblical tragedies and comedies" at Frankfort-on-Main but had been refused the privilege of staging "sacred and profane comedies" in Strasbourg. In 1606, he was allowed to give at the Hôtel de Bourgogne "*jeux* and honest comedies for the contentment of the public," while in 1609 his proposed offerings were to be made up of "tragicomedies, comedies, pastorals, and other *jeux*." "Comi-tragedy" was not a combination that lasted, though "pastoral tragicomedy" had some application during the seventeenth century. In 1610, and two years later in 1612, papers signed by Valleran show that his company was prepared to present, with an occasional variant in the order of listing, "comedies, tragicomedies, pastorals, and other *jeux*." It will be noted that during this period no specific mention was made of tragedies, though fifteen or twenty years before they had been named first in the great actor's repertory. The vague inclusion of tragedies in "other *jeux*" is a further suggestion that Valleran was having no success with them in Paris during these decades when the farce-players were in command at the Hôtel de Bourgogne. Nor were farces named separately by Valleran on the documents of this interval in his career; but this would not have been necessary, since his troupe never had any success in competing with Gros Guillaume and Gautier Garguille in the rough genre of the farce. Outside Paris, the actor Antoine Cossart and company between 1615 and 1620 presented in Lille a series of "comedies, pastimes, and trage-dies," for the entertainment of the general public as well as for the officialdom of the city. Back in Paris, Gautier Gar-guille himself made a generalized dumping of all things dra-matic into one pot when he spoke in 1634 of "the comedy" and "those who love the comedy" at the Hôtel de Bourgogne. "Comedy," then, in the first years of the seventeenth century could refer to any type of drama that was staged, just as "comedian" could indicate any kind of actor.[3]

The only writer of serious plays from the sixteenth century to be used freely by the early professional performers, as well as by the amateurs, was Robert Garnier. Garnier wrote a number of tragedies based on Greek and Roman antiquity, but his preferred play, as far as any public representation was concerned, was probably the tragicomedy, *Bradamante*. The Frères Parfaict, who had a number of good things to say about Garnier, thought very highly of *Bradamante*. Lemazu-rier stated that the Hôtel de Bourgogne had first been peopled by some "ignoble farce-players" who were then joined by "a few actors accustomed to play the tragedies of Garnier." Later critics, including Germain Bapst and Eugène Rigal, have thought that the plays of Garnier, along with those of Jodelle, Montchrétien, and others, never had the "honors of the stage." But there are arguments of considerable potency on the other side. One of the earliest bands of traveling comedians in Scarron's *Roman comique* presented for an audi-ence of provincial aristocracy "*Roger et Bradamente* by the poet Garnier." * Roger, the suitor of the equestrian heroine,

* For details on this performance, see Chapter X, note 15.

Bradamente, was in this case given equal billing with her. Irrefutable proof of the fact that Garnier's plays (several of his tragedies, in particular) were staged by the early professional troupes was found recently in the archives of the Belgian city, Tournai. Raymond Lebègue has summarized this evidence, which shows the repertory of the troupe of the actor-manager, Adrien Talmy, from 1594 to 1599 as he gave performances in cities like Arras, Mons, and (in 1598) Paris. Garnier's great religious tragedy, Les Juives, as well as his tragedies from Greek antiquity, La Troade and Hippolyte, were on Talmy's list. These plays were presented "not before a chosen audience, but before a public as mixed as that of the Hôtel de Bourgogne." The writings of Garnier were undoubtedly the dramatic legacy from the sixteenth century most favored by the first of the professional actors.[4]

The gaps in the serious repertory of the actors on the early public stage were filled in by Alexandre Hardy, the most prolific writer in the history of French drama and the first composer to aim his plays at a seeing rather than a reading audience. He was recognized by seventeenth- and eighteenth-century commentators on the theatre, and modern scholars have given his life and works a full treatment. Despite all this attention many details in his career still remain obscure. In any case, the fact that he was born around 1572 and died in 1632 put him in an ideal chronological spot to participate in the development of the professional theatre. Beauchamps said that eight hundred plays were attributed to him, which was an "unbelievable" number even if it were reduced to five hundred — a figure, incidentally, which is nearer to modern critical estimates. Hardy was one of the first, if not the first, auteurs de troupe, a position that was not very lucrative as the sixteenth century was ending, and not considered sufficiently important to merit putting the author's name on the occasional poster advertising the play. In the words of Beauchamps, Hardy was "reduced to making his living by furnishing six plays a year to the comedians"; but in doing this he "cleared the way" for later writers like Corneille, Scudéry, and others. Of all the hundreds of plays that Hardy wrote only thirty-four have survived, a pessimistic commentary on contemporary opinion concerning their literary worth but a sufficiently long list to show what the professional comedians were offering their audiences, other than farces, in the early decades of the seventeenth century. In the Hardy collection, then, are: one "secular history" (the *Théagène et Chariclée*), twelve tragedies, fourteen tragicomedies, five pastorals, and two "dramatic poems" (these were spectacle plays based on stories from mythology). The tragedies most likely belong to the first decade of the century and were not popular with Paris theatregoers; therefore, a shift to tragicomedies and pastorals was made in an effort to please the public. In all the Hardy plays there is emphasis on action as well as on spectacular and, at times, harrowing scenes in the hope of attracting the interest of the spectators. He did not bother with such niceties as smoothness of versification or obedience to the unities of time and place; the unity of action was observed in an effort toward audience appeal.[5]

Hardy, despite his assistance around 1600 in getting serious plays out of the schoolrooms onto the public stage, did not receive later in the century the full approbation of those who were closer to the great epoch of Corneille and Racine. The Abbé d'Aubignac, in great lack of appreciation, said: "Hardy was the one who provided most abundantly to our comedians material for diverting the people; and it was he without doubt who suddenly stopped the progress of the theatre by giving a bad example for the disorders which we have seen happen in our time." Marolles, in making an analysis of several dramatic pieces, felt that Hardy suffered in comparison with some of the dramatists who followed him immediately: "I did not understand those [the plays] of Alexandre Hardy, who composed more than eight hundred, because they were rather an-

tiquated; and their quite rough versification rendered them
disagreeable at the moment when the *Bergeries* of monsieur
de Racan, the [*Pyrame et*] *Thisbé* of Théophile [de Viau],
and the *Sylvie* of monsieur Mairet were coming out." On the
other hand, Tallemant des Réaux, in speaking of Racan, intimated that the author of the popular pastoral, *Les Bergeries*,
was quite kindly disposed toward Hardy: "He [Racan] said
that the comedies of Hardy which he saw presented at the
Hôtel de Bourgogne, where he entered without paying, excited him very much." The Frères Parfaict devoted considerable space to Hardy and his period; he wrote some seven
hundred plays, according to their figures, and of them "happily only forty-one remain." In general, the writings of
Hardy were placed by the Frères Parfaict in the category
of "feeble" and ridiculous pieces.[6]

   Despite the criticism lavished on Hardy in regard to his
artistic inadequacies, no one denied during his time or later
that he was the first dramatist to be attached to the evolving
professional companies of actors; as such he was paid a
fee for his plays, "a custom which was unknown before him."
It was not a large amount, possibly three to nine livres of
Tours a play before 1600, and the author got no further
financial return from his composition; only later in the century did he begin to receive a portion of the house receipts
and sell his writings to a publisher. By the end of 1597, or
early in 1598, Hardy became *poète à gages*, or composer of
plays under contractual agreement, for the troupe of Valleran
le Conte. This arrangement gave him some slight financial
security and also recognized the fact that his varied types of
plays had gained for him some reputation in the provinces.
That his income was precarious, however, is suggested by
the 1612 agreement in which Hardy is listed as an actor,
rather than as a poet, in Valleran's company. Conditions had
improved by 1625 when Hardy was to receive from Bellerose one hundred livres of Tours for a comedy entitled *Le*

Jaloux — a tremendous increase over the fees that were being expended for a play some thirty years before. And on January 5, 1627, Hardy signed a paper with another company in Paris, that of Claude Deschamps, by which he was to get a percentage of the receipts from performances. Succeeding dramatists in the 1630's, who were paid as much as six hundred livres of Tours by a company for the rights (exclusive for a number of months) to produce a play, owed a large debt to Alexandre Hardy who blazed the financial way for the professional playwright. No large monetary returns came to any author during the century from the publication of plays, though the actors allowed a drama to be printed after it supposedly had no further appeal to an audience. The author, with permission from the manager of the troupe, sold his composition to a publisher for a nominal sum.[7]

For Henry IV's reign from 1589 to 1610, a recent count has catalogued a total of "approximately" 159 dramatic compositions: 76 tragedies, 21 pastorals, 13 eclogues, 19 tragicomedies, 11 to 13 farces, and a few miscellaneous pageants, moralities, and colloquies. Many of these writings could be considered plays only in the very broad sense that they contained dialogue; and from the listing all the writings of Hardy have been excluded. During Henry IV's period references were made to 256 representations, professional and amateur, of plays: 67 productions of tragedies, tragicomedies, comedies, and pastorals; and 189 productions of mysteries, farces, Latin plays, pageants, histories, or other unclassified *jeux*. The accounting is impressive, although no distinction has been possible between a single reading for family and friends, and a full-scale production by a professional troupe. In another computation, Raymond Lebègue has found the titles of 133 tragédies that were written between 1573 and 1610. Most of these, in all likelihood, were not even accorded an amateur staging, but it is still a surprising figure for a period when tragedy was scarcely given any consideration in Paris as public or Court entertainment. Tragedy, tragicomedy, and pastoral drama all got their early acceptance as stageable material from support outside Paris. The frequently quoted statement made by the dramatist, Troterel, in 1615 would indicate that serious drama was being performed at the time in the land of France: Troterel said that he had seen a "thousand tragedies" put on in a "variety of spots." Most of the places in Troterel's somewhat exaggerated claim would have been away from the capital city. Also, well on into the first decades of the seventeenth century, other cultural areas (Rouen, for example) were genuine rivals of Paris in publishing as well as in producing plays.[8]

From the period between 1610 and 1618 around 45 plays have survived, aside from the compositions of Hardy. They are all crude and rough in texture, and have little refinement of verse or situation. Deeds of violence on stage are acceptable in them even as they were with Hardy, who depicted such things as young girls being murdered and their bodies thrown in a well,* all in front of the spectators. Plays in this group — 19 of which, incidentally, had their first printing in Rouen — consisted of tragedies, tragicomedies, pastorals, a very few comedies and farces, and political plays. All of them were written for production rather than reading, and they all probably received some sort of staging, with the possible exception of historical dramas on Henry IV and the Maréchal d'Ancre. Between 1619 and 1624, some elements of greater elegance in verse and situation began to be visible in plays; the two best dramatic creations of the period were Racan's pastoral, *Les Bergeries*, in 1620 and Théophile de Viau's tragedy, *Pyrame et Thisbé*, in 1621. Some farces were popular, but only one or two tragicomedies have survived from these years. Jean de Mairet and others put the pastoral in vogue between 1625 and 1628, from which time 17 plays are extant; Paris became again during these years the center

* In his tragedy, *Scédase*.

of dramatic publication. Around 1628, tragicomedy began to receive more attention, as did the pastoral. From 1630 to 1634, 16 pastorals appeared and 37 tragicomedies. Tragedy was for the moment in an eclipse, but the comedy of manners (under the influence of Corneille's *Mélite*) was coming into being. An indication of the neglect of tragedy during this time can be noted from the *Mémoire* of Mahelot: of the 71 plays included by the decorator as a part of the repertory of the Hôtel de Bourgogne in 1634, only 2 were tragedies. The masterpieces of Corneille and Racine were yet to come; they would hardly have been appreciated by the audiences of the early public theatre. At any rate, according to the record of H. C. Lancaster, from the death of Henry IV until 1634, a minimum of 255 plays appeared in France. Of these a large number received professional staging and several were accorded public acclaim.[9]

To the question as to what type of plays were preferred by the spectators in the Hôtel de Bourgogne, the Abbé d'Aubignac had a simple answer: the nobles, with their more highly developed sensibilities, liked tragedy while the rabble in its crudeness wanted farce. Such a critical estimate would hardly give a complete picture, any more than would the conclusion that the greatest musical appreciation resides today in the diamond-studded occupants of the center boxes at the opera. At the turn of the seventeenth century in Paris, everybody in the public theatre seemed to prefer farce; and a trifle later tragicomedy and the pastoral were well received. Although many tragedies continued to be written, it was not until the 1630's that they were given a full accolade by the theatre-going public. In the early 1600's, it is true, the artistic quality of dramatic composition in France was a long way from that of England and Spain during the same period. Alexandre Hardy could hardly have been called a French Lope de Vega and even less a French Shakespeare. But the delay in the development of a cultivated theatre in France was as much the result of a lack of taste in the nobility as it was in the lower classes; Henry IV enjoyed a farce possibly more than did his most ignorant lackey. Even if the King's preferences in drama had been more lofty, it would have been rather difficult to have a writer of the caliber of Corneille, Molière, or Racine appear on the literary horizon simply by royal command. It is probably just as well that none of France's great dramatic trio reached the peak of his powers before there was a public capable of appreciating him. Fortunately, much of the spade work had been done by Alexandre Hardy and his immediate successors.[10]

Before the 1630's many of the concepts of rules and decorum that were standard for later plays were not yet in operation. This lack of regulation applied to tragedy as well as to the most unbridled farce. No play as yet fitted into the classical unities of time and place, though some of them were well knit as to action. Hardy's tragedies, for example, sought to present one major problem to which the fifth act gave a solution. But the actors were not interested in the twenty-four-hour rule nor in the logic of on-stage action's being limited to a palace or to a public square. The "rigors of the rules" had no appeal either for the performers or composers, and one theory had it that the necessity of writing regular pieces would "stop the small authors completely and interfere with the work of others." This diagnosis was partially correct, since the great Corneille had trouble in compressing the action of such a play as Le Cid into twenty-four hours, and would have been happy with a general agreement to extend the temporal limits of a tragedy to thirty hours. On the other hand, Corneille belittled his early and irregular pieces, and asked that critics not take them too seriously. A rather provocative comment on rigidly controlled drama was made by a young counselor of the Parlement of Rennes in Scarron's Roman comique, where the lawyer was discussing matters theatrical with the little traveling troupe: all the regular plays, said the counselor, have already been written, and "finally one would be reduced to dispensing with the rule of twenty-four hours; people in the greater part of the world have not known what was the good of severe rules in the theatre, and they have found greater pleasure in seeing things presented on stage than in hearing recitals about them." It should be possible, then, to write some very good plays outside the limits of the Aristotelean code, "without falling into the extravagance of the Spaniards." Such an unrestricted type of drama did not receive approval in the golden years of the French theatre, although Jean Racine stated in 1676 that the primary aim of a play was "to please and to move," and the spectators should not bother themselves with technical elements of structure.[11]

Until after 1630, then, nobody was greatly concerned with the rules in drama, smooth versification and proper words, or refinement of action on the stage. Father Garasse, in too severe an outburst, said in 1623 that dramatists like Théophile de Viau were "parasites of Plautus" who soiled with their immodesties the whole interior of the Hôtel de Bourgogne. This blast came soon after the success of Théophile's play based on Ovidian legend, *Pyrame et Thisbé*, a piece of ultra-refinement when compared with the farces and comedies that preceded it, and one which was later to be lampooned by Boileau because of its preciosity. The popularity of Théophile's play in its time was indicated in the *Roman comique* of Scarron where an old actor sought to show his histrionic ability by reciting "some verses from *Pyrame et Thisbé*," as he rode a mule across country. Some peasants along the road thought he was preaching the word of God and listened with bowed heads. As for violence in language and action in tragedy before Théophile's sad story of Pyramus and Thisbe, nothing could have been much worse than two plays published in Rouen around 1612. In one, called *Tragédie Mahommétiste* or a "tragedy involving Mohammed," a Sultana with full

26. *The front curtain for Mirame, Richelieu's theatre, 1641*

27. *A festival for Louis XIII and Anne of Austria in the Place Royale, 1612*

description of the gory details cuts out a man's heart and gloatingly drinks the blood. The second of these tragedies, *Le More cruel*, shows a Moorish slave, upon being released from his chains, raping his master's wife and throwing one of her children off a tower of the master's château. The erstwhile master, in a gesture of appeasement, cuts off his own nose, at the Moor's request, whereupon the Moor sneeringly tells him that he "will have no further need for a handkerchief" — and the remaining children are thrown off the tower. In the *Philarchie des Dieux*, published in Paris in 1612 and written by one Oudineau, there is considerable rough action among the gods and few of even the earthly proprieties are observed. The goddess Rhea is delivered of a child on stage, accompanied by a full discussion of all the symptoms and problems of pregnancy. The language is a far cry from what might be expected to be heard on Mount Olympus; in 1612, obviously, a consideration for the amenities was not even required of the gods when they appeared on the French scene.[12]

In comedy and in farce during the early years of the seventeenth century there was, as can well be imagined, little restriction of language and situation. In farce it was primarily a matter of grossness of words, while in comedy it was a question of crudeness of situation in amorous relationships — though in a comedy like Troterel's *Les Corrivaux* of 1612 the dialogue is far from being lofty. Mairet's *Les Galanteries du duc d'Ossone* carried on the fashion of immoral bedroom escapades into the 1630's. As for the amount of amorous exchange that could be made by two lovers in front of the spectators, during this period it was undoubtedly enough to make clear the intentions of the boy and girl. The Frères Parfaict quoted Fontenelle, the nephew of Corneille, as saying that with Hardy "the first caresses were made on the stage, and what went on between two lovers was as completely exposed as possible to the audience." By the time of

Corneille restriction on amorous scenes had not yet been sufficiently applied: "The stage was still rather licentious, and there was great familiarity between persons who were in love. In the *Clitandre* * of monsieur Corneille, Caliste comes to find Rosidor in bed; it is true that they are to be married soon, but a polite spectator should not be bothered with these preludes to marriage. . . . One of the greatest obligations due monsieur Corneille is the one owed him for purifying the stage. He was at first led on by custom already established, but he changed soon afterward; and since his play, *Clitandre*, no more licentiousness has been found in his works." [13]

The prologue as a formalized introduction to an afternoon of drama had disappeared by 1630, when the audience was beginning to show signs of being a little more tractable. Bruscambille was one of the last of the clever prologuists to harangue a restive and heterogeneous group impatient for the play to begin. Throughout the century from time to time, indeed, the *orateur de troupe* would still have to come out on stage to placate the mob if there was any inordinate delay in presenting the entertainment; but Bruscambille ended the tradition of a planned beguiling of the customers while "our actors" made preparations for the "tragedy" or other species of drama. As a generality, the program before the 1630's consisted of the tragedy, or tragicomedy, or pastoral or comedy, and then a farce. The sequence was a result of long tradition, since the semiprofessional societies of the fifteenth century had offered regularly at a single dramatic session a morality, a fool's play, and a farce, with the farce coming last. As the forces of refinement made themselves more and more apparent by 1630, there was developing pressure to drop the rough and vulgar farce from the dramatic schedule. Bruscambille, it will be remembered, had said earlier that the comedians would have gladly eliminated the farce from their day's activities if their clientele had not insisted, for the full value of the

* A rather wild comedy dating from 1632; it ends in a double wedding.

price of admission, that it be retained. The farce did last on
into the 1630's, both in the public theatre and in private representations, even though its great vogue had passed. As has
been seen, the tremendous and lofty audience for the triple
wedding at the Arsenal in 1634 was diverted by a comedy in
prose, three dancing interludes, a comedy in verse, and a
farce.

By the second half of the seventeenth century it was accepted practice that the "heroic pieces" should be given in
the winter season (in spite of the barn-like frigidity of the
halls), while the lighter dramatic fare was reserved for the
summer time. This has come to be the standard procedure in
Paris and New York today, but it was not the case with the
public theatre as it began in France. Anything was tried that
might attract the people of Paris into the parterre and loges,
whether it was farce or a stilted tragedy. For in-between
material, Bruscambille, during his moments at the Hôtel de
Bourgogne, approved of the pastoral as an instrument for
expressing the delicate sentiments of love: a "rural rhetoric"
was better for emotional nuances than the "flattering language
of the Court." With Le Cid, which had its première during
the last days of December 1636, or the first week of January
1637, the great plays began a routine of winter openings;
later in the century the first performances of the finest of
all French tragedies, Racine's Phèdre, occurred in January
1677. These noble spectacles would have in them lofty maxims, heroes and heroines with tragic flaws, and reflect "some
tincture of moral virtues." But, in the first years of the professional theatre both the plays and the public that saw them
were somewhat motley and unclassified; the drama of this
period had variety, but little grandeur.[14]

RICHELIEU AND REFORM

THE "GRAND CARDINAL DE RICHELIEU, one of the most enlightened of all men," duke and peer of France, prince of the Church, and all-powerful prime minister of possibly the greatest nation of his age, caused Europe to tremble when his classic features were creased in a frown; but he spent his moments of relaxation in the make-believe of the theatre. Richelieu, though he had been called into the royal council in 1624, did not become principal minister of state until 1629, and it was after this important milestone in his career that he, rather miraculously, found time for the world of dramatic illusion. By this moment a great deal of the spade work for the establishment of the professional theatre had been done. Bellerose and the royal comedians were at the Hôtel de Bourgogne, and Montdory with his companions were gaining a foothold in the Marais quarter. The new generation of playwrights like Racan, Théophile de Viau, Mairet, Rotrou, and Corneille had already appeared or were just beginning to make their reputation. The greatest of all epochs in French drama, as far as creative artistry was concerned, was just around the corner in the triumvirate of Corneille, Molière, and Racine. It remained for Richelieu, with his exceptional leverage of power and authority, to bring to the institution of the theatre the position necessary for this fabulous trio of composers to come into full blossom. There were still to be on the stage in the early 1630's farces which had not had all the dirt washed out of them, as well as comedies full of doubtful situations and double meanings. Nevertheless, under the influence of the Cardinal — who, incidentally, was not himself a regular patron of the Hôtel de Bourgogne or the Théâtre du Marais — the professional theatre attained a degree of politeness and prestige that it had not known before.[1] Richelieu's support of drama and dramatists was in some ways a symbol of the nation's recognition of the theatre as a part of its structure. Louis XIII, who should have been the primary spokesman for things dramatic, was not, even though the principal edicts concerning actors, acting companies, and theatrical halls went out over his signature. Louis, it is true, did make adjustments in the personnel of the dramatic troupes from time to time, frequently in opposition to marks of patronage displayed by the Cardinal; but the King did not have the intellectual interest in plays that Richelieu had, nor was he particularly concerned with their production. The prime minister, therefore, was something of the official spokesman for and regulator of dramatic affairs in France during the decade of the 1630's. No preliminary underwriting of the theatre by some wealthy nobleman had been done in France as had happened in Italy and other countries. There was no French Duke of Mantua with his own company, and there was no French equivalent, in regard to the encouragement of actors, of the Prince of Orange of the Dutch house of Nassau; neither was there in any city of France, Paris included, a hall of drama comparable to the splendid Olympic theatre of Palladio in the Italian town of Vicenza. Before the 1630's no theatrical Maecenas existed, either inside or outside the orbit of royalty, in France to give actors and the stage a much-needed boost. To Richelieu, the busiest man in Europe, fell the task of making the theatre a fully recognized part of the French nation.

Much of the assistance given the professional theatre by Richelieu was indirect. An aristocrat down to the marrow of his bones, he would never have lent his presence to the farcical antics of Gros Guillaume or Gautier Garguille at the

Hôtel de Bourgogne. On the other hand, he was much interested in the new crop of dramatic authors that appeared during the late 1620's, with their more finished type of composition. He liked verse and became intrigued with the idea of the classical unities, possibly under the persuasion of the bleak Jean Chapelain, who came to be known as the oracle of Aristotle. Men of letters were able to get the Cardinal's ear, particularly after the noonday meal as he took a constitutional stroll on his estates at Rueil; and the writer who had easiest access to him was the pleasant and facile Boisrobert, an abbé whose religion weighed on him very lightly. Boisrobert, who had considerable histrionic ability, amused the Cardinal with stories, verses, and posturings. Also, through Boisrobert many poor poets got a hearing from Richelieu and an eventual pension. The august French Academy, election to which is still today the greatest distinction that can come to a French man of letters, germinated in Boisrobert's fertile brain and was later officially brought into being by the Cardinal. Boisrobert may have, too, had something to do with Richelieu's formation of a quintet of authors to write plays, the famous Committee of Five.

The Committee of Five was made up of Corneille, Rotrou, Boisrobert, Claude de l'Estoile (the son of the chronicler Pierre de l'Estoile), and Guillaume Colletet (known for his biographies of several poets of the late Renaissance). The latter two writers had little reputation for creating drama — nor did Boisrobert, for that matter — but in Corneille and Rotrou, Richelieu adopted the two most gifted playwrights of the period. The five poets were given an impossible task by the Cardinal: each one of them was to write an act of a play which would then be examined by Richelieu for revision or possible changes in plot or versification. Whether he ever wrote any verse of his own is still an argument among critics; no incontrovertible evidence has been discovered to prove that he composed any poems or plays. The literary works with which he was concerned were always signed by somebody else, and Richelieu assumed no responsibility of authorship. The scheme of having five workmen busy simultaneously at the same task was, according to Pellisson in his *Histoire de l'Académie* of 1653, an efficient one: in this way the Cardinal could have a whole "comedy" finished in a month. The first dramatic composition of the Committee of Five was the *Comédie des Tuileries*, which was presented at the Arsenal on March 10, 1635, with Montdory and his cohorts handling the acting chores. It was a five-act verse play of which Corneille had done the third act; but the stubborn Norman did not like to function under the supervision of Boisrobert and managed to get out of the collaboration after this single effort. Corneille's own plays were beginning to attract more and more attention, so he was allowed to concentrate on them. Mairet, who had gained fame with his tragedy, *Sophonisbe*, in 1634, joined the Committee for *La Grande Pastorale* which was presented before Richelieu and Their Majesties on January 10, 1637. The last of the Committee's combinations was *L'Aveugle de Smyrne*, five acts and in verse like the other two, though created by only four authors; Mairet was now the missing man. It was produced, as had been *La Grande Pastorale*, at the "Hôtel de Richelieu" with the King, Queen, Monsieur (Gaston d'Orléans), and other distinguished guests in attendance. The date was February 22, 1637, less than six weeks after the previous spectacle, so the Committee had had a busy time fitting their couplets together into a harmonious play. The two troupes of the Hôtel de Bourgogne and of the Marais combined their talents on this occasion to make *L'Aveugle de Smyrne* a brilliant affair.[2]

After the dissolution of the Committee of Five, which the astute Richelieu must have recognized as an unsatisfactory method for getting plays written, Desmarets de Saint Sorlin became the Cardinal's dramatic handyman. Desmarets had gained for himself considerable notoriety in 1637 with his successful comedy of manners, *Les Visionnaires*, a clever satire on preciosity and fanciful ideas. The genteel sophistication of Desmarets appealed to Richelieu and caused the Cardinal to extend to the poet his patronage. The last of Richelieu's plays, then, came out under the name of Desmarets de Saint Sorlin: *Roxane* in 1639, *Mirame* in 1641, and *Europe* in 1642. None of these plays was a literary masterpiece, though they all had splendor of spectacle and obtained dramatic effects through the complication of theatrical machines. In them may have been concealed references to historical events and intimations of high-level intrigue: *Europe* was a political allegory of the Cardinal's career and the triumph of France over her enemies on the Continent. The play was in its final rehearsals in the great theatre of the Palais Cardinal when Richelieu died on December 4, 1642.

The plays written under the direction of Richelieu were purified as to language and situation, but they were sufficiently flamboyant. In order to mount them the Cardinal built appropriately ornate theatres in his extending domain. A small theatre was available in his town house by 1634 and, with the acquisition of enough terrain to complete the elaborate Palais Cardinal, space was found in it for a much larger hall of drama, which was officially dedicated with the spectacle of *Mirame* on January 14, 1641. The Cardinal also had a theatre on his property at Rueil; it was used generally for rehearsals and informal presentations. The historian Sauval has left a good deal of information on the two halls in Paris — which, unfortunately, are no longer in existence. Sauval had several words to say about Richelieu's interest in plays and the theatres he built: "Everyone knows the passion the Cardinal de Richelieu had for the comedy. . . . Certainly this passion, if it should be called that, exercised such tyranny over him that the troupe of royal comedians not being sufficient for him, he wished to have another one which might follow him into the country and which could give him at his home in Paris the pleasure of comedy even at the time the King was enjoying the same amusement at the Louvre. And, furthermore, one theatre was not enough for him in his palace; he had to have two, a small one and a large one, the small one capable of containing six hundred persons and the large one with a capacity of more than three thousand." Sauval's story would give some explanation of the fact that Richelieu favored more specifically the actors at the Théâtre du Marais than those in the Hôtel de Bourgogne; the inhabitants of the Bourgogne were officially the *comédiens du Roi*, so the Cardinal turned to the Marais as the group of performers upon which he could have first call. Sauval gave further details on the architecture of the large theatre in the Palais Cardinal: it had twenty-seven tiers of seats that gradually rose as they went back from the stage, two superimposed galeries along each side of the hall, and a colonnade of pillars above painted in trompe l'oeil.* It was the finest theatrical structure in Paris and rivaled the theatres in Italy; whether it would contain three thousand persons or not is a moot question. The hall was used later by Molière and the Académie Royale de Musique. The most striking feature of it was the series of gently rising tiers of seats, an indication that the arguments of the Abbé d'Aubignac favoring a structure with the seating plan modeled on a Greek amphitheatre had had some influence on Richelieu. Regrettably, the Cardinal's impressive theatre burned down before the end of the eighteenth century.[3]

The grand opening of the Cardinal's splendid hall was done

* See Figure 21, which is an engraving from a collection at the Bibliothèque Nationale depicting the activities of royalty. It gives a very good idea of the interior of the theatre in the Palais Cardinal, with the rows of seats removed. The engraving was evidently based on a painting in the Musée des Arts Décoratifs; the details in each are the same, except the central figure of the cortier in the engraving is, in the painting, the Cardinal de Richelieu, who is carrying on an animated conversation with Louis XIII as is the case with the courtier in the engraving.

in a festival honoring the Queen, Anne of Austria, and was signalized by the superlatively ornate staging of *Mirame*. It was for this presentation that, as has been noted, the front curtain was certainly used, probably to enhance the effect of the elaborate theatrical machines, which were terribly expensive and caused the whole production to cost around one hundred thousand crowns. All this expenditure for mechanisms could not disguise the feebleness of the romanesque piece wherein the daughter of a king (Mirame) spends five acts being devoted to a feeble suitor (Arimant) instead of accepting the attentions of a strong one (Azamor) — all carried on to the accompaniment of weak versification, pseudo-poisonings, and the supposed death of the hero in the fourth act. The play failed miserably, while an elegant audience looked on, in spite of the complex mechanics and grandeur of its décor. The Abbé de Marolles had a comment to make on the play and the way the machines worked: "That same year (1641) there were many magnificences in the Palais Cardinal for the grand comedy of *Mirame*, which was represented before the King and the Queen, with some machines that made the sun and moon rise, and which could bring up in the distance the sea covered with ships." Marolles did not care for the performance, particularly the overworking of the machines which for him became tiresome. On this point he offered a pretty good bit of dramatic criticism: "The principal attraction of plays, in my opinion, is the diction of good actors, the inventiveness of the poet, and the beauty of the versification." The author of *Mirame*, Marolles said he had understood, had done better in some other plays wherein there was not "so much apparatus." After *Mirame*, in further dazzling of his royal and noble guests, the Cardinal gave a big party in the theatre, with excellent music, food, and drink. The whole program of entertainment for Their Majesties, especially for the Queen, would hardly have been done so lavishly if Richelieu, as was suggested by Tallemant des

Réaux, had been hostile at this time to Anne of Austria and had sought to embarrass her by having in *Mirame* a situation (claimed by Tallemant) that would recall the Duke of Buckingham's visit to the Court of France and the rumored amorous episode between him and Anne of Austria. Desmarets, said Tallemant, created *Mirame* "contrary to the rules," and Richelieu "forced her [the Queen] to come to see it." All of which is a quite unlikely story, since *Mirame* and the celebrations in connection with the play were more in a gesture of reconciliation of past differences with the Queen — and it was done in the great Palais Cardinal theatre, the roof of which covered a "vast expanse" and was supported by timbers cut from the tallest and strongest trees in France.[4]

The little theatre with a seating capacity of six hundred, which had been built in the Cardinal's smaller town house before he extended his palace over adjacent terrain, was destined for plays that "the comedians represented ordinarily in the Marais of the [rue Vieille du] Temple." This would imply that plays with the relatively simple staging demands of the professionals, who could not yet afford the machinery necessary to make suns and moons rise on their scene, would be set up in the more intimate theatre. Montdory and company could have given there, for example, a drama like Tristan l'Hermite's *Mariamne* for the relaxation of the Cardinal, his household, and a restricted number of friends. The smaller area must have been used also for private and amateur performances, with even fewer spectators on hand to view the proceedings. One of the auditors on December 14, 1634, was the King's brother, Gaston d'Orléans, who ended a busy day by going to the Cardinal's little hall of drama where ". . . during the evening . . . he heard the comedy, which was attended also by the Cardinal Duke." The performers in this instance were most probably the Marais troupe, though the title of their offering is not known. On the amateur level, there was the story concerning Jacqueline Pascal (the sister of the scientist and philosopher, Blaise Pascal), who wrote a play and acted in it with some other girls when she was only twelve years old, in 1636. The affair evidently attracted some attention because "the Cardinal de Richelieu during that time got the notion of having *Le Prince déguisé* * performed by some children. Boisrobert took charge of the arrangements. He chose to be in the cast, as can well be imagined, the little Pascal girl." The play was quite a success at the Hôtel de Richelieu and pleased the Cardinal greatly, "but it was the petite Pascal who won the honors of the day." Richelieu, clearly, participated in the general fashion of the time of having children act grown-up roles on the stage, even though he had no offspring of his own.[5]

There is still some argument as to whether Richelieu removed his favor from Corneille because of *Le Cid*, which had such a popular success in spite of features in it that Richelieu did not like: the glorification of dueling (ignoring Richelieu's recent decrees against it), the portrayal of weak governmental controls at a time of military crisis, and other details. Recent scholarship has tended to minimize Richelieu's part in the literary quarrel over *Le Cid* and his supposed hostility toward its author. Nevertheless, after the triumph of *Le Cid* in 1637, a parody, which would suggest the Cardinal's disapproval of the play, was staged in the Cardinal's own little theatre for his delectation. It should be remembered, incidentally, that the parodying of a successful play has long been in France an indirect, and sometimes unintended, compliment to a well-received theatrical venture. For *Le Cid*, the amiable and ubiquitous Boisrobert took charge of arranging the satiric version in the Hôtel de Richelieu: "In order to divert the Cardinal and at the same time satisfy the hostility that he bore against *Le Cid*, he [Boisrobert] had it played by some lackeys and kitchen boys. Among other features, in that spot where Don Diègue said to his son, 'Rodrigue, do

* A play of Georges de Scudéry, first presented in 1634.

you have any heart [courage],' Rodrigue replied, 'No, I have only a weak stomach.' " * Such a satirizing of a serious moment in Corneille's work would have been more pleasing to the Cardinal if he had disliked the original.[6]

However serious may have been Richelieu's irritation at Corneille because of *Le Cid*, there was no question concerning the Cardinal's general patronage of writers, in particular of those who wrote drama. He extended his financial consideration also to the actors who performed the plays: in order to make their position more secure he envisaged before his death a combination of the professional companies in Paris under some form of state subvention, which would allow the actors to enjoy a greater feeling of economic security. He anticipated, therefore, the government-supported Théâtre Français, which did not come into existence until 1680, but which carries on still today the great tradition of French classic drama. Men like Boisrobert and Jean Chapelain, who were primary advisors to the Cardinal on matters of literary policy, were almost members of Richelieu's household and therefore in a position to help pick out the recipients of his largesse. The Abbé d'Aubignac was also very close to the Cardinal, although D'Aubignac fell a bit from grace after 1639 when he criticized Desmarets de Saint Sorlin, the later favorite of Richelieu. Boisrobert, according to Tallemant des Réaux, helped Mairet get a pension of two hundred crowns (or six hundred livres) from the Cardinal. Boisrobert approved of the grant with the remark: "Monseigneur, if this were done only because of [the play] *Sylvie*,† all the ladies will bless

---

* The episode which these lines parody occurs in the first act of *Le Cid*: Don Diègue has been slapped by the father of Chimène, whom Rodrigue loves. Diègue because of age and infirmity cannot defend his honor against this insult; he therefore asks his son to do it for him. Diègue's original question to Rodrigue — *Rodrigue, as-tu du coeur?* — was kept in the parody. Rodrigue's fiery reply, *Tout autre que mon père l'éprouverait sur l'heure!* ("Any other but my father would have proof of it right now!"), was changed to *Je n'ai que du carreau*.

† A pastoral play, presented in 1628.

you for having given a hand to poor Mairet." The Frères Parfaict said apropos of Mairet that "the reputation that he had acquired by his works gained for him entrée to the Cardinal de Richelieu who became fond of him and gave him a pension of one thousand livres." Six hundred livres must have been the beginning figure of the Cardinal's generosity, since in 1633 on the basis of a play called *Occasions perdues*, Rotrou was assigned an annual pension of this amount. Richelieu was fond of music and ballet, though not nearly so much as he was of "the comedy"; but on one occasion he gave a certain madame de Saint-Thomas eight hundred crowns for her splendid rendition of some Italian melodies.[7]

Montdory and his company were accorded financial assistance by Richelieu, though the actors undoubtedly contributed in return an adequate amount of private entertainment for the Cardinal in his own theatres. After his tragic paralysis of the tongue in 1637, Montdory wrote later in the year, on November 13, a very moving letter to Boisrobert stating his gratitude for the "kindnesses of His Eminence" and wishing that he could try one more time to act in "the theatre of His Eminence where the true Apollo (and consequently, the god of remedies) presides." Richelieu began in 1634 to grant to Montdory a pension of fifteen hundred livres. The Frères Parfaict stated that after the very sad effort Montdory made to return to the boards in *L'Aveugle de Smyrne*, where he was able to finish only two acts, Richelieu gave him a pension of two thousand livres. This grant was augmented by the gifts of other noblemen until it reached the figure of eight or ten thousand livres, which Montdory "enjoyed until his death." Louis XIII extended most of his assistance to the Hôtel de Bourgogne: Floridor, it will be recalled, was able to leave the Théâtre du Marais and buy Bellerose's wardrobe at the other theatre because of Floridor's share in "the pension that the King gives to the Hôtel de Bourgogne."[8]

The Cardinal definitely enjoyed being in an atmosphere of

drama and dramatists, of plays being made or performed. On one occasion he had the writer, Gombaud, stand up a long time, by a candle that burned lower and lower, reading a comedy aloud to him. He supposedly said to Desmarets de Saint Sorlin that he found more pleasure in poetry than in seeking the well-being of France; and when His Eminence was in the process of overseeing the construction of a play, no foreign or domestic minister of state was able to get his ear. Boisrobert, who did not like Desmarets, was the most versatile of the Cardinal's coterie of literary men; the "pleasant abbé" could act in plays as well as write them. Richelieu "overwhelmed him with favors," and Boisrobert, in return, amused the Cardinal and gave him diversion from weighty and official matters. The physicians of the Cardinal said that drugs never brought any relief to his pain-wracked body unless they were mixed with "a little Boisrobert." In regard to his histrionic ability, Tallemant des Réaux said of Boisrobert: ". . . there is no better comedian in the world. He is attractive in appearance. He said that once for amusement the Cardinal in his palace ordered him and Montdory to play an emotional scene and that the Cardinal found he did better than the most celebrated actor, perhaps, that has lived since Roscius." Boisrobert was passionately fond of acting in private productions and imitated the technique of Montdory — to such a degree, in fact, that the poet was called the "abbé Montdory." Richelieu could remove his favors as well as grant them; as will be recalled, Boisrobert himself fell into disgrace because he invited a former actress of the Montdory troupe to be his guest at a rehearsal of *Mirame*.[9]

Other noble patrons assisted Richelieu in bringing about an era of politeness in the theatre. The duc de Montmorency, from his beautiful château of Chantilly outside Paris, lent his patronage to Mairet and was an early supporter of regular plays obeying the unities. Montmorency did not see the great years of preclassic theatre, however, since he was decapitated in 1632 on orders from Richelieu. The comte de Belin, who died in 1638, was a benefactor of the Marais troupe as well as an admirer of actresses. Belin's affection for the company of the Marais was suggested in a letter to Belin in Le Mans from Chapelain in Paris on December 8, 1636: "On your return, if things do not change, you will find that the great comedians [the Hôtel de Bourgogne] have regained the upper hand over the little ones [the Marais], notwithstanding the support you have given monsieur de Montdory among the powers that be; and the reestablishment of his position will be an accomplishment worthy of the affection you have for him." Chapelain's famous letter to Belin on January 22, 1637, which mentioned how the public had been diverted "for fifteen days" by *Le Cid* and a play of Rotrou, also conveyed the fact that "monsieur and mademoiselle de Scudéry" were grateful for Belin's generosity. It was too bad, said Chapelain, that Belin could not have seen these two plays, since that would have contributed greatly to the comfort of his "maladies," just as they had for those of a certain "general." The comte de Belin, according to Tallemant, "in order to put that troupe [the Marais] in reputation begged madame de Rambouillet to allow them to play at her home the *Virginie* * of Mairet. The Cardinal de La Vallette was there and was so pleased with Montdory that he gave him a pension." [10]

One of the strong influences for reform in the theatre was the salon of Catherine de Vivonne, marquise de Rambouillet. The gifted and intelligent madame de Rambouillet early in the century retired from what she considered the uncouth ceremonials at the Louvre and began to receive at her town house a short distance from the royal palace on the rue Saint Thomas du Louvre (a street now absorbed in the rue de Rivoli and the spacious open terrain around the Louvre). The marquise, who was charming and rich and cultivated, set up as a necessary prerequisite for admission to the Hôtel de

* Tallemant gives the date of this play as 1631, but it should be 1633.

Rambouillet a sense of politeness and good manners; a noble if he conducted himself as a boor was not welcome there. On the other hand, madame de Rambouillet, with her knowledge of languages and literatures, welcomed to her salon men of letters who had no title of nobility but who did possess qualities of refinement. Her assemblies were pervaded with an aura of preciosity, gallantry, and feminity — all of which was satirized later in the century by Molière in his clever one-act play, *Les Précieuses ridicules*. In any case, the triumph of woman in seventeenth-century French society, once the Rabelaisian coarseness of Henry IV's court had been removed, was progressive and uncontested. It began with the popular pastoral novel, the *Astrée*, which sought in its lengthy installments over a period of twenty years up to 1627, to teach young men to be polite to young ladies. The high priestess in the movement for the glorification of woman was madame de Rambouillet. She started receiving in her "blue room" after 1618 and was therefore ready to welcome the improved crop of authors which began to appear in the 1620's. Most of them paid their homage to the marquise who, in return, provided a sophisticated audience to listen to their works. Men like Chapelain and Desmarets de Saint Sorlin from the Richelieu group were there, along with the superrefined salon lyric poet, Vincent Voiture. Among other articles in madame de Rambouillet's bill of rights for women was the following: the public theatre must be cleaned up both in language and atmosphere so that sensitive ladies might attend it without being shocked. The habituées of the Hôtel de Rambouillet functioned on a rather lofty pinnacle of linguistic delicacy: it was considered bad form, for example, when a collation was being offered by the hostess — and there many intervals at the Hôtel de Rambouillet for eating and drinking — to say "I like the melon"; the proper phrasing was "I esteem the melon." The playwrights and actors had a problem in avoiding what might be considered vulgarisms by the precious ladies of the rue Saint Thomas du Louvre. However that might have been, madame de Rambouillet exercised until around 1648 a primary and personal influence on the manners, literature, and theatre of Paris.

Even as was done for Mairet, the marquise de Rambouillet opened her doors to other dramatists and performers. According to Tallemant, "Montdory always felt a debt of gratitude to madame de Rambouillet since it was from that day * that he began to gain some renown." Madame de Rambouillet assisted Scudéry in obtaining a governmental post at Marseille. A certain monsieur de Brienne, in connection with the incident, wrote to her saying "that it was a dangerous matter to give an official position to a poet who had written some pieces for the Hôtel de Bourgogne and had put his name on them." Madame de Rambouillet replied that she had discovered that Scipio Africanus had composed some comedies — but, as a matter of fact, "they had not been performed at the Hôtel de Bourgogne." Corneille was also a frequenter of the Hôtel de Rambouillet when he was in Paris, though it is hard to see how the stubborn and somewhat awkward Norman would have been at ease in a salon environment. Nevertheless, Corneille read his great religious tragedy of the early 1640's, *Polyeucte*, before a gathering at the Hôtel de Rambouillet, "the sovereign tribunal over literary matters at that time." Voiture did not like it and Corneille was so impressed by the trivial poet's opinion that he wanted to get the manuscript back from the actors before the play was given a public staging. Fortunately, this did not happen, but the incident does show the effect upon the theatre exercised by the Hôtel de Rambouillet and its inhabitants. The elegant mistress of this salon, then, joined with Richelieu in bringing about several refinements in the theatre during the 1630's.[11]

It was to the Cardinal de Richelieu that most people in the

* A performance of Mairet's *Virginie* at the Hôtel de Rambouillet.

seventeenth century gave the greatest amount of credit for bringing prestige to the public theatre. Corneille in his comedy of 1636, *L'Illusion comique*, said: ". . . at present the theatre is at such a high point of perfection that everyone idolizes it"; and in the letter of dedication to Richelieu of his tragedy of 1640, *Horace*, Corneille admitted to the Cardinal that "if I have any reputation today I owe it all to you," and quoted a few verses in Latin from Horace to prove it. Chapelain in writing to Boisrobert on January 24, 1635, agreed that in matters theatrical or literary everyone might profit "from the inspiration of the great genius of Monseigneur." The year 1635, said Mathieu Molé in his memoirs, had a fine lot of entertainment to which the King and "people of quality" might go, since the King knew that "the comedy, now that everything has been banished from the theatre which could soil the most delicate ears, is one of the most agreeable diversions in his city of Paris." Chappuzeau stated a little later in the century that he would like to defend the theatre and show what the nature of comedy is "since it came into its bloom through the esteem granted it by Armand de Richelieu, and the finish accorded it by Pierre Corneille." Scarron also had some things to say about plays and actors in the time of Richelieu: "In our days recognition in some ways has been given to their [the actors'] profession, and they are more highly regarded than was formerly the case. Also it is true that people find in the comedy one of the most innocent of diversions which can at the same time instruct and delight. It is cleansed today, at least in Paris, of all the licentiousness it used to have. One could wish also that it might be cleared of pickpockets, pages, lackeys, and other human scum whom the facility of stealing cloaks attracts to the theatre more than did formerly the dirty jokes of the farce-players; but today farces are abolished, and I dare say there are private parties where there is hearty laughter at foul and low stories which would shock the first loges of the Hôtel de Bourgogne." The parterre, clearly, was still a problem, though the writer, Charles Sorel, said in 1642 that the open and unseated area had its points, since it was possible in it to get closer to the stage — and "at times you find very genteel persons there; and the greater part of the poets, who are the most capable judges of plays, are unwilling to go anywhere else." [12]

If "the comedy came into honor after the Cardinal de Richelieu took charge of it," it was only after other problems associated with the theatre had received attention. Tabarin in his *Decrees* of 1623 said that the constabulary should take the responsibility of checking on "all the infamous lodgings located on the rue Saint Antoine, in the Marais du Temple quarter and surroundings areas, where from one day to the next so many unlucky people are tricked and robbed." All this region (prime terrain for the developing public theatre) was, said Tabarin, filled with "canaille, which does nothing but infect, corrupt, and spoil this whole city of Paris." The nobles were as much of a problem as the rabble as far as general conduct was concerned. Their dueling and sword play was on a higher level of social interchange, but it was more destructive than the disturbances of the less well-armed lower classes. Richelieu's journalist, Théophraste Renaudot, reported in his *Gazette* of February 1, 1634, that the marquis du Pont de Courlay and the baron de Bole met on the rue de la Ferronnerie and immediately started fighting. One of Richelieu's hopes for the developing theatre was that it would provide the young nobles with a more courteous and amiable diversion than dueling. On February 11, 1634, several official decrees were issued in an effort to establish better controls over the people of Paris. There would be no manufacturing or sale of pistols, and students were not to be permitted to carry any kind of weapons. In the wintertime taverns were to close at seven o'clock in the evening, and at eight o'clock in the summer; and the police were supposed to make "a careful search for all thieves, and sellers of or users of tobacco." In matters of social improvement, by October 26, 1636, the position of actors had risen to such a degree that in a marriage contract between the farce-player, Guillot-Gorju, and Gabrielle le Messier, the sister of Bellerose, both Guillot-Gorju and Bellerose, a witness to the agreement, were called "bourgeois of Paris." [13]

One of the most notable decrees concerning the theatre was that issued by Louis XIII, at the probable instigation of Richelieu, on April 16, 1641. In it the King said: "The fear that we have that the comedies, which are being represented effectively for the diversion of the people, may sometimes be accompanied by ignoble pieces, causes us to give the required orders to prevent such an eventuality. We have made and do make very express prohibitions . . . to all comedians against presenting any low action on stage, or using any lascivious words or *double-entendres* which can insult public morals, under threat of being declared infamous." On the other hand, if the "said comedians regulate in such manner their productions in the theatre so that they are exempt from impurity, we wish that the profession of the comedians (which can divert our people from various bad occupations) not be considered worthy of blame nor prejudicial to their reputation in society." Thus, before Richelieu's death the theatre was adjudged an acceptable public amusement and the actor, if he conducted himself correctly, a legitimate dweller in the social sphere. Later in the century there were to be further arguments concerning the professional theatre and whether or not the comedian could be a first-class citizen.[14]

But the land of France, while the public theatre was working its way up toward respectability, had grown stronger and more solid as the reign of Louis XIII drew near its end. Her capital city of Paris had continued to break through the stone restraint of medieval walls into the muddy fields beyond, although when one sipped a liqueur during the entr'acte at one of her theatres, it was easy to forget the

rough extensions and to say that "Paris was never so beautiful nor so splendid as she is today." There were some who
thought that Paris was not so new and fresh as certain towns
in Germany or the Low Countries, and some wished lugu-
briously to "speak of the muds of Paris, the old walls, and
of the rather ugly gates of this great city, its badly paved
streets, its fords, and its poorly maintained docks on the
river." But such conditions were inevitable, said the Abbé
de Marolles, in the growth of a spreading metropolis; and
everybody would have to admit that the new construction
in Richelieu's quarter and in that of the Marais had been
splendid. Also, if construction continues in the city as it
has been going on for the last forty-five years,* "there is
every indication that a century from now Paris will be the
most beautiful thing in the world" — a prophecy that has
come near to being fulfilled. The scarred and battle-weary
Paris found by Henry IV gave way before increasing
beauties of line and building. And the early public theatre,
with its grossness and gropings, was a steppingstone to an
era of theatrical magnificence.[15]

* This was written in 1656.

Notes

Bibliography

Index

NOTES

INTRODUCTION

1. Brantôme, Pierre de Bourdeille, seigneur de, *Oeuvres complètes*, publiées par Ludovic Lalanne (Paris, 1864–82), VII, 346. The longer quoted passage in its original form is: ". . . (elle) aymoit fort à veoir jouer des commédies et tragédies; mais depuis *Sofonisba* . . . elle eust opinion qu'elle avoit porté le malheur aux affaires du royaume, ainsi qu'il succéda; elle n'en fist plus jouer, mais ouy bien des commédies et tragi-commédies, et mesme celle des *Zani* et *Panthalons*." The Zanni and Pantalone, types rather than individuals in the *commedia dell' arte*, were favorites because of their "zany" antics and slapstick comedy. As a generality, the traveling companies of *commedia dell' arte* employed much improvisation, clowning, and buffoonery in their performances. This was different from the more stylized and formalized *commedia sostenuta*.

2. See Pierre de l'Estoile's *Mémoires-Journaux* (éd. Gustave Brunet *et al.* Paris, 1875–93), I, 189, 201–202.

I. THE SETTING

1. See Pierre de l'Estoile, *Mémoires-Journaux*, V, 32 ff. In describing the suffering of Paris in 1590, L'Estoile says: "La chair de cheval estoit si chère que les petits n'en pouvoient acheter: si qu'ils estoient contraints de chasser aux chiens et les manger." Butter had risen from four and one half to seven francs a pound. In August 1590, people were dying in the streets from hunger. Obviously, no great interest in the theatre was possible under these conditions.

2. Louis Batiffol, *Le Siècle de la Renaissance* (10th ed.), p. 327. Much of the material of this chapter, which is summative and rather general, comes from several works of Batiffol, from Lavisse, Auguste Bailly, Victor L. Tapié, and Jacques Boulenger's *Le grand Siècle* (Paris: Hachette, 10th ed., s.d.). I have had reference also to contemporary sources like Brantôme, Pierre de l'Estoile, D'Aubigné's *Histoire universelle*, the *Lettres missives* of Henry IV, the *Mémoires* of Bassompierre, the *Journal* of Jean Héroard, and the *Gazette* of Théophraste Renaudot, as well as others.

3. Jean Héroard, *Journal sur l'enfance et la jeunesse de Louis XIII, 1601–1628* (2 vols., edited by Eudore Soulié et Ed. de Barthélemy. Paris: Picot, 1868). For many of these points, see vol. I, pp. 91 ff.

4. Cardinal de Retz' *Mémoires*, second part, second chapter, contains a fine description of Richelieu, wherein the statement is made: "Il avoit assez de religion pour ce monde."

5. The "inexorable Cardinal" is a phrase of Boulenger's.

6. The Maréchal de Bassompierre, *Mémoires* (Paris: Société de

l'Histoire de France, 1870–77), I, 286: "... Mr le prince de Conty querella Mr Le comte de Soissons, son frere, parce que leurs carrosses, en passant, s'estoient choqués, et leurs carrossiers battus."

II. EARLY ACTORS AND THEIR COMPANIES

1. See Beauchamps, *Recherches sur les théâtres de France* (Paris, 1735), II, 2–3; and Emile Campardon, *Les Comédiens du roi de la troupe italienne* (Paris, 1880), *passim*, as well as Armand Baschet, *Les Comédiens italiens à la cour de France* (Paris, 1882), *passim*.

2. Pierre de l'Estoile's opinion of *I Gelosi* has been mentioned in the Introduction. For the Battista Lazzaro episode, see Eugène Rigal, *Esquisse d'une histoire des théâtres de Paris de 1548 à 1635* (Paris, 1887), 19 and Baschet, *Les Comédiens*, 89. They base their evidence on Eudore Soulié, *Recherches sur Molière et sa famille* (Paris, 1863), 153.

3. Victor Fournel, *Les Contemporains de Molière* (Paris, 1863–75), I, xxvi repeats the story of turning the Hôtel de Bourgogne into a *collège*; see Soulié, *Recherches*, 153 ff. for the Italians' difficulties with the Confrérie in 1599, and Baschet, *Les Comédiens*, 106 ff. for Tristano Martinelli.

4. Baschet, *Les Comédiens*, 122 ff.

5. For Cola, see the Héroard *Journal*, I, 346 and L'Estoile, *Mémoires-Journaux*, XI, 231; and for general details Baschet, *Les Comédiens*, 152 ff.

6. See the Héroard *Journal*, I, 421–422 and II, 62 for the episodes concerning the Dauphin Louis, and Baschet for other material mentioned here. The last quotation is from the Frères Parfaict, *Histoire du théâtre français depuis son origine jusqu'à présent* (Paris, 1745–9), III, 236: "Ceux-ci [the Italians] introduisirent des Pantomimes dans leurs pieces, en sorte qu'à l'imitation des anciens Histrions, c'etoit un mélange de récits et de gesticulations, ou de tours de souplesse: cela leur attira d'abord un fort grand concours mais l'ordre public ne pût pas les souffrir longtemps."

7. See *Félix et Thomas Platter à Montpellier* (Montpellier, 1892), 391 ff.

8. L'Estoile, *Mémoires-Journaux*, VII, 299–302.

9. This story comes from Tallemant des Réaux, *Les Historiettes* (Paris, 1932–34), I, 16.

10. See Bassompierre's *Mémoires*, I, 50, and Héroard, *Journal*, I, 382 ff.; II, 130 ff.

11. In the *Première Harangue de Midas*, Bruscambille talks about the Italians — see his *Oeuvres* (Rouen, 1626), 18. See Claude d'Esternod, *L'Espadon satyrique* (Paris, 1922), 45 and 90 for the familiar use of Arlequin, and the Sieur de Sigogne, *Les Oeuvres satyriques com-*

plètes (Paris, 1920), 316 ff. for *Les Comédiens de la Cour*. The quotation from Sorel is taken from Eugène Rigal, *Alexandre Hardy* (Paris, 1889), 108.

12. For these happenings in the provinces, see Louis de Gouvenain, *Le Théâtre à Dijon, 1422–1790* (Dijon, 1888), 36–38; Georges Lecocq, *Histoire du théâtre en Picardie depuis son origine jusqu'à la fin du XVIe siècle* (Paris, 1880), 117 ff.; Henri Tribout de Morembert, *Le Théâtre à Metz, du Moyen Âge à la Révolution* (Paris and Metz, 1952), 17. The archives of the provincial cities in France have yielded considerable information about the theatre.

13. Tribout de Morembert, *Le Théâtre à Metz*, 11 ff.; Gouvenain, *Le Théâtre à Dijon*, 39; for the performance of the mystery of John the Baptist in Bordeaux, see Jean de Gaufreteau, *Chronique bordelaise* (Bordeaux, 1876), I, 212–214, from which comes the story of the drenching of the priests: ". . . plusieurs prestres et religieux désirant voir ce baptesme, se mettoyent tout joignant les theatres, les heretiques faisoyent, avec l'argent qu'ils donnoyent, que ces belistres, qui estoyent sur le theatre, les arrosoyent abundamment avec les sceaux pleins, qui estoyent preparés pour le susdict mystere, avec une très grande mocquerie."

14. See L.-V. Gofflot, *Le Théâtre au collège du Moyen Âge à nos jours* (Paris, 1907), 31 ff. for the prohibitions of the Parlement de Paris, and *ibid.*, 62–63, for performances in Poitiers. Etienne Pasquier, who says he was there, gave a good description in his *Recherches de la France* of Jodelle's *Cléopâtre* at the Collège de Boncourt. The student presentation of Terence in Metz is told in Gofflot, *Le Théâtre*, 47 and Tribout de Morembert, *Le Théâtre à Metz*, 14.

15. For details on *Bradamante*, *Clytemnestra*, and the students in Aix, see Gofflot, *Le Théâtre*, 59 ff. — and P.-D. Lemazurier, *Galerie historique des acteurs du théâtre français depuis 1600 jusqu'à nos jours* (Paris, 1810), 7–8 for an opinion that *Bradamante* was used by the early professional actors, which idea is shared by contemporary scholars like Raymond Lebègue. The story about the "blood of Abel" is in Tallemant, *Historiettes*, II, 236.

16. See Gofflot, *Le Théâtre*, 89 ff. and Ernest Lavisse, *Histoire de France*, VI-2, 97 ff. for the Jesuits and general conditions in the schools of France at the end of the sixteenth century. The Héroard *Journal*, II, 219 and elsewhere mentions Louis XIII and the Jesuits.

17. L'Abbé d'Aubignac, *La Pratique du Théâtre* (Paris, 1927), 389–390 and Bruscambille, *Oeuvres*, 328–329. The story of the *bâteleurs* of Metz is in Tribout de Morembert, *Le Théâtre à Metz*, 14–6. The incident concerning Jean de Pontalais is found in the thirtieth *Nouvelle* of Bonaventure des Périers.

18. See E. Gosselin, *Recherches sur les origines et l'histoire du théâtre à Rouen avant Pierre Corneille* (Rouen, 1868), 41 ff. for the

story on Lepardonneur. The quoted excerpts from the Rouen archives I have taken from this work. As for more recent investigations, see Raymond Lebègue, "La Vie dramatique à Rouen de François Ier à Louis XIII," *Bull. phil. et hist.* (Paris: Imprim. Nat., 1957), 399–422.

19. See Georges Lecocq, *Histoire du théâtre*, 145 ff. and Louis de Gouvenain, *La Théâtre à Dijon*, 42 for excerpts on Amiens and Dijon; and Francisque Habasque, *Documents sur le théâtre à Agen* (Agen, 1893), 9 ff. and E. Charvet, *Recherches sur les anciens théâtres de Beauvais* (Beauvais, 1881) 30 ff. for the details on Agen and Beauvais.

20. Les Frères Parfaict, *Histoire du théâtre*, III, 329. Marcel Poète, *Une Vie de cité. Paris da sa naissance à nos jours* (3 vols. Paris, 1925–31), II, 271 tells the story of the Confrérie's stopping the farces.

21. The inventory of the papers of the Hôtel de Bourgogne is in Soulié, *Recherches*, 151 ff. It is a basic example of the rewarding information that can come from examining the archives. The bit of doggerel, which is in the *Muses gaillardes* . . . of 1609 is quoted from Rigal, *Esquisse*, 17. Tallemant, *Historiettes*, VII, 121 ff. starts his story of French actors with Agnan Sarat.

22. The Frères Parfaict, *Histoire du théâtre*, III, 235–6; the quoted remarks concerning the Hôtel de Cluny come from the sixth edition of Germain Brice's seventeenth-century *Description nouvelle de la ville de Paris* (2 vols. Paris, 1713), II, 428–429.

23. Les Frères Parfaict, *Histoire du théâtre*, III, 236 ff.

24. See Emile Campardon, *Les Spectacles de la Foire* (Paris, 1877), I, viii–x for the Courtin and Poteau privilege; and the Soulié inventory for the 1596 and 1597 documents.

25. The Soulié inventory has the two decrees concerning the company of Jehan Sehais. See the Héroard *Journal*, I, 88 ff. for the English company at Court, and J. Fransen, *Les Comédiens français en Hollande* (Paris, 1925), 11 ff. for English companies traveling over Europe; and Gosselin, *Recherches*, 64 for the English company's experience in Rouen.

26. Gaufreteau, *Chronique*, I, 306–308.

27. For this period in the life of Valleran le Conte, see Fransen, *Les Comédiens français*, 43 ff. as well as Fransen's "Documents inédits sur l'Hôtel de Bourgogne," *Rev. d'Hist. litt. de France*, XXXIV (1927), 321–323; also, K. Trautman, *Französische Schauspieler am bayrischen Hofe* (Munich, 1888) and Pantaléon Deck, *Histoire du théâtre de Strasbourg* (Strasbourg-Paris, 1948).

28. Much of the information in this section is based on the documents discovered in the archives of Paris some years ago by Madame S. Wilma Deierkauf-Holsboer and included in the Appendix of her *Vie d'Alexandre Hardy, poète du roi* (Philadelphia, 1947). H. C. Lancaster, *French Dramatic Literature of the Seventeenth Century* (Baltimore, 1929), part I, vol. I, 15 suggests that as early as 1592

Valleran le Conte's troupe may have been known as the "comédiens du Roi."

29. See the Soulié inventory and Deierkauf-Holsboer, *Alexandre Hardy*.

30. *Ibid*.

31. See Deierkauf-Holsboer, *Alexandre Hardy*, Appendix.

32. Deierkauf-Holsboer, *Alexandre Hardy* and Fransen, "Documents inédits."

33. The Deierkauf-Holsboer Appendix and Fransen, "Documents inédits," 321. I have borrowed the last quoted phrase from Madame Deierkauf-Holsboer.

34. Tallemant, *Historiettes*, VII, 121 ff. and Michel de Marolles, *Mémoires* (Amsterdam, 1755), I, 58–59.

35. See Thomas Platter le jeune, *Description de Paris* (Paris, 1896), 33 ff.

36. Tallemant, *Historiettes*, I, 27; Fransen, "Documents inédits," 331; and several excerpts from the Soulié inventory.

III. *FARCE-PLAYERS AND STREET ENTERTAINERS*

1. See D'Aubignac, *Pratique du théâtre*, book II, chs. I and X for his opinion on farces. Jean Bodin in his *Six livres de la république* (Geneva, 1629), 848 said: "Maintenant on met tousiours à la fin des tragédies (comme une poison és viandes) la farce, ou comédie." I have taken this quotation from Lancaster in the passage cited in note 3, below.

2. L'Estoile, *Mémoires-Journaux*, tome VIII, 277 ff.; Tallemant, *Historiettes*, I, 27.

3. See Frères Parfaict, *Histoire du théâtre*, IV, 254–264 for the farce and comments on it. For the *Farce de Perrine*, see Emile Magne, *Gaultier-Garguille, comédien de l'Hôtel de Bourgogne* (Paris, 1911), 184–190. Lancaster, *French Dramatic Literature*, part I, vol. I, 145 ff. discusses several of the farces of his period. Edouard Fournier published two of the *farces tabariniques* in his collection of preclassical plays in France.

4. These points are made by Bruscambille in his *En Faveur de la comédie*, 393 ff.

5. See Henri Sauval, *Histoire et recherches des antiquités de la ville de Paris* (Paris, 1724), III, 36–37.

6. *Ibid.*, 38–39.

7. See Lemazurier, *Galerie historique*, I, 29 ff. and Tallemant, *Historiettes*, VII, 121, 127.

8. *Ibid.*, VII, 17 ff., 47.

9. The Du Ryer prologue is quoted from Lancaster, *French Dramatic Literature*, I, 204. For other quotations see Sigogne, *Oeuvres*, 111 and Esternod, *L'Espadon*, 25, 39. Le Père François Garasse in his

Doctrine curieuse des beaux esprits de ce temps, ou prétendus tels (Paris, 1624), 72–73, lambastes the *farceurs* and their language. Gabriel Guéret in *Les Auteurs en belle humeur* (Amsterdam, 1723), 12–13, includes the complaint of Vergil.

10. This material has been gleaned for the most part from the Soulié *Inventaire* and the Deierkauf-Holsboer, *Alexandre Hardy*, Appendix.

11. Tallemant, *Historiettes*, VII, 126; IV, 231, for Jodelet. Théophraste Renaudot in his *Recueil des Gazettes nouvelles* (Paris, 1634), 564, tells the famous story of the transfer of the actors.

12. See the delightful *Testament de feu Gautier Garguille, trouvé depuis sa mort* (Paris, 1634) for these details and others.

13. Platter, *Description de Paris*, 34.

14. Sauval, *Histoire*, III, 37; Gautier Garguille, *Testament*, 9–10.

15. Most of these points will be found in the first volume of the *Oeuvres complètes* of Tabarin, edited by Gustave Aventin (2 vols. Paris, 1858).

16. Tabarin, *Oeuvres*, I, 41–43; II, 193 ff., for the *Farce des bossus*; and I, 8–9, for the persons to whom the book will appeal.

17. From *Les Fantaisies plaisantes et facétieuses du chappeau à Tabarin*, II, 337–338: "... nos comédiens et facessieux françois ... ont pris autant de peine que l'on pourroit imaginer de contenter de leurs rares comédies et fameux prologues ceux qui les ont assistez de leur présence. Mais je puis dire ... que le chappeau de Tabarin, assisté de celuy qui le porte, a plus fait rire de peuple en un jour que les comédiens n'en sçauroient avoir fait pleurer avec leurs feintes et regrets douloureux en six, quelque comédie, tragicomédie, pastourelle ou autre subjet qu'ils puissent jouer dans l'hostel de Bourgogne ou autres lieux semblables." Other details on Gautier Garguille, *et al.*, and the chambermaids follow on the succeeding page of this work.

18. For *Les Tromperies des charlatans*, see Tabarin, *Oeuvres*, II, 207 ff.

19. The *Discours de l'origine des moeurs fraudes et impostures des Ciarlatans . . . par* J.D.P.M.O.D.R. is in Tabarin, *Oeuvres*, II, 231 ff. I know of no further mention of Grisigoulin.

20. See Tabarin, *Oeuvres*, II, 221–224, for the *Réponse* to the doctors.

21. The *Juste Plainte de sieur Tabarin contre l'un des ministres de Charenton* is in Tabarin, *Oeuvres*, II, 471 ff.

iv. *THE ACTOR'S PROFESSION*

1. For this quotation see Bruscambille, *Oeuvres*, 332.

2. In *Sur la considération qu'on doit aux gens de lettres*, the

twenty-third of Voltaire's *Lettres Anglaises*, he speaks of the "barbare et lâche injustice" of Mademoiselle Lecouvreur's being thrown on the *voirie* when she died.

3. See Bruscambille, *Oeuvres*, 170–171 (*Des Pythagoriens*); 327 ff. (*Des Accidens comiques*); 387–394 (*En Faveur de la comédie*); 464 ff. (*En Faveur de la scène*).

4. Emile Campardon, *Les Comédiens du Roi de la troupe française pendant les derniers siècles* (Paris, 1879), 281–282, includes this *lettre patente* on Laporte's rehabilitation. The document is in the Archives Nationales in Paris.

5. Valleran was called a *bouffon* by L'Estoile, *Mémoires-Journaux*, VIII, 301. For the confusion over Valleran's name, see Peiresc's *Lettres* (Paris, 1893), IV, 135–137. Chapelain spoke of Rotrou's connection with the theatre in a letter to M. Godeau on October 30, 1632, and in one to Balzac on February 17, 1633 — see Jean Chapelain, *Lettres* (Paris, 1880), I, 6, 27. For Esternod's comment on the position of a comedian, see *L'Espadon satyrique*, 145.

6. See D'Aubignac, *Pratique du théâtre*, 25, 390–391; and Sauval, *Histoire*, III, 36–37.

7. Bellerose defends his profession in the introductory speech of Gougenot's play; Beauchâteau's statement comes from the third act of this play, p. 292 of the Fournier edition. See Gautier Garguille, *Testament*, 8, for his quip at Beauchâteau; and Chappuzeau, *Théâtre*, 88, and Brice, *Description*, II, 278, for other opinions on actors.

8. Gaufreteau, *Chronique*, I, 306–308.

9. Gautier Garguille, *Testament*, 9; La Beausoleil's defense of actresses is in Act I, scene 3 of Scudéry's play, *La Comédie des Comédiens*.

10. From Scarron, *Roman comique*, part II, ch. 1, comes the comment on actresses' *vertu*: "Ce n'est pas à dire qu'il n'y en ait de la profession qui n'en manquent point; mais dans l'opinion du monde, qui se trompe peut-être, elles en sont moins chargées que de vieilles broderies et de fard."

For the Tallemant's low opinion of actors and actresses, as well as the comment on Boisrobert, see *Historiettes*, VII, 121 and II, 245–246.

11. Tristan's letter, *A une belle comédienne en l'année 1620, expressions de pitié de sa condition*, begins: "Toute la France ne se peut lasser de vous admirer, mais, pour moi, je ne fais autre chose que vous plaindre, et de mêler secrètement des larmes aux ordinaires applaudissements que vous exigez des peuples." (Tristan l'Hermite, *Les Amours*, etc., Ad. van Bever edition, 178.)

See Lemazurier, *Galerie historique*, I, 29–32, for the remarks on Gautier Garguille's wife. Sestiane is described in the cast of characters of Scudéry's play as being "amoureuse de la comédie." Leopold

Lacour speaks of actresses being "hors classe" in his *Les premières actrices françaises* (Paris, 1921), 160.

12. La Caverne tells her story in the second part, the third chapter, of Scarron's novel.

13. Many of these contracts with apprentices are included in Deierkauf-Holsboer, *Alexandre Hardy*, Appendix; in particular, documents 9, 17, 18, 23.

14. *Ibid.*, documents 24, 25, 26, 27.

15. This discussion comes from the first scene of the first act of the Gougenot play.

16. See D'Aubignac, *Pratique du théâtre*, 389 ff.

17. Scudéry, *La Comédie des Comédiens*, Act II, scene 1.

18. Deierkauf-Holsboer, *Alexandre Hardy*, Appendix, documents 28, 30, 41.

19. *Ibid.*, 128 ff.; Gautier Garguille, *Testament*, 3, leaves to his comrades the privilege "d'amasser de l'argent pour acheter des maisons aux champs et à la ville."

20. *Ibid.*, 7; Chappuzeau, *Théâtre*, 115; Scarron, *Roman comique*, part I, ch. 5; Tallemant, *Historiettes*, VII, 125–127; Lemazurier, *Galerie historique*, II, 45–46; Les Frères Parfaict, *Histoire du théâtre*, V, 24–28. The story told about madame de Montbazon was taken, say the Frères Parfaict, from the *Mémoires* of the Cardinal de Retz.

21. See Deierkauf-Holsboer, *Alexandre Hardy*, Appendix, document 38; Elie Cottier, *Le Comédien auvergnat Montdory* (Clermont-Ferrand, 1937), *passim*; Tallemant, *Historiettes*, VII, 122–124.

22. For many of these details, see J. Fransen, *Les Comédiens français en Hollande*, 51 ff. and his "Documents inédits," 342 ff. The quotation from the duchesse de La Trémoille comes from the *Société archéologique de Nantes*, tome IX, 4e trim., 1869. For the comment on Montdory's presence in Rouen, see E. Gosselin, *Recherches* (Rouen, 1868), 70.

23. The paralysis of Montdory's tongue was referred to by many persons in the seventeenth and eighteenth centuries. The 1637 letter of Montdory to Boisrobert is in the Bibliothèque de l'Arensal in Paris, and has been carefully reproduced by Georges Mongrédien in *Les Grands Comédiens du XVIIe siécle* (Paris, 1927), 51–54.

24. See Gautier Garguille, *Testament*, II; Balzac in a letter said that Montdory added graces to "poètes vulgaires" and "le son de sa voix, accompagné de la dignité de ses gestes, annoblit les plus communes et les plus viles conceptions." Tristan said in the *Avertissement* of *Panthée* that Montdory was an "illustre acteur." Corneille praised Montdory in his *Discours de l'utilité des trois unités*. Cottier has in his book on Montdory a large collection of *éloges* given to the actor by his contemporaries. For Tallemant's opinions, see his *Historiettes*, VII, 121 ff. For later opinions, see Marolles, *Mémoires*,

235–236; Chappuzeau, *Théâtre*, 115–116, 121–122, 163; Lemazurier, *Galerie historique* I, 420 ff.; and les Frères Parfaict, *Histoire du théâtre*, IV, viii; V, 96 ff.

25. See D'Aubignac, *Pratique du théâtre*, IV, 279–281; and Gabriel Guéret, *Le Parnasse réformé* (Amsterdam, 1723), 41, 74 ff.

26. Scarron, *Roman comique*, part I, chs. 1, 2; part III, ch. 9.

27. For these points, see Gautier Garguille, *Testament*, 12; Fransen, "Documents inédits," 354; Soulié, *Inventaire*, 154; Emile Campardon, *Les Spectacles de la Foire* (Paris, 1877), I, viii-x — on the question of actors doing things which could "émouvoir le peuple à la sédition."

28. See Campardon, *Comédiens du Roi*, 279–280, for the *lettre patente* removing the actors' banishment; the document is in the Archives Nationales. For the theft of Des Oeillet's baggage, see Henri Chardon, *Nouveaux documents sur les comédiens de campagne et la vie de Molière* (Paris, 1886–1905), I, 19–21.

29. See Gautier Garguille, *Testament*, 12, for the "petites douceurs" of madame le Noir; and Théophraste Renaudot, *Recueil des Gazettes nouvelles . . . 1634* (Paris, 1635), 564, for the transfer of the actors. Tallemant mentions it briefly in *Historiettes*, VII, 124 ff.

30. These details are mentioned in Campardon, *Comédiens du Roi*, 278–279, and in Soulié, *Inventaire*, 150 ff.

31. See Soulié, *Inventaire*, and Fransen, "Documents inédits."

32. Deierkauf-Holsboer, *Alexandre Hardy*, Appendix, documents 1, 21, 29, 34, 38.

33. This scene comes from the second act of Gougenot's play.

34. Tallemant, *Historiettes*, VII, 121 ff.; Scarron, *Roman comique*, part II, ch. 3; Deierkauf-Holsboer, *Alexandre Hardy*, Appendix, documents 2, 5, 19, 34.

35. This story of Charles le Noir's wardrobe and house is told by Madame S. Wilma Deierkauf-Holsboer in *Le Théâtre du Marais* (Paris, 1954), I, 57 ff., 70. Tallemant, *Historiettes*, VII, 126 speaks of Floridor's purchase of Bellerose's clothes and position. The actresses complain in the third act of Gougenot's play of the stinginess of their husbands in the matter of clothes. Chappuzeau, *Théâtre*, 111–112, mentions the money actors spend on dress.

36. See Deierkauf-Holsboer, *Alexandre Hardy*, Appendix, document 30.

v. *THE THEATRICAL QUARTER OF PARIS*

1. Chappuzeau, *Théâtre*, 121–122 speaks of the Théâtre du Marais being in "une extrémité de Paris, et dans un endroit de rue très incommode." Beauchamps, *Recherches*, I, 93 repeats the statement: the Marais troupe had some excellent performers, but the theatre was in

"une extrémité de Paris." For all this discussion of terrain, the many plates of portions of Paris city maps will be helpful to the reader.

2. Louis Batiffol in *La Vie de Paris sous Louis XIII* (Paris, 1932), 14, speaks of the Marais quarter's being filled with "beaux hôtels habités par une quantité de noblesse et de personnages illustres." The complaint of the occupants of the rue Michel-le-Comte was cited by the Frères Parfaict, and is treated in detail in Chapter VII. Sauval, *Histeire*, I, 163 mentions the fact that the rue Vieille du Temple "passait le long d'un grand marais."

3. See Chapelain, *Lettres*, I, 131–132 for Belin and the "grands comédiens" [the Hôtel de Bourgogne] who have "regagné le dessus sur les petits" [the Marais]. Boulenger, *Le grand Siècle*, 85–86 refers to "Messieurs du Marais" and Cinq-Mars.

4. For Rotrou in the Marais quarter, see Chardon, *Nouveaux Documents*, I, 120–121; Chardon speaks of the poet's living "rue Neuve-Saint François," which would be "rue Françoise" as marked on the Rochefort map of Paris. For the details on the streets inhabited by Valleran le Conte and Alexandre Hardy, see Deierkauf-Holsboer, *Alexandre Hardy*, Appendix, documents 5, 30, 39.

5. See Henri Sauval, *La Chronique scandaleuse de Paris* (Paris, 1910), 113 for the prostitutes on the rue de la Perle. Sauval, famous for the ponderous tomes on the antiquities of Paris, is scarcely known at all for this rather brief bit of down-to-earth information. The remark of Jodelet about the size of the imagined fountain of purification in the Marais quarter comes from Tallemant, *Historiettes*, VII, 126.

6. This 1622 document on the parrot episode, taken from the *Grands jours tenus de Paris*, is quoted by Batiffol, *La Vie de Paris*, 115–116.

7. These comments on the Foire Saint Germain come from Claude Malingre, *Les Antiquités de la ville de Paris* (IV livres. Paris, 1640), livre II, 205; le sieur Dechuyes, *Le Guide de Paris* (Paris, 1656), 151–152; Germain Brice, *Description nouvelle de la ville de Paris* (2 vols. Paris, 1698), II, 244–245.

8. Sauval, *Histoire*, I, 664 gives a colorful and detailed description of the Foire Saint Germain. From this exposition I have translated the word *travée* as "section."

9. Sauval's wording on the fair's popularity is worth quoting in the original: "De jour on dirait qu'elle n'est ouverte que pour le peuple qui y vient en foule, et la nuit pour les personnes de qualité, pour les grandes dames, et pour le roi même. Les riches rues se font admirer à la clarté des lustres et des flambeaux, surtout celles des orfèvres, et tous viennent là pour jouer et se divertir; de sorte qu'alors ce lieu est moins une foire qu'un palais enchanté, où tout le beau monde se trouve assemblé, comme à un rendez-vous."

The collection of "comedians, clowns, etc." is taken from Batiffol, *La Vie de Paris*, 246.

10. For these comments, see L'Estoile, *Mémoires-Journaux*, VIII, 176; VIII, 276; XI, 231. The original of the first quatrain of the sonnet is:

C'est un plaisir quand la Foire commence:
Borgnes, bossus, farcineux sont aimés;
Lourdauds, badins et veaux sont estimés,
Et, comme aux saints, on leur fait révérence.

11. All these points may be noted in Héroard, *Journal*, 382; the *Mémoires* of Bassompierre, I, 293; II, 110–111; III, 14–15; Marolles, *Mémoires*, II, 21–22; Tallemant, *Historiettes*, III, 28; Esternod, *L'Espadon satyrique*, xlviii; Sigogne, *Oeuvres*, 256.

12. For the 1595 and 1618 companies at the Foire Saint Germain, see Campardon, *Les Spectacles de la Foire*, viii–x, xi–xii.

13. The *Gazette* of Renaudot has been previously mentioned; Madame Deierkauf-Holsboer makes extensive use of it in her *Théâtre du Marais*. The *jeu de longue paume*, just east of the Abbaye de Saint Germain, is shown on the Rochefort plan of Paris and may be seen dimly in figure 11.

14. The play, *La Foire de Saint Germain*, is mentioned by Rigal in *Alexandre Hardy*, 183 and by Lancaster, *French Dramatic Literature*, II, 621. It was described in *L'Ouverture des jours gras*, published in 1634. Mahelot's requirements for setting the play are detailed in his *Mémoire*, 100–101.

vi. *THE HÔTEL DE BOURGOGNE*

1. The term, "maison appellée vulgairement l'Hôtel de Bourgogne," seems to have been used in the early leases of the property, and appears in 1632 on a collection of papers concerning the theatre.

2. See Claude Malingre, *Les Antiquitez de la ville de Paris* (Paris, 1640), 562–563, for the dimensions of the *salle* in the Hôpital de la Trinité and the offerings of the Confrérie. In this important series of dimensions, Malingre says that the "belle grande salle" was "vingt-une toises et demy de long, et six toises de large." For the Marais theatre, see Deierkauf-Holsboer, *Le Théâtre du Marais*, the first of two volumes on the history of the Marais. For the Petit Bourbon, etc. see Germain Bapst, *Essai sur l'histoire du théâtre* (Paris, 1893), 150. The long story of the Bourgogne is told by Charles Niemeyer, "The Hôtel de Bourgogne, France's First Popular Playhouse," *The Theatre Annual*, *1947*, 64–80.

3. For the question of stools, benches, macaroons, etc. in the parterre, see Fransen, "Documents inédits," 325 ff., 342. The dimensions of the Bourgogne stage have been mentioned by Laumann, Deierkauf, and others, without citations of authority.

4. Fransen, "Documents inédits," 328–329, 342, 348. Rigal intimated that the second gallery might run around the three house walls, which idea has been copied by T. E. Lawrenson, *The French Stage in the Seventeenth Century* (Manchester, 1957), 164.

5. Platter le jeune, *Description de Paris*, 33 ff.; Beauchamps, *Recherches*, 92.

6. The maps of Paris which have been used for the Hôtel de Bourgogne are the 1676 Rochefort Plan de Paris, the 1652 Gomboust Plan de Paris, and the 1707 retouching of the 1676 Bullet Plan de Paris. If the Gomboust and Bullet plans agree on the general outline of the Hôtel de Bourgogne, it seems obvious that the Rochefort plan simply left off the ell-shaped appendage extending toward the rue Française. For a general treatment of maps of Paris, see A. Bonnardot, *Etudes archéologiques sur les anciens plans de Paris du XVIe, XVIIe et XVIIIe siècles* (Paris, 1851). The departure of the Italians as shown in the 1697 drawing is reproduced by Mme Horn-Monval in the *Revue d'histoire du théâtre*, I (1948–9), 184 ff. The Hôtel de Bourgogne in this same number is shown on a 1733 Plan de Paris, completely surrounded by other buildings.

7. For all these details, see Chappuzeau, *Théâtre*, 115–116; D'Aubignac, *Pratique du Théâtre*, 324; the Frères Parfaict, *Histoire du théâtre*, III, 224–225; François Colletet, *La Ville de Paris* (Paris, 1677), 103; Marquis de Rochegude et Maurice Dumolin, *Guide pratique à travers le vieux Paris* (Paris, 1923), 173; Michel Félibien, *Histoire de la ville de Paris* (5 vols. Paris, 1725), II, 1023–1025; Antoine de Léris, *Dictionnaire portatif des théâtres* (Paris, 1754), xiii; Poète, *Une vie de cité*, II, 267–268. Jean Lemoine in "La Première du Cid," *Revue des questions historiques* (November 1936), 131–149 and "Pièces relatives à la Première du *Cid*," *ibid.*, 207–221 concluded that there was a *grande porte* in the little building on the rue Française; the customers for the loges went through it into a courtyard and from there entered the Hôtel de Bourgogne through a door on its east side. Patrons going into the parterre used a door on the rue Mauconseil. Niemeyer agrees with Lemoine's point of view. This suggested arrangement might well have existed in the seventeenth century.

8. Chappuzeau, *Theatre*, 116; Beauchamps, *Recherches*, préface; Frères Parfaict, *Histoire du Théâtre*, III, 257.

9. The title in French of the famous brochure is *Recueil des principaux tiltres concernant l'acquisition de la propriété des masure et place où a été bastie la Maison (appellée vulgairement l'Hostel de Bourgogne), sise en cette ville de Paris ès rues de Mauconseil et neuve S. François faicte par les Doyen, Maistres et Gouverneurs de la Confrérie de la Passion. . . . Chartres et Confirmations de Rois tres-Chrestiens Charles VI, François I, Henry II, François II, Charles*

IX, Henry III, Henry IV et Louys le Iuste XIII . . . pour mon-strer que lesdits Doyen, etc. . . sont . . . vrais et legitimes acque-reurs, proprietaires et possesseurs dudit Hostel de Bourgogne, et justifier. . leur innocence. . . Alencontre des convices et calomnies theatrales de Robert Guérin, dict la Fleur, Hugues Guéru, dict Fleschelles, Henry le Grand, dict Belle-ville, Pierre Messier, dict Belleroze, et autres comediens leurs associés, soy disans Comédiens du Roy de l'Eslite Royale: accusans tres-faussement (sauf correction) lesdicts Doyen, Maistres, Gouverneurs, et confrères, d'estre usur-pateurs d'iceluy Hostel de Bourgogne (71 pages. Paris, 1632).

10. *Ibid.,* 3–30.

11. *Ibid.,* 33–41, 47–53.

12. *Ibid.,* 42–47. Soulié, *Recherches,* 151 spoke of the original tract of the Confrérie's holdings as being 17 by 15 *toises,* but earlier documents say 17 by 16 *toises.* Lancaster, *French Dramatic Literature,* like Soulié, gives the dimensions as 17 by 15 *toises.* Lemoine, quoted above, has found evidence that the Confrérie sold *four* small lots from their original tract.

13. *Recueil,* 57–59.

14. *Ibid.,* 59–63.

15. *Ibid.,* 63–66, 70. See also Fransen, "Documents inédits," 337.

16. *Recueil,* 64–66, 71.

17. *Ibid.,* 69–70. Soulié, *Recherches,* lists other instances of actors being fined for performing outside the Hôtel de Bourgogne.

18. See the Frères Parfaict, *Histoire du théâtre,* III, 258 ff. and Bapst, *Essai,* 171. I have not seen this 1631 document. Victor Fournel in his *Les Contemporains de Molière* (3 vols. Paris, 1863–75), I, xxiv-v, says that it is in the third volume of the Frères Parfaict, but it is not there.

19. For the difficulties of seeing and hearing in the Bourgogne, see Lemazurier, *Galerie historique,* 4–5. For other points, see Héroard, *Journal,* 382–384 and Chappuzeau, *Théâtre,* 112–113.

20. Brice, *Description,* 227 ff.

VII. *A JEU DE PAUME CAN BECOME A THEATRE*

1. The quotation on the terms, *jeu de paume* and *tripot,* comes from Edouard Fournier, *Notice sur le jeu de paume, son histoire et sa description* (Paris, 1862), 4. Fournier draws from the seven-teenth-century writer, Furetière, for the theory on the origin of *tripot.* Throughout the sixteenth and seventeenth centuries, the game was called the *jeu royal de la paume.*

2. See Platter le jeune, *Description de Paris,* 42; and Albert de Luze, *La magnifique histoire du jeu de paume* (Bordeaux and Paris, 1933), 118 ff. Luze's book shows him to be a great lover of the game of the palm.

3. Marolles, *Mémoires*, II, 11, speaks of the entrance to the Louvre being "dans le pinacle d'un jeu de paulme." See Fournier, *Notice*, 10–11, for the comment on Henry IV's oiling the springs of his muscles by playing court tennis; Fournier includes several quotations from Pierre de l'Estoile on Henry IV's activities in jeux de paume in 1594 and 1597. For other comments by L'Estoile on Henry IV's interest in the game, see *Mémoires-Journaux*, V, 19; VII, 120–121.

4. For the young Dauphin Louis's playing *à la paume*, see the Héroard *Journal*, I, 251. Modern devotees of jeu de paume, as illustrated at the Racquet and Tennis Club in New York, have continued all the traditions of the game.

5. In Charles Hulpeau, *Le Jeu royal de paume* (Paris, 1632) will be found all these details on the rules of the game, courtesies (no swearing), prizes, etc. For the young man's being killed in a jeu de paume, and the quarrel that led to a duel, see L'Estoile, *Mémoires-Journaux*, VIII, 16, 2. For the decline in interest in the game, see D'Aubignac, *Pratique du Théâtre*, I, 13. The tax on racquet strings is listed in Thoisy, *Recueil* (of seventeenth-century public documents), III, 86.

6. For the edict against further construction of jeux de paume in Paris, see the *Registres des déliberations du Bureau de la ville de Paris, 1598–1602*, in the *Histoire générale de Paris*, XII, 603.

7. For the sentence against Estienne Robin, see Soulié, *Recherches*, 150 ff.

8. The blueprint of the division of an area of Paris into lots and houses, as well as the report of the *censier* in the year 1757, are in the collection of documents concerning the Fief du Clos aux Bourgeois in Paris — Archives Nationales, N III, Seine 109.

9. Details on the Mestayers will be found in Auguste Vitu, *Le jeu de paume des Mestayers ou l'Illustre Théâtre, 1595–1883* (Paris, 1883).

10. See Scarron, *Roman comique*, part I, chs. 1–3; and Henri Chardon, *Nouveaux documents sur les comédiens de campagne et la vie de Molière* (2 vols. Paris, 1886–1905), I, 37, for the limitation on the number of jeux de paume in Le Mans.

11. For these points on provincial jeux de paume, see Tribout de Morembert, *Le Théâtre à Metz*, 32; Gosselin, *Recherches*, 79–81; Gouvenain, *Le Théâtre à Dijon*, 43; and Félix et Thomas Platter, *Notes de Voyage*, 391 ff. Molière used the *Braques* in Rouen in 1658; a description of it, with dimensions, is given in *Le Moliériste*, VIII, 27.

12. The Frères Parfaict, *Histoire du Théâtre*, III, 244, and Antoine de Léris in his *Dictionnaire portatif des théâtres, contenant l'origine des différents théâtres de Paris* (Paris, 1754), xvii, both

speak of the actors being in a jeu de paume on the Vieille rue du Temple, "au-dessus de l'égout."

13. Soulié, *Recherches*, 150 ff., includes the sentence against Charles le Noir and company for performing in the Jeu de Paume de Berthault instead of the Hôtel de Bourgogne. Madame Deierkauf-Holsboer in assembling material for *Le Théâtre du Marais* found in the Archives Nationales evidence of the contract on the Jeu de Paume de la Sphère. Some details on the Sphère have been taken from her study. The Frères Parfaict, *Histoire du Théâtre*, V, 49 ff. speak of the actors' presence in the Jeu de Paume de la Fontaine, and include an official paper concerning dramatic activities in la Fontaine. Madame Deierkauf-Holsboer used this document to indicate that the Montdory company was occupying the Jeu de Paume de la Fontaine in March 1632. The paper is dated, however, March 22, 1633. In the Appendix of her book, Madame Deierkauf-Holsboer has included the deed of sale of the Jeu de Paume du Marais on October 26, 1633. This is a most valuable piece of information, and some excerpts have been taken from it.

14. See Deierkauf-Holsboer, *Le Théâtre du Marais*, I, 152–155.

15. *Ibid.*, 25 ff.

16. The fire at the Théâtre du Marais was described by Olivier Lefèvre d'Ormesson, *Journal* (2 vols. Paris, 1861), I, 138.

17. The indefatigable Madame Deierkauf-Holsboer tells at length the story of the reconstructed Marais in *Le Théâtre du Marais*, I, 98 ff. In the Appendix is printed the master builder's *mémoire* of specifications employed in the erection of the new Marais. On the basis of this listing, Madame Deierkauf-Holsboer, with the assistance of some professional architects, has drawn a blueprint of the new building to scale, and also made a sketch of what it must have looked like.

18. *Ibid.*, 100 ff.

19. For a remark on Beauchâteau and the game of the palm, see Gautier Garguille, *Testament*, 8; for the *jeu royal de paume*, its halls, and its players later in the century, see Abraham du Pradel (Nicolas de Blegny, his real name), *Le Livre commode des adresses de Paris pour 1692* (2 vols. Paris, 1878), 260, 274. The statement that players of jeu de paume advertise "comme les comédiens" is attributed to Dangeau.

VIII. *THE STAGE IS SET*

1. See E. M. Laumann, *La Machinerie au théâtre depuis les Grecs jusqu'à nos jours* (Paris, 1898), 42. Laumann's work is inclusive of too many phases of theatrical history to treat any one of them in detail. Professor H. C. Lancaster's critical edition of the Mahelot memoir — *Le Mémoire de Mahelot, Laurent et d'autres décorateurs*

de l'Hôtel de Bourgogne (Paris, 1920) — has long been of great value to those interested in the seventeenth-century French stage.

2. The quotation is taken from the Lancaster edition of the Mahelot *Mémoire*, page 73; Laumann's ideas are on page 42 of *La Machinerie*.

3. For these details, see Deierkauf-Holsboer, *Le Théâtre du Marais*, I, 108–110; Vitu, *Le Jeu de Paume des Mestayers*, 42–43; Henri Clouzot, *L'ancien théâtre de Poitou* (Niort, 1901), 333 — for the theatre at Fontenay-le-comte, which is considered in Lancaster, *French Dramatic Literature*, part I, II, 712 ff. Madame S. Wilma Deierkauf-Holsboer, *Histoire de la mise en scène en France de 1600 à 1657* (Paris, 1933), 109, reverses the Laumann estimated dimensions of the Bourgogne stage and makes it "7 mètres de long, sur 5 mètres de large."

4. See Fransen, "Documents inédits," 341, and H. Liebrecht, *Histoire du théâtre à Bruxelles* (Paris, 1923), 38.

5. For these matters, see Deierkauf-Holsboer, *Le Théâtre du Marais*, I, 108–110.

6. *Ibid.;* and Soulié, *Recherches*, 150–151.

7. See Charles Perrault, *Parallèle des anciens et des modernes*, III, 191 (Paris, 1692): ". . . le théâtre fut orné de tapisseries qui donnaient des entrées et des issues aux acteurs par l'endroit où elles se joignaient l'une à l'autre. Ces entrées et sorties étaient fort incommodes et mettaient souvent en désordre les coiffures des comédiens"; Lemazurier, *Galerie historique*, 4 and Bapst *Essai*, 144–145. Troterel's *Les Corrivaux* is in Viollet-le-Duc, *Ancien théâtre français*, VIII, 227–292.

8. The miniature of the stage set of the Passion of Valenciennes has been reproduced many times in various histories of French medieval dramatic literature. It is also in the Bédier and Hazard general history of French literature.

9. See Mahelot, *Mémoire*, 67–68.

10. These agreements are to be found in Deierkauf-Holsboer, *Alexandre Hardy*, Appendix, documents 10, 12, 19, 20; and Fransen, "Documents inédits," 344.

11. *Ibid.*, 349; and Gautier Garguille, *Testament*, 10.

12. See D'Aubignac, *Pratique du théâtre*, 104, 107, for an objection to the *Pyrame et Thisbé* wall, and to the Louvre and the Palais Royal being on the same stage set. Jean Chapelain used the figure of "deux temps et deux lieux" in a picture in his *Lettre sur la règle des vingt-quatre heures* — to oppose the violation of the unity of place.

13. Montdory's famous letter to Balzac has been carefully reproduced in Georges Mongrédien's *Le grands Comédiens au XVIIe siècle* (Paris, 1927), 45–47. I have borrowed from this copy.

14. D'Aubignac, *Pratique du théâtre*, 106: ". . . le théâtre ne

devrait jamais être vide ni jamais les acteurs ne devraient disparaître
. . . on devrait toujours voir les acteurs." I have modernized the
spelling in D'Aubignac's treatise.

15. The question of the curtain used with ballets is taken up by
Henry Prunières, *Le Ballet de cour en France avant Benserade et
Lully* (Paris, 1914), 156. Niccolò Sabbattini's *Pratica di fabricar
scene e machine ne' teatri* came out in Ravenna in 1638; his discussion of the curtain is in chapter XXXVII of the first book. Serlio's
earlier study of stage sets had been translated from Italian into
French by 1545. Mahelot needed a "night" for Du Ryer's *Lisandre
et Caliste* — see his *Mémoire*, 68. Jean Lemoine, "La Première du
Cid," 218–220, examined the document concerning the repairs to the
Hôtel de Bourgogne in 1647. Georges Védier in his *Origine et
évolution de la dramaturgie néo-classique* (Paris, 1955) took up the
general question of the front curtain.

16. For the quotation, see Perrault, *Parallèle*, III, 192.

17. Sabbattini, *Pratica di fabricar*, book I, chs. XXXVIII, XXXIX;
Fransen, *Les Comédiens français*, 329; Deierkauf-Holsboer, *Alexandre Hardy*, Appendix, document 14.

18. This advice on the staging of *Bradamante* and the placing of
the musicians is in Les Frères Parfaict, *Histoire du Théâtre*, III, 454–
455, footnote. Pujade's *Jacob* is discussed in Lancaster E. Dabney's
French Dramatic Literature in the Reign of Henri IV (Austin, Texas,
1952), 16–17.

19. Deierkauf-Holsboer, *Alexandre Hardy*, Appendix, documents
5, 22, 31, 38; Perrault, *Parallèle*, III, 192; Tallemant, *Les Historiettes*,
VI, 162. For the poverty-stricken theatre of earlier days, see D'Aubignac, *Pratique du Théâtre*, 15, 393 ff. For the opinion on the proper
settings for comedies, see Marolles, *Mémoires*, I, 133 ff.

IX. THE AUDIENCE

1. See the Frères Parfaict, *Histoire du théâtre*, III, 237–238, where
is cited a portion of the *Remonstrances très-humbles au Roy de
France et de Pologne, Henry III de nom*. In this pamphlet of 1588
is mentioned "une cloaque et maison de Satan, nommée l'Hôtel de
Bourgogne."

2. For these points, see Beauchamps, *Recherches*, I, 92; II, 6–7;
Soulié, *Recherches*, 151 ff.; Platter, *Description de Paris*, 33 ff.

3. See Tallemant, *Historiettes*, VII, 122; l'Abbé d'Aubignac, *Dissertation sur la condamnation des théâtres* (Paris, 1666), 243, for
ladies wearing masks at the theatre; L'Estoile, *Mémoires-Journaux*,
VIII, 271 ff., for Henry IV and retinue at the farce.

4. Pierre Martino, in his edition of D'Aubignac's *Pratique du*

théâtre, p. ii, speaks of ladies and gentlemen around 1620 having a "goût de la crapule"; for the *Avertissement au lecteur* and the *Prologue* of Troterel's *Les Corrivaux*, see Viollet-le-Duc's *Ancien théâtre français*, VIII, 277 ff.; Bruscambille's prologue addressed to "mesdames" is in his *Oeuvres*, 484–488.

5. Gaufreteau, *Chronique*, II, 204.

6. Mairet, in his dedicatory epistle to *Les Galanteries du duc d'Ossone*, says: "les plus honnêtes femmes fréquentent maintenant l'Hôtel de Bourgogne avec aussi peu de scrupule et de scandale qu'elles feraient celui du Luxembourg." The lady's defense of her husband in the Scudéry play comes from the third scene of the first act. Véroneau's *Impuissance*, with the references to specific details on the husband's impotence, is in the *Ancien théâtre français*, VIII, 297–392. Discret's *Alizon* is in the same collection, VIII, 393–495; in this play the old soldier, looking for his lady, says:

> *Tantôt un président l'emmène promener,*
> *Tantôt un conseiller vient chez elle dîner;*
> *Souvent elle est au cours ou à la comédie.* (p. 407)

The little story about Ninon de l'Enclos is in Tallemant, *Historiettes*, VI, 12.

7. Lemazurier, *Galerie historique*, I, 5; D'Aubignac, *Pratique du théâtre*, 36–39.

8. See Bruscambille, *Oeuvres*, 70–75; the rapid patter comes from his *Prologue sur un habit* (135 ff.), a portion of which might be worth citing in the original: "Messieurs et Dames, je désirerais, souhaiterais, voudrais, demanderais, et requerrais désidérativement, souhaitativement, volontativement, demandativement, et requisitativement avec les désidératoires, souhaitatoires, volontatoires, demandatoires, et requisatoires, que vous fussiez enluminés," etc. A similar piece of banter, in mixed French and Latin, is the prologue of Adrien de Montluc's *La Comédie de proverbes*, which dates from 1616 (pp. 192–227 of the Fournier collection of sixteenth" and seventeenth-century French plays). It is addressed to "Messieurs les auditeurs" and to "Mesdames les auditrices."

9. Soulié, *Recherches*, 151 ff.; Gautier Garguille, *Testament*, 12.

10. For the wounding of the actor Laroque, see Deierkauf-Holsboer, *Le Théâtre du Marais*, I, 77–78, where she tells the full story from the Archives Nationales. The episode on Battistino is from the correspondence of the Duke of Mantua — see Baschet, *Les Comédiens italiens*, 169–170. For the other disorders, see D'Aubignac, *Pratique du théâtre*, 393–4.

11. Tallemant, *Historiettes*, VII, 128.

12. This document concerning the troubles around the Jeu de Paume de la Fontaine can be found in the Frères Parfaict, *Histoire du théâtre*, V, 50–51.

13. The 1609 edict is quoted by Michel Félibien, *Histoire de la ville de Paris* (5 vols. in fol. Paris, 1725), II, 1025. It is repeated by both Beauchamps and Lemazurier. For other details, see Soulié, *Recherches*, 151 ff.; the Frères Parfaict, *Histoire du théâtre*, III, 233, for the 1572 decree; Fransen, "Documents inédits," 348, for the "heures licites et accoutumées."

14. See Héroard, *Journal*, I, 382, 384; II, 78. John Lough in the first chapter of *Paris Theatre Audiences in the 17th and 18th Centuries* (London, 1957), mentions many other instances of the Dauphin Louis' visiting the Hôtel de Bourgogne, based upon unpublished sections of the Héroard diary in the Paris manuscript. All of these examples show, too, that young Louis returned home around six-thirty in the evening; but it does not seem to occur to Lough that these must have been private performances for the royal court. The quotation concerning the play's beginning at five o'clock comes from Scudéry's *La Comédie des Comédiens*, act I, scene 3.

15. *Ibid.*, act I, scenes 1, 2.

16. The *Lygdamon et Lydias* poster is in the Bibliothèque de l'Arsenal, in Paris. For other details, see Deierkauf-Holsboer, *Alexandre Hardy*, Appendix, document 5; Marolles, *Mémoires*, II, 25, 67; Chappuzeau, *Théâtre*, 139 ff.

17. Deierkauf-Holsboer, *Alexandre Hardy*, Appendix, document 14.

18. Scudéry, *Comédie des Comédiens*, act I, scene 1, and *passim*; Guéret, *Les Auteurs*, 23. V. Fournel in his *Curiosités théâtrales* (Paris, 1878), 159–60, relates several stories of the dangers to life and limb endured by *portiers* during the seventeenth century.

19. See Bruscambille, *Oeuvres*, 18, and Gautier Garguille, *Testament*, 5; Fransen, "Documents inédits," 330, for the free performance on Mardi gras. For the "surplus de deniers," see the *Registres . . . de la ville de Paris*, XIV, 41.

20. Fransen, "Documents inédits," 325; Soulié, *Recherches*, 151 ff.; Rigal, *Alexandre Hardy*, 105, for details on the shops "au-dessous du théâtre." Most of the information on the annual leases of the Hôtel de Bourgogne is in Soulié.

21. For the pleasant hours in the theatre, see D'Aubignac, *Pratique du théâtre*, 10. The agreement to play three times a week "au moins" is in Deierkauf-Holsboer, *Alexandre Hardy*, Appendix, document 35. For other details, see Chappuzeau, *Théâtre*, 70, and Abraham du Pradel, *Le Livre commode des adresses de Paris pour 1692* (2 vols. Paris, 1878), I, 270.

22. Chappuzeau, *Théâtre*, 151–152.

23. See Gougenot's *La Comédie de Comédiens*, the introductory speech of Bellerose; Beauchamps, *Recherches*, II, 6–7. Desmarets de

Saint Sorlin's opening lines of *Les Visionnaires* show his opinions of the rabble; he even quotes some verses, which he does not identify:

Ce n'est pour toi que j'écris (sic),
Indocte et stupide vulgaire:
J'écris pour les nobles esprits,
Je serais marri de te plaire.

For Tristan's remarks on the merchants of Saint-Denis, see Guéret, *Les Auteurs*, 39 ff. These bourgeois are not to be trusted in their judgments on the dramatic poets producing for the Hôtel de Bourgogne, says Tristan.

x. COURT AND PRIVATE ENTERTAINMENTS

1. For the effect of gambling on all classes, see Emile Magne, *Scarron et son milieu* (Paris, 1905), 44, from which the quotation has been taken. The comment on Henry IV's winning at dice comes from L'Estoile, *Mémoires-Journaux*, VII, 83.

2. Sec Bassompierre, *Mémoires*, I, 200, 214, 218; II, 110–111; L'Estoile, *Mémoires-Journaux*, IX, 241–242; Tallemant, *Historiettes*, III, 23, for Voiture.

3. D'Aubignac, *Pratique du théâtre*, 14 speaks of the "magnificence" of the seventeenth-century ballet when compared to the dancing routines of the ancients. Sauval, *Histoire*, II, 209–210 describes the salle du Petit-Bourbon.

4. See L. C. Dabney, *French Dramatic Literature in the Reign of Henri IV* (Austin, 1952), 339 ff.; and Bassompierre, *Mémoires*, I, 196, 269.

5. For these ballets and the complications attached to them see L'Estoile, *Mémoires-Journaux*, VIII, 4, 111; IX, 215; Tallemant, *Historiettes*, III, 10.

6. Marolles, *Mémoires*, II, 167 ff.; Sigogne, *Oeuvres*, 287.

7. For Louis XIII's dancing in ballets, see Tallemant, *Historiettes*, II, 148–149. Héroard, *Journal*, I, 392 ff. describes fully the representation of *Bradamante* at Fontainebleau. Gustave Lanson thought this production was a ballet — see his "Etudes sur les origines de la tragédie classique en France," *Revue d'histoire littéraire de la France*, X (1903), 223.

8. See Marolles, *Mémoires*, I, 51, for the masks thrown out the window. For the ballets concerning the history of France and the American Indian, see Henri Bouchot, *Catalogue de dessins relatifs à l'histoire du théâtre conservés au départment des Estampes de la Bibliothèque Nationale* (Paris, 1896). For the other comments, including the "machine representant la musique en gros," see Marolles, *Mémoires*, 114–116, 132, and Bassompierre, *Mémoires*, III, 14–15.

9. C. Lemaire, *Paris ancien et nouveau* (3 vols. Paris, 1685), III,

210 comments on the hall for comedies in the Arsenal. For other de-
details, see Tallemant, *Historiettes*, I, 95–96, 250–251, and Renaudot,
Recueil, 1634, 32.

10. Fransen, *Les Comédiens français*, 34 ff. mentions the "théâtre
de société" in Europe, and the little Dutch princess' learning by heart
Corneille's *Médée*. The details on Louis XIII will be found in Héroard,
Journal, I, 392 ff.; II, 71 ff. See Bassompierre, *Mémoires*, I, 196 for the
performance at the home of the marquis de Coeuvres.

11. For the comments on Gaston d'Orléans, Gros Guillaume, and
Gautier Garguille, see Magne, *Gaultier-Garguille*, 48–49, 78. Magne
quotes Bruscambille's statement to the effect that Gautier Garguille
used to "frotter l'échine aux piliers du Louvre." For other points, see
Bassompierre, *Mémoires*, I, 336, 341; Renaudot, *Recueil, 1634*, 48.

12. *Ibid.*, 525–528. A portion of Renaudot's description of this
spectacle (in his unmodernized French) might be of interest: "La
Reine ne fut pas plustost assise sur le haut dais qui luy estoit préparé
à dix pas du théâtre (dont la lumière artificielle éclairoit et faisoit
voir à nud toute la scène, sans estre elle mesme vue) que la troupe
de Mondori, qui fut choisie en cette occurrence pour donner du plaisir
à Sa Majesté, commança par ces trois entrées qu'ils ne voulurent nom-
mer que boufonneries: encor qu'elles meritassent bien le nom de
ballets."

13. This story is told by Tallemant, *Historiettes*, VI, 66–67.

14. Marolles, *Mémoires*, I, 235–236; Tallemant, *Historiettes*, V, 17
ff.

15. Bassompierre, *Mémoires*, I, 50; III, 158; Scarron, *Roman comique*, part I, chs. 20, 21, and part II, ch. 3, where the actors
were presenting for the baron de Sigognac "Roger et Bradamante,
du poète Garnier." A page had been called into service to recite two
lines in the play:

> *Monsieur, rentrons dedans; je crains que vous tombiez:*
> *Vous n'êtes pas trop bien assuré sur vos pieds.*

The "sot de page" said *jambes* for *pieds*, and everybody laughed.

16. See Dabney, *French Dramatic Literature*, 372 ff. for a sum-
mary of, and excerpts from, this pastoral.

17. L'Estoile, *Mémoires-Journaux*, IX, 392, for Henry IV and the
cow; Tallemant, *Historiettes*, VII, 122 ff.

xi. *TYPES OF PLAYS*

1. See the Frères Parfaict, *Histoire du théâtre*, III, 228, for "les
barbarismes de Ronsard" and "le style enflé de Sénèque." The Frères
Parfaict, despite their many errors on the dating of plays, are not
without critical judgment.

2. For all these details on terminology, see Gofflot, *Théâtre au*

collège, 62–63, 91; Gosselin, *Recherches*, 41–44; Lecocq, *Histoire du théâtre*, 146; Habasque, *Documents*, 9–11; Gaufreteau, *Chronique*, 306.

3. See Holsboer-Deierkauf, *Alexandre Hardy*, Appendix, documents 5, 7, 12, 24, 37; Fransen, *Les Comédiens français*, 51, 71, and "Documents inédits," 321–323, 328; Gautier Garguille, *Testament*, 3–6.

4. For these theories concerning Garnier and the performance of his plays, see the Frères Parfaict, *Histoire du théâtre*, III, 454 ff.; Lemazurier, *Galerie historique*, I, 7–8; Bapst, *Essai sur l'histoire*, 142–143 (for "les honneurs du théâtre"), and Eugène Rigal, *Le Théâtre français avant la période classique*, (Paris, 1901), *passim*; Scarron, *Roman comique*, part II, ch. III. Raymond Lebègue of the Sorbonne, the best scholar today in the field of the French theatre of the Renaissance, assembled a great deal of material on the repertory of Adrien Talmy in his article, "Le Répertoire d'une troupe française à la fin du XVIe siècle," *Revue d'histoire du théâtre*, I (1948), 9–24. Lebègue in this treatise pays homage to the Belgian archivist, Verriest.

5. Beauchamps, *Recherches*, II, 61 ff. Beauchamps may have taken from the Abbé de Marolles the figure of around 800 plays attributed to Hardy; Marolles is cited below in note 6. Eugène Rigal has devoted a large tome, *Alexandre Hardy* (Paris, 1889), to the life and works of the dramatist. Here he first stated that Garnier was not performed professionally. Lancaster added some information on Hardy in his *French Dramatic Literature*, part I, 1610–1634; and Madame Deierskauf-Holsboer's *Alexandre Hardy* has provided further documentation. Hardy's *Théagène et Chariclée*, a dramatized version of a Greek romance, was called an *histoire profane*.

6. See D'Aubignac, *Pratique du théâtre*, 117, where it is said of Hardy that "ce fut lui sans doute qui tout d'un coup arrêta le progrès du théâtre." Scarron, *Roman comique*, part I, ch. 5, speaks of being "réduit aux pièces de Hardy." For other details, see Marolles, *Mémoires*, II, 241; Tallemant, *Historiettes*, II, 218, note; the Frères Parfaict, *Histoire du théâtre*, IV, preface and ff.

7. The Frères Parfaict, *Histoire du théâtre*, IV, 18: ". . . il [Hardy] a introduit l'usage de recevoir de l'argent de ses pièces, usage inconnu avant lui." For other points, see Deierkauf-Holsboer's *Alexandre Hardy*, 337, and her *Le Théâtre du Marais*, I, 64; also, the Appendix, documents 35, 42.

8. These figures have been taken from Dabney, *French Dramatic Literature*, and from Lancaster's *French Dramatic Literature*. Raymond Lebègue's count of tragedies was made in his "Tableau de la tragédie française de 1573 à 1610," *Bibliothèque d'Humanisme et Renaissance*, V, 373–393. Troterel's estimate of "mille tragédies" was

cited by Lanson, "Etudes sur les origines," *RHLF*, X (1903), 177–231, 413–436.

10. For many of these details, see Lancaster, *French Dramatic Literature*.

10. D'Aubignac, *Pratique du théâtre*, 74–75.

11. D'Aubignac, *Pratique du théâtre*, 25 speaks of "la rigueur des règles," which "rebuterait les petits auteurs, et retarderait de beaucoup le travail des autres." For the opinion of the counselor from Rennes on the rules in drama, see Scarron, *Roman comique*, part I, ch. 21. Racine said in a perface to *Bérénice* that the primary aim of a tragedy is "de plaire et de toucher," and all other rules are subordinate to this dual purpose.

12. See Garasse, *Doctrine curieuse*, 72; Scarron, *Roman comique*, part II, ch. 2; and for the gruesome tragedies, see further details in Lancaster, *French Dramatic Literature*, ch. III.

13. For the quotations from Fontenelle on Corneille, see the Frères Parfaict, *Histoire du théâtre*, IV, 9, 546.

14. Chappuzeau, *Théâtre*, 69 said that the winter season is the time for "pièces héroiques." Bruscambille, *Oeuvres*, 478 ff. in his prologue "Pour Pastoralles" made a defense of the speech of shepherds on stage, saying that love preferred an *houlette* to a *sceptre*. D'Aubignac, *Pratique du théâtre*, said spectacles should be useful and give to the people "quelque teinture des vertus morales."

XII. RICHELIEU AND REFORM

1. Chappuzeau, *Théâtre*, 26 spoke of "le grand Cardinal de Richelieu, un des plus éclairés de tous les hommes," who honored writers and favored "la comédie."

2. All these theatrical events in the Cardinal's *hôtel* or palace were chronicled by Théophraste Renaudot in his weekly *Gazette*, the beginning of what might be called journalistic writing in France. Richelieu controlled the publication. Léopold Lacour in his *Richelieu dramaturge* (Paris, 1926) has told the story of the Cardinal's dramatic productions.

3. See Sauval, *Histoire*, II, 161. The long passage begins: "Chacun sait la passion que le Cardinal de Richelieu avait pour la comédie." Full details are given by Sauval on the structure of the large theatre in the Palais Cardinal. Louis Batiffol, *Richelieu et Corneille* (Paris, 1936), 11 ff. has added further information on the Cardinal's large hall from a plan in the Cabinet des Estampes at the Bibliothèque Nationale.

4. Lacour, *Richelieu*, 108 ff. has told the story of *Mirame* and has offered a theory that it symbolized a reconciliation between Richelieu and the Queen, Anne of Austria. See Marolles, *Mémoires*, I, 236–237

for his opinions on the machines and his theories on drama. For Tallemant's ideas on *Mirame*, see *Historiettes*, I, 10; Sauval in the passage cited above speaks of the vast roof of Richelieu's theatre being supported by the tallest timbers in France.

5. Sauval, *Histoire*, II, 161 said that the little hall was for plays that "les comédiens représentaient ordinairement au Marais du Temple." For Gaston d'Orléans' visit to the Cardinal's town house, see Renaudot, *Recueil*, *1634*, 572; for details on "la petite Pascal," see Tallemant, *Historiettes*, V, 78–79.

6. Batiffol, *Richelieu*, has minimized the hostility of Richelieu for Corneille. For the performance of *Le Cid* by the lackeys and kitchen boys, see Tallemant, *Historiettes*, II, 244.

7. For these points, see Tallemant, *Historiettes*, II, 240; the Frères Parfaict, *Histoire du théâtre*, IV, 341; Lacour, *Richelieu*, 20, 84; Batiffol, *Richelieu*, 13.

8. Mongrédien, *Les grands Comédiens*, 51 ff. quotes in full this letter of Montdory to Boisrobert. For other details, see Batiffol, *Richelieu*, 18; the Frères Parfaict, *Histoire du théâtre*, V, 96 ff.; Tallemant, *Historiettes*, VII, 125–126.

9. Emile Magne in his *Le plaisant abbé de Boisrobert, fondateur de l'Académie Française, 1592–1662* (Paris, 1919) gives a good treatment to Richelieu's favorite. For the stories on Gombaud and Desmarets de Saint Sorlin, see Tallemant, *Historiettes*, II, 50 ff.; for the material on Boisrobert, see the Frères Parfaict, *Histoire du théâtre*, V, 10 ff. and Tallemant, *Historiettes*, II, 244 ff.

10. See Chapelain, *Lettres*, I, 131–132, 133–135; Tallemant, *Historiettes*, VII, 123, said: "Le comte de Belin, pour mettre cette troupe en réputation, pria Mme de Rambouillet de souffrir qu'ils jouassent chez elle la *Virginie* de Mairet. Le cardinal de la Vallette y était, qui fut si satisfait de Montdory qu'il lui donna pension."

11. Tallemant, *Historiettes*, VII, 37–38; for the reading of *Polyeucte*, see the Frères Parfaict, *Histoire du théâtre*, VI, 124 ff.

12. In *L'Illusion comique*, Act V, scene 5, is the statement:
... *A présent le théâtre*
Est en un point si haut que chacun l'idolâtre.
For other details, see Chapelain, *Lettres*, I, 89–90; Molé, *Mémoires*, II, 292; Chappuzeau, *Théâtre*, 9; Scarron, *Roman comique*, part 2, ch. 8. A defense of the parterre was made by Sorel in *Maison des jeux*; the Frères Parfaict quote this passage from him, *Histoire du théâtre*, VI, 128 ff.

13. Tallemant, *Historiettes*, VII, 122; Tabarin, *Oeuvres complètes*, II, 447–448; Renaudot, *Recueil*, *1634*, 40, 55; Campardon, *Les Comédiens*, 123–124, for the marriage contract.

14. This famous decree was reproduced by the Frères Parfaict, *Histoire du théâtre*, VI, 131–134.

15. Chappuzeau, *Théâtre*, 152 said very optimistically: ". . . mais tout va en ce monde de bien en mieux, et de quelque côté que l'on tourne, Paris ne fut jamais si beau, ni si pompeux qu'il est aujourd'hui." For Marolles's opinions of the city, see *Mémoires*, II, 10–11. It is from this passage that come the prophetic words, "il y a apparence que dans un siècle d'ici, Paris sera la plus belle chose du monde."

BIBLIOGRAPHY

(This is a selected bibliography of material referred to either in the main body of the book or in the notes.)

Aubignac, Abbé d'. *Dissertation sur la condamnation des théâtres.* Paris: Chez N. Pepingue, 1666. pp. 250.

—— *La Pratique du théâtre* . . . . éd. par Pierre Martino. Alger-Paris: Carbonel et Champion, 1927. pp. xxx, 439.

Auerbach, Erich. *Vier Untersuchungen zur Geschichte der Französischen Bildung.* Bern: A. Francke ag Verlag, 1951. pp. 127.

Bapst, Germain. *Essai sur l'histoire du théâtre.* Paris, 1893. pp. 693.

Baschet, Armand. *Les Comédiens italiens à la cour de France sous Charles IX, Henri III, Henri IV et Louis XIII.* Paris: Plon, 1882. pp. 367.

Bassompierre, Maréchal de. *Mémoires (Journal de ma vie).* 4 vols. Paris: Société de l'Histoire de France, 1870–1877.

Batiffol, Louis. *Richelieu et Corneille.* Paris: Calmann-Lévy, 1936. pp. 197.

—— *Le Siècle de la Renaissance.* 10th edition. Paris: Hachette, n.d. pp. 368.

—— *La Vie de Paris sous Louis XIII.* Paris: Calmann-Lévy, 1932. pp. 252.

Beauchamps, P.-F. Godard de. *Recherches sur les théâtres de France depuis l'année onze cents soixante-un, jusques à présent.* 3 vols. bound in one. Paris, 1735.

Bonnardot, A. *Etudes archéologiques sur les anciens plans de Paris des XVIe, XVIIe et XVIIIe siècles.* Paris: Deflorenne, 1851. pp. 253.

Bonnassies, Jules. *La Comédie française. Notice historique sur les anciens bâtiments.* Paris: Aubry, 1868. pp. 32.

Bouchot, Henri. *Catalogue de dessins relatifs à l'histoire du théâtre conservés au département des Estampes de la Bibliothèque Nationale.* Paris: Bouillon, 1896. pp. 82.

Boulenger, Jacques. *Le grand Siècle.* 10th edition, revised. Paris: Hachette, n.d. pp. 426.

Brice, Germain. *Description nouvelle de la ville de Paris.* 2 vols. Paris: Nicolas le Gras, 1698. pp. 402, 381 plus tables.

Bruscambille (Des Lauriers). *Les Oeuvres de Bruscambille, contenant ses Fantaisies, Imaginations et Paradoxes, et autres discours comique* (sic). Rouen: Martin de la Motte, 1626. pp. 468.

Campardon, Emile. *Les Comédiens du Roi de la troupe française pendant les derniers siècles.* Documents inédits recueillis aux Archives Nationales. Paris: H. Champion, 1879. pp. 336.

Chapelain, Jean. *Lettres.* . . . publiées par Tamizey de Larroque. 2 vols. Collection des Documents Inédits sur l'Histoire de France. Paris: Imprimerie Nationale, 1880–1883.

Chappuzeau. *Le Théâtre français*, accompagné d'une préface et de notes par Georges Monval. Paris: Jules Bonnassies, 1876. pp. 183.

Chardon, Henri. *La Troupe du Roman comique dévoilée et les comédiens de campagne au XVIIe siècle*. Le Mans: Monnoyer, 1876. pp. 171.

Charvet, E. *Recherches sur les anciens théâtres de Beauvais*. Beauvais: Imprimerie D. Père, 1881. pp. 189.

Colletet, François. *La Ville de Paris*. Paris: Antoine de Raffle, 1677. pp. 183.

Cottier, Elie. *Le Comédien auvergnat Montdory*, Clermont-Ferrand: Imprimeries Mont Louis, 1937. pp. 265.

Dabney, Lancaster E. *French Dramatic Literature in the Reign of Henri IV*. A Study of the Extant Plays Composed in French between 1589 and 1610. Austin (Texas): The University Cooperative Society, 1952. pp. 472.

Dechuyes, Le Sieur. *Le Guide de Paris*. Paris: Jean Prome, 1656. pp. 191.

(Deierkauf)-Holsboer, S. Wilma. *L'Histoire de la mise en scène dans le théâtre français de 1600 à 1657*. Paris: E. Droz, 1933. pp. 335.

Deierkauf-Holsboer, S. Wilma. "Vie d'Alexandre Hardy, poète du roi." *Proceedings of the American Philosophical Society*, vol. 91 (1947), pp. 328–404.

——— *Le Théâtre du Marais*. 2 vols. Tome I, La Période de gloire et fortune, 1634–1648. Paris: Nizet, 1954; Tome II, Le Berceau de l'Opéra et de la Comédie Française, 1648–1675. Paris: Nizet, 1958.

Desmarets de Saint Sorlin. *Mirame*. Paris: Chez Henri le Gras, 1641. pp. 100, in-fol.

——— "Les Visionnaires," in *Le Théâtre français au XVIe et au XVIIe siècles*, éd. par Edouard Fournier, pp. 430–457.

Discret, L.-C. "Alizon," comédie, in Viollet-le-Duc's *Ancien théâtre français*, VIII, 393–495.

Dulaure, J.-A. *Histoire civile, physique et morale de Paris*. 10 vols. plus atlas. 3rd edition. Paris: Baudouin Frères, 1825–1826.

Du Pradel, Abraham (Nicolas de Blegny). *Le Livre commode des adresses de Paris pour 1692*. . . . éd. par Edouard Fournier. 2 vols. Paris: Daffis, 1878. pp. 321, 399.

Esternod, Claude d'. *L'Espadon satyrique*, édition critique, d'après l'édition originale de 1619 . . . par Fernand Fleuret et Louis Perceau. Paris: Librairie de Bon Vieux Temps, 1922. pp. 225.

Félibien, Michel. *Histoire de la ville de Paris*. 5 vols., in-fol. Paris: Desprez et Desessarts, 1725.

Fontenelle, Bernard de. "Vie de Pierre Corneille," pp. 1–50 in *Chefs-d'oeuvre de P. Corneille*. Paris: Petite Bibliothèque du Théâtre, 1785.

Fournel, Victor. *Les Spectacles populaires et les artistes des rues.* Paris: E. Dentru, 1863. pp. 420.
——— *Les Contemporains de Molière.* 3 vols. Paris: Didot, 1863–1875.
Fournier, Edouard. *Notice sur le jeu de paume, son histoire et sa description.* Paris: Didier et Cie, 1862. pp. 71.
———*Le Théâtre français au XVIe et au XVIIe siècles.* Paris: Laplace, 1871. pp. 583.
Franklin, Alfred. *La Vie privée d'autrefois.* 27 vols. Paris: E. Plon, Nourrit et Cie, 1887–1902.
Fransen, J. *Les Comédiens français en Hollande au XVIIe et au XVIIIe siècles.* Paris: Champion, 1925.
——— "Documents inédits sur l'Hôtel de Bourgogne," *Revue d'Histoire Littéraire de la France,* XXXIV (1927), 321–355.
Garasse, Le Père François. *La Doctrine curieuse des beaux esprits de ce temps, ou prétendus tels.* Paris: Chez Sebastien Chappilet, 1624. pp. 1025 plus tables.
Gaufreteau, Jean de. *Chronique bordelaise.* 2 vols. Ed. par Jules Delpit. Bordeaux: Imprimerie Gounouilhou, 1876. pp. 335, 478.
Gautier Garguille. *Le Testament de feu Gautier Garguille, trouvé depuis sa mort, et ouvert le jour de la réception de son fils adoptif Guillot-Gorju.* Paris, 1634. pp. 14.
——— *Chansons de Gaultier* [sic] *Garguille.* Nouvelle édition . . . . avec introduction et notes par Edouard Fournier. Paris: Jannet, 1858. pp. 256.
Gofflot, L.-V. *Le Théâtre au collège du moyen âge à nos jours.* Paris: Champion, 1907. pp. 336.
Gosselin, E. *Recherches sur les origines et l'histoire du théâtre à Rouen avant Pierre Corneille.* Rouen: E. Cagniard, 1868. pp. 81.
Gougenot, Le Sieur. "La Comédie des comédiens," in *Le Théâtre français au XVIe et au XVIIe siècles,* éd. par Edouard Fournier, pp. 285–318.
Gouvenain, Louis de. *Le Théâtre à Dijon, 1422–1790.* Dijon: Jobard, 1888. pp. 171.
Guéret, Gabriel. *Les Auteurs en belle humeur.* Amsterdam: L'Honoré et Chatelain, 1723. pp. 78, 80 — in one vol. Contains *Le Parnasse réformé,* from the second edition of 1669.
Habasque, Francisque. *Documents sur le théâtre à Agen (1585–1788).* Agen: Lamy, 1893. pp. 40.
Héroard, Jean. *Journal de Jean Héroard sur l'enfance et la jeunesse de Louis XIII (1601–1628).* 2 vols. Ed. par Eudore Soulié et Ed. de Barthélemy. Paris: Picot, 1868.
Hulpeau. Charles. *Le Jeu royal de la paume.* Paris, 1632. pp. 39.
Lacour, Léopold. *Les premières Actrices françaises.* Paris: Librairie Française, 1921. pp. 229.
——— *Richelieu dramaturge.* Paris: Ollendorf, n.d. (1926?) pp. 169.

Lancaster, H. C. *A History of French Dramatic Literature in the Seventeenth Century. Part I: The Pre-Classical Period, 1610–1634.* 2 vols. Baltimore: The Johns Hopkins Press, 1929. These are the first volumes in Lancaster's great series.

Lanson, Gustave. "Etudes sur les origines de la tragédie classique en France," *Revue d'Histoire Littéraire de la France,* X(1903), 177–231, 413–436.

Lawrenson, T. E. *The French Stage in the Seventeenth Century. A Study in the Advent of the Italian Order.* Manchester (England): Manchester University Press, 1957. pp. 209.

Laumann, E.-M. *La Machinerie au théâtre depuis les Grecs jusqu'à nos jours.* Paris: Firmin-Didot, 1898. pp. 158.

Lavisse, Ernest. *Histoire de France depuis ses origines jusqu'à la Révolution.* Paris: Hachette, 1905.

Lebègue, Raymond. *La Tragédie française de la Renaissance.* Revised edition. Bruxelles: Office de Publicité, 1954. pp. 120.

——— "Tableau de la tragédie française de 1573 a 1610," *Bibliothèque d'Humanisme et Renaissance,* V (1944), 373–393.

——— "Le Répertoire d'une troupe française à la fin du XVIe siècle," *Revue d'Histoire du Théâtre,* 1948, 9–24.

——— "La Vie dramatique à Rouen de François Ier à Louis XIII," *Bulletin philologique et historique* (Paris: Imprimerie Nationale, 1957), 399–422.

Lecocq, Georges. *Histoire du théâtre en Picardie depuis son origine jusqu'à la fin du XVIe siècle.* Paris: H. Memi, 1880. pp. 223.

Lemaire, C. *Paris ancien et nouveau.* 3 vols. Paris: Girard, 1685.

Lemazurier, P.-D. *Galerie historique des acteurs du théâtre français depuis 1600 jusqu'à nos jours.* 2 vols. Paris: Joseph Chaumerot, 1810. pp. 563, 411.

Lemoine, Jean. "La Première du *Cid;*" "Pièces relatives à la Première du *Cid,*" *Revue des Questions Historiques* (November 1936), 131–149, 207–221.

Léris, Antoine de. *Dictionnaire portatif des théâtres, contenant l'origine des différents théâtres à Paris* . . . Paris: Jombert, 1754. pp. 557.

L'Estoile, Pierre de. *Mémoires-Journaux,* édition . . . publiée par MM. G. Brunet, A. Champollion, E. Halphen, Paul Lacroix, Charles Read et Tamizey de Larroque. 12 vols. Paris: Librairie des Bibliophiles, 1875–1896.

Lough, J. "French Actors in Paris from 1612 to 1614," *French Studies,* IX (1955), 218–226.

———*Paris Theatre Audiences in the 17th and 18th Centuries.* London: Oxford University Press, 1957. pp. 293.

Luze, Albert de. *La magnifique Histoire du jeu de paume.* Bordeaux et Paris, Delmas et Bossard, 1933. pp. 415.

Magne, Emile. *Gaultier-Garguille, comédien de l'Hôtel de Bourgogne.*

Suivi des Chansons de Gaultier-Garguille et de la Farce de Perrine. Paris: Louis Michaud, 1911. pp. 192.

Mairet, Jean. *Les Galanteries du duc d'Ossone, vice-roy de Naples.* Paris: Chez Pierre Rocolet, 1636. pp. 128.

Malingre, Claude. *Les Antiquitez de la ville de Paris.* Paris: Chez Pierre Rocolet, 1640. 4 *livres* in 2 vols. pp. 798, 145 plus tables.

Marolles, Michel de (Abbé de Villeloin). *Mémoires.* 3 vols. Amsterdam, 1755.

Molé, Mathieu. *Mémoires,* publiés pour la Société de l'Histoire de France . . . par Aimé Champollion-Figeac. 4 vols. Paris: Renouard, 1855–1857.

Mongrédien, Georges. *Les grands Comédiens du XVIIe siècle.* Paris: Société d'Edition "Le Livre," 1927. pp. 309.

——— "Chronologie des troupes qui ont joué à l'Hôtel de Bourgogne (1598–1690)," *Revue d'Histoire du Théâtre* (1953), 160–174.

Montluc, Adrien de. "La Comédie de proverbes," in Edouard Fournier's *Le Théâtre français au XVIe et au XVIIe siècles,* pp. 192–227.

Mouhy, Le Chevalier de. Journal du théâtre français. Ms. 9229, fonds français, Bibliothèque Nationale.

Niemeyer, Charles. "The Hôtel de Bourgogne, France's First Popular Playhouse," *The Theatre Annual,* 1947, pp. 64–80.

Nuitter, Ch. et Fr. Thoinon. *Les Origines de l'Opéra français.* Paris: Plon, 1886.

Ormesson, Olivier Lefèvre d'. *Journal* . . . publié par M. Chéruel. 2 vols. Paris: Imprimerie Impériale, 1860–1861.

Parfaict, Les Frères. *Histoire du théâtre français depuis son origine jusqu'à présent.* 12 vols. Paris: Lemercier et Saillant, 1745–1749.

Peiresc. *Lettres,* publiées par Philippe Tamisey de Larroque. 4 vols. Paris: Imprimerie Nationale, 1893.

Perrault, Charles. *Paralelle des anciens et des modernes, en ce qui regarde les arts et les sciences.* 4 vols. Paris: Chez Jean Baptiste Coignard, 1688–1697.

Plans de Paris: Quesnel, 1609; Quesnel-Vellefaux of Clos Francs Bourgeois, 1615; Gomboust, 1652; Rochefort, 1676; Bullet, 1676, retouché par Jaillot fils, 1707; N. de Fer, 1697.

Platter, Félix et Thomas. *Félix et Thomas Platter à Montpellier. Notes de voyage de deux étudiants bâlois.* Montpellier: Coulet, 1892. pp. 505.

Platter, Thomas le jeune. *Description de Paris par T. P. le jeune de Bâle (1599).* Traduite de l'allemand par L. Sieber . . . Extraits des Mémoires de la Société de l'Histoire de Paris et de l'Ile de France. Paris, 1896. pp. 62.

Poète, Marcel. *Une Vie de cité. Paris de sa naissance à nos jours.* 3 vols. Paris: Picard, 1925–1931.

Pougin, Arthur. *Dictionnaire historique et pittoresque du théâtre.* Paris: Firmin-Didot, 1885. pp. 775.

Recueil des principaux tiltres concernant l'acquistion de la propriété des masure et place où a été bastie la Maison appellée vulgairement l'Hostel de Bourgogne . . . Paris, 1632. pp. 71.

Registres des delibérations du Bureau de la ville de Paris. Histoire Générale de Paris. Tome 12, 1598–1602.

Renaudot, Théophraste. *Recueil des Gazettes nouvelles* . . . , *1633.* Paris: Au bureau d'Adresse, 1634. pp. 532. *Recueil des Gazettes.* . . . *1634.* Paris: Au bureau d'Adresse, 1635. pp. 596.

Rigal, Eugène. *Esquisse d'une histoire des théâtres de Paris de 1548 à 1635: Hôtel de Bourgogne et Marais.* Paris: Dupret, 1887. pp. 116.

——*Alexandre Hardy et le théâtre français à la fin du XVIe et au commencement du XVIIe siècle.* Paris: Hachette, 1889. pp. 715.

——*Le Théâtre français avant la période classique.* Paris: Hachette, 1901. pp. 363.

——"Bruscambille fabuliste," *Revue des Langues Romanes,* 1886, pp. 305–308.

Rochegude, le Marquis de, et Maurice Dumolin. *Guide pratique à travers le vieux Paris.* Paris: Champion, 1923. pp. 600.

Sabbattini, N. *Pratica di fabricar scene e machine ne' teatri* . . . ristampata di novo . . . Ravenna, 1638. In-fol. pp. 12, 168.

Sauval, Henri. *Histoire et recherches des antiquités de la ville de Paris.* 3 vols. Paris: Moette et Chardon, 1724.

—— *La Chronique scandaleuse de Paris.* Paris: Daragon, 1910. pp. 142.

Scarron, Paul. *Le Roman comique.* Nouvelle édition. Paris: Garnier, 1909. pp. 412.

Scherer, J. *La Dramaturgie classique en France.* Paris: Nizet, n.d. pp. 488.

Scudéry, Georges de. *La Comédie des comédiens.* Paris, 1635.

——*L'Apologie du théâtre.* Paris: Chez Augustin Courbé, 1639. pp. 99.

Sigogne, Le Sieur de. *Les Œuvres satyriques complètes* . . . par Fernand Fleuret et Louis Perceau. Collection des Satiriques Français. Paris: Bibliothèque des Curieux, 1920. pp. 355.

Sorel, Charles. *La Bibliothèque française.* Paris: Compagnie des Libraires du Palais, 1664. pp. 399.

Soulié, Eudore. *Recherches sur Molière et sa famille.* Paris: Hachette, 1863. pp. 385.

Tabarin. See Fournier, *Le Théâtre en France au XVIe et au XVIIe siècles,* pp. 228–229.

——*Farces tabariniques,* in Fournier, pp. 229–234.

—— *Œuvres complètes,* éd. par Gustave Aventin. Bibliothèque Elzévirienne. 2 vols. Paris: Jannet, 1858. pp. 290, 502.

——— *Œuvres.* La Bibliothèque Précieuse. Paris: Nilsson, 1933. pp. 253.

Tallemant des Réaux. *Les Historiettes,* édition documentaire établie par Georges Mongrédien. 8 vols. Paris: Garnier, 1932–1934.

Tapié, Victor L. *La France de Louis et de Richelieu.* Paris: Flammarion, 1952. pp. 561.

Thoisy. *Recueil, droit public et civil,* tome III. A collection, half manuscript and half printed pamphlet, of legal processes and disputes during the 17th century.

Tribout de Morembert, Henri. *Le Théâtre à Metz.* Tome I. Du Moyen Age à la Révolution. Publications de la Société d'Histoire du Théâtre. Paris et Metz, 1952. pp. 118.

Tristan l'Hermite. *Poésies galantes et héroïques.* Paris. Chez Jean Baptiste Loyson, 1662. pp. 368.

———*Les Amours.— La Lyre.— Les Vers héroïques.— Les Heures de la Vierge.— La Mariamne.— Le Parasite.— Lettres amoureuses.* . . Notice de Ad. van Bever. 2ième édition. Paris: Mercure de France, 1909. pp. 320.

Troterel, Pierre. "Les Corrivaux," in Viollet-le-Duc's *Ancien théâtre français,* VIII, 227–292.

Valmy-Baysse, Jean. *Naissance et vie de la Comédie Française.* Paris: Floury, 1945.

Védier, Georges. *Origine et évolution de la dramaturgie néo-classique.* Paris: Presses Universitaires de France, 1955. pp. 196.

Vianey, Joseph. "Bruscambille et les poètes bernesques," *Revue d'Histoire Littéraire de la France,* VIII (1901), 569–576.

Vitu, Auguste. *Le Jeu de paume des Mestayers ou l'Illustre Théâtre, 1595–1883.* Paris: Lemerre, 1883. pp. 73.

INDEX